Texas Instruments Technology Resource Manual

Calculus
Graphical, Numerical, Algebraic
Third Edition

Ross L. Finney

Franklin D. Demana
The Ohio State University

Bert K. Waits
The Ohio State University

Daniel Kennedy
Baylor School

PEARSON
Prentice Hall

Boston   San Francisco   New York
London   Toronto   Sydney   Tokyo   Singapore   Madrid
Mexico City   Munich   Paris   Cape Town   Hong Kong   Montreal

Pearson Prentice Hall™ is a trademark of Pearson Education, Inc.
Pearson® is a registered trademark of Pearson plc.
Prentice Hall® is a registered trademark of Pearson Education, Inc.

0-13-201415-7
1 2 3 4 5 6 7 8 9 10 BB 10 09 08 07 06

C O N T E N T S

Chapter 5 Exploring Calculus with the TI-86   103

C H A P T E R

1

Overview

1.1 Introduction

This manual is designed to be used with current calculus textbooks that incorporate the technology of graphing calculators and computers, such as the textbook *Calculus: Graphical, Numerical, Algebraic* by Finney, Demana, Waits, and Kennedy.

1.2 Using Technology in a Graphing Calculator or Computer Intensive Calculus Course

Graphing calculators and computers can be used effectively to enhance the teaching and learning of calculus. Our philosophy of using graphing calculator and computer numerical and visual methods to enhance the teaching and learning of calculus can be summarized as follows:

1. Do a problem analytically (with paper and pencil or using the computer algebra facility of a computer algebra system), then SUPPORT numerically and/or graphically with a graphing calculator or computer.

2. Do a problem numerically and/or graphically (with a graphing calculator or computer), then CONFIRM analytically (with paper and pencil or using the computer algebra facility of a computer algebra system).

3. Do a problem numerically and/or graphically because other methods are IMPRACTICAL or IMPOSSIBLE, including using computer algebra!

1.3 Toolbox Programs

Each brand of graphing calculator has not only an introductory chapter but also a chapter of useful calculus "toolbox" programs (or utilities) and examples of their use that can be applied to calculus. For example, there is a program called RAM for use on graphing calculators that applies a rectangle approximation method (RAM) for estimating area under a curve. (For example, if you use a TI-84 Plus Silver Edition, the RAM program is in Chapter 4.)

A complete list of 22 toolbox utilities follows. Many of the calculators require little programming because the needed toolbox programs are built-in features of the calculator. Other calculators require more programming; however, once programmed, these toolbox programs can be used to easily enhance the learning of calculus.

Following are the 22 program names and their functions:

1. **NDER**   Computes the numerical derivative.
2. **NDERGRAF**   Graphs the numerical derivative.
3. **TANLINE**   Draws a tangent line to a curve.

4. **NINT**   Computes the numerical definite integral.

5. **NINTGRAF**   Graphs an indefinite integral (an antiderivative) using numerical methods.

6. **SOLVE**   Finds a root of $f(x) = 0$ numerically.

7. **RAM**   Applies a rectangle approximation method for estimating area under a curve or a definite integral.

8. **TRAP**   Applies a trapezoidal approximation method for estimating a definite integral.

9. **SIMP**   Applies Simpson's method for estimating a definite integral.

10. **EULERT**   Applies Euler's method of solving an initial value problem and provides table output.

11. **EULERG**   Applies Euler's method for solving an initial value problem and provides graphical output.

12. **IMPEULT**   Applies an "improved" Euler's method for solving an initial value problem and provides table output.

13. **IMPEULG**   Applies an "improved" Euler's method for solving an initial value problem and provides graphical output.

14. **RUNKUTT**   Applies a Runge-Kutta method for solving an initial value problem and provides table output.

15. **RUNKUTG**   Applies a Runge-Kutta method for solving an initial value problem and provides graphical output.

16. **PARTSUMT**   Calculates the partial sums of a series.

17. **PARTSUMG**   Graphs the partial sums of a series.

18. **PSUMRECT**   Calculates the partial sums of a series defined recursively.

19. **PSUMRECG**   Graphs the partial sums of a series defined recursively.

20. **GRAPHSUM**   Graphs the partial sums of a power series.

21. **SLOPEFLD**   Graphs a slope field for the differential equation $dy/dx = f(x, y)$.

22. **AREA**   Provides a visual geometric interpretation of the RAM (see above).

1.4 Graphing Utilities

Devices that automatically produce graphs are called **graphing utilities** or **graphers**. The most practical graphing utilities today are graphing calculators. Larger computers with graphing software also are graphing utilities.

Calculus books that incorporate the technology of a graphing utility generally assume you have a grapher to use at all times, but the choice of grapher is up to you. This creates a bit of a problem in that different graphers use different terminology and different keying or menu selection steps. In this manual, we try to cover the differences among graphing calculators. Nevertheless, we still had to choose a single set of terminology to use.

Following is a list of that terminology. In each instance, we considered the possibilities and used what we felt is the best "generic" definition even though it sometimes matches what is used by a particular grapher. Other than implying our preferences for terminology in those individual instances, we make no recommendation of one grapher over another. Indeed, most we have used are fine products and owners of any of them should be able to develop the necessary grapher expertise fairly efficiently. Computer algebra systems also have graphing utilities built in.

1.4.1   Basic Terminology

(For the terms we use, you might want to note equivalent terminology for your grapher next to the term.)

Viewing window (or **view**, or **window**)—The portion of the coordinate plane shown in the display screen of the grapher. The **standard viewing window** has view dimensions $[-10, 10]$ by $[-10, 10]$.

View dimensions (or **window dimensions**)—The minimum to maximum x-values and the minimum to maximum y-values in the viewing window. We often speak of a viewing window with view dimensions $[x\text{min}, x\text{max}]$ by $[y\text{min}, y\text{max}]$.

Pixel—A small rectangle on the display screen that can be illuminated to represent a point in the coordinate plane. In a rectangular viewing window, the pixels are arranged in a rectangular array of rows and columns.

xmin, xmax—The minimum and maximum x-values, respectively, in a viewing window. The first screen coordinate of each pixel in the left-most pixel column is $x$min. The first screen coordinate of each pixel in the right-most pixel column is $x$max. When a function $y = f(x)$ plots across the N pixel columns of the viewing window, x takes on values from $x$min to $x$max in Δx increments, where

$$\Delta x = \frac{x\text{max} - x\text{min}}{N} - 1$$

ymin, ymax—The minimum and maximum y-values, respectively, in a viewing window. The second screen coordinate of each pixel in the bottom pixel row is $y$min. The second screen coordinate of each pixel in the top pixel row is $y$max.

Scale unit—The unit length on a coordinate axis.

xscale, yscale—The distance between scale marks on the x-axis and y-axis, respectively. If $x$scale $= 1$, the marks on the x-axis will show the scale unit.

Screen coordinates—The coordinate pair that names a screen pixel. If a viewing window has N pixel columns and M pixel rows, then, from left to right, the pixel columns have

$$x_i = x\text{min} + (i - 1)\Delta x, i = 1, 2, ..., N$$

as their first screen coordinates. From bottom to top, the pixel rows have

$$y_i = y\text{min} + (j - 1)\Delta y, j = 1, 2, ..., M$$

as their second screen coordinates, where

$$\Delta x = \frac{x\text{max} - x\text{min}}{N} - 1 \text{ and } \Delta y = \frac{y\text{max} - y\text{min}}{M} - 1$$

TRACE y-coordinate—If a pixel is part of the graph of $y = f(x)$, its first screen coordinate is x_i as computed above. Its second coordinate is $f(x_i)$, not the screen coordinate y_i.

Cursor-movement keys—The device(s) we use to move the screen cursor from pixel to pixel.

tmin, tmax—In Parametric mode, the minimum and maximum values, respectively, of the parameter t.

tstep—The increment used as the parameter t changes from $t$min to $t$max.

1.4.2   Terms Related to Grapher Procedures

You can consider each term we use here simply as a name for *any* toolbox procedure that does the indicated task. The procedure might be one that is already built into your grapher or that can be programmed into it. (For the terms we use, you might want to note equivalent terminology for your grapher next to the term.)

GRAPH (or **PLOT**)—Draws a graph in the specified viewing window.

SQUARE—Makes the scale unit appear to be the same length on each axis. This results in a graph with no scale distortion. Circles look like circles, etc.

TRACE—Allows you to move the cursor from pixel to pixel along a graph. The coordinates of the selected pixel will show on the screen, usually as the screen's first coordinate, with the *function value* (of the first screen coordinate) as the second coordinate.

ZOOM-IN, ZOOM-OUT—Zoom-In magnifies a portion of the coordinate plane so that you can see finer detail. Zoom-Out enlarges a portion of the coordinate plane. The effects are much like those of zooming in and zooming out with a camcorder.

SOLVE (or **ROOT**)—Finds a real-number solution of an equation of the form $f(x) = 0$ or equivalently, finds a real-number zero of f, or an x-intercept of its graph. Applied to $(f - g)(x) = 0$, this procedure finds the x-coordinate of a solution of $f(x) = g(x)$ or, equivalently, finds the x-coordinate of a point of intersection of the graphs of f and g.

INTERSECT—Finds a real-number solution of the system $y = f(x)$ and $y = g(x)$.

STORE—Stores a constant, a variable, an expression, and so on, in an assigned internal location.

1.4.3 Terms Related to Screen Formats

(If a particular format is unavailable you may skip activities using that format.)

Dot and **Connected**—In dot format, only computed pixels are illuminated. In connected format, computed pixels are illuminated and "in-between" pixels are also illuminated to give the graph more of a visual "connected" effect, an effect that might be desirable with a continuous function.

Sequential and **Simultaneous**—For two functions y_1 and y_2, the graph of y_1 can be plotted first, followed by the graph of y_2 (sequential), or the graphs of y_1 and y_2 can be plotted at the same time (simultaneously).

Axes On and **Axes Off**—"Axes on" displays coordinate axes in the viewing window. "Axes off" displays no axes, which might be desirable when we want to see better what happens along an axis.

1.5 Text and Calculator Keying Sequences

Following is a list of some of the text formatting used in this manual:

- Calculator keystrokes, with the exception of numbers and alphabet characters, are always shown as buttons or in custom brackets. Numbers and alphabet characters are shown **bold-face** without a box.

- Commands, features, applications, operations, and menus are shown in capital letters.

- Menus that are within menus and options on numbered menus that are to be selected as part of an input are shown in brackets.

- A minus sign appears as $\boxed{-}$ and a negative sign appears as $\boxed{(-)}$.

1.6 Using New TI Calculators

Chapters 2 and 4 contain instructions for the TI-84 Plus Silver Edition graphing calculator. The reader will find that the TI-83 Plus, the TI-83 Plus Silver Edition, and the TI-84 graphing calculators have many of the same keystrokes, menus, and screens. Throughout the text, the TI-84 Plus Silver Edition graphing calculator will be referred to simply as the TI-84.

Chapters 6 and 7 contain instructions for the TI-89 Titanium graphing calculator. The reader will find the TI-89, the TI-92, and the Voyage 200 graphing calculators have many of the same keystrokes, menus, and screens. The TI-89 Titanium will be referred to simply as the TI-89 throughout the rest of the text.

CHAPTER

2

Graphing with the TI-84 Plus Silver Edition

The TI-84 Plus Silver Edition calculator includes several preloaded applications, and is easily connected to a computer or classroom presentation device with a built-in USB port. The TI-84 Plus Silver Edition is compatible with the TI-83 calculator. The following aspects of working with the calculator are covered:

- Section 1—the keypad and major features and functions
- Section 2—graphing techniques
- Section 3—parametric graphing
- Section 4—polar graphing
- Section 5—sequence graphing
- Section 6—tables to represent functions
- Section 7—finding accurate approximations to solutions
- Section 8—piecewise functions
- Section 9—graphical databases
- Section 10—drawing pictures
- Section 11—working with increments and screen coordinates

2.1 Getting Started on the TI-84 Plus Silver Edition

The front of the calculator can be divided into two sections: the viewing screen in the upper third and the keys in the lower two-thirds. We discuss both of these in the following sections.

2.1.1 Turning the TI-84 On and Off

To turn on the calculator, press

ON

which is located in the far lower left-hand corner of the keypad.

To turn off the calculator, press

2nd   ON

On the TI-84, 2nd is the blue key in the upper left-hand corner of the keypad. (See Section 2.1.4 for more information about 2nd .) This manual will give keystrokes by their function on the keypad, not by the name of the button. For example, we show the keystrokes for turning off the calculator as 2nd [OFF], not 2nd ON . Note that the word OFF is in blue above the ON .

When you first turn on the calculator, you see the **Home screen**, which is the calculator's primary viewing screen, and the **entry cursor**, a blinking rectangle (**▮**) that is the calculator's basic cursor for entering data (other cursors are shown in Table 2.1 in Section 2.1.6). On the Home screen, you see the results of the data and instructions you entered at the keyboard. When you turn off the calculator, all data shown on the Home screen are retained in memory and reappear when you again turn on the calculator. If you are in any other screen or in a menu, turning off the calculator removes you from both and when you turn on the calculator again, you will see the Home screen. ***Note:*** *The calculator includes a power-saver feature that results in the calculator turning itself off after approximately three to four minutes of nonuse. To reactivate the calculator when it has powered-off on its own, press*

$$\boxed{\text{ON}}$$

When the calculator turns itself off under the power-saver feature, any data on the screen at the time of power-off reappears just as it was before the calculator shut down. If you were in another screen or in a menu, you are returned to your original location.

2.1.2 Exploring the Keypad

The keypad is divided into parts according to the position and color of the keys.

The keys are grouped according to position as follows:

- Row 1—the **Graphing keys**
  Used to access the calculator's interactive graphing features.

- Rows 2 and 3 (the first three keys of Row 2 and the first two keys of Row 3)—the **Editing keys**
  Used to edit expressions and values.

- Row 4—the **Advanced Function (menu) keys** (left four keys)
  Used to access the calculator's advanced functions through various full-screen menus.

- Rows 5–10—the **Scientific Calculator keys**
  Used to access the capabilities of a standard scientific calculator.

The keys are grouped according to color as follows:

- Cursor-movement keys (gray)
  Notice the triangles on these four keys. Each triangle points in the direction in which the cursor moves when the key is pressed. For information on the types of cursors the calculator's display, see Table 2.1.

- Basic mathematical operator keys (gray)
  The four basic arithmetic keys—$\boxed{\div}$, $\boxed{+}$, $\boxed{-}$, and $\boxed{\times}$—are set out for easy access.

- Number pad (white)
  The numbers 0–9 are set out in white, as is the negative sign $\boxed{(\text{--})}$ and the decimal point.

- $\boxed{\text{ENTER}}$
  Notice that unlike on some calculators, the TI-84 does not have an equals (=) key. Instead it has the $\boxed{\text{ENTER}}$ (gray) key. Pressing this key causes the calculator to calculate the function you entered. In some cases, it also is used to accept certain variable information and performs other duties, as we will see in this manual.

- All other keys (except $\boxed{\text{2nd}}$ and $\boxed{\text{ALPHA}}$) are black and represent the various features and functions available on the TI-84. Of those, we discuss in detail $\boxed{\text{CLEAR}}$, $\boxed{\text{2nd}}$ $\boxed{\text{QUIT}}$, $\boxed{\text{2nd}}$ $\boxed{\text{INS}}$, and $\boxed{\text{DEL}}$ in the next several sections.

Erasing Data from the Screen and Leaving a Screen or Menu. Generally, pressing either $\boxed{\text{CLEAR}}$ or $\boxed{\text{2nd}}$ $\boxed{\text{QUIT}}$ enables you to clear the Home screen of data, such as expressions and the results of evaluating expressions, and quit a screen or menu by returning you to the previous screen on which you were working or to the Home screen. What the key does depends on what screen you are in. $\boxed{\text{CLEAR}}$ also serves other purposes, described as needed in these instructions.

Deleting and Inserting Data. [DEL] and |INS| (the latter accessed by pressing [2nd] followed by [DEL]) enable you to edit data you have entered on the Home screen and on screens such as the Y = edit screen that call for you to enter values.

You can always "delete" data by entering new data over it. The new entry replaces the old, character for character. For example, to delete the number 123233 and replace it with 243556, position the entry cursor over the left-most character of 123233 and key in the new value, 243556. However, for those occasions when you need to delete data entirely, this method won't work. For example, if you want to delete the number 123233 entirely, use [DEL] instead. [DEL] deletes the character on which the entry cursor is sitting. To use [DEL], do the following:

1. a. To delete one character, position the entry cursor on the character you want to delete.
   b. Press

[DEL]

The character is erased.

2. a. To delete more than one *consecutive* character, position the entry cursor on the left-most character by using the arrow keys.
   b. Press and hold

[DEL]

until all characters you want deleted are erased.

[2nd] |INS| enables you to insert additional data between characters already on the screen. Suppose you have entered the following on the Home screen:

5 [×] 36

You realize it should read 5 * 316. To insert a 1 between the 3 and 6, do the following:

1. Position the entry cursor on the 6.
2. Press

[2nd] |INS|

3. Type a 1.

The number 1 is inserted **to the left** *of the 6.*

2.1.3   Resetting the Calculator

Resetting the calculator erases all previously entered data and programs. Before beginning the sample problems in these instructions, reset the calculator.

To reset the TI-84, do the following:

1. Turn the calculator on by pressing

[ON]

2. Press [2nd] |MEM| to display the MEM (memory) menu.

3. Select

[7:Reset...]

The RESET menu appears.

4. Select

[1:All RAM...]

5. Select

[2:Reset]

The calculator returns a "Mem cleared" message.

6. To return to the Home screen, press

[CLEAR]

2.1.4 Accessing the Calculator's Features and Functions

The calculator offers numerous features and functions, so many that if each were assigned a separate key, the size of the keypad would more than double. Therefore to keep the size of a keypad manageable, most of the keys perform double or triple duty. This capability resembles that of a typewriter or computer keyboard on which each key can be used to access more than one character, number, or function.

On the TI-84, the first level of features or functions is represented by the names or symbols printed on the keys. As on a typewriter, to access one of these, simply press the key. For example, to enter the number 5, press 5. Or to calculate the square of 5, press

$$5 \boxed{x^2} \boxed{\text{ENTER}}$$

The second level of features or functions is represented by names or symbols printed in blue directly above the first level. To access this level, press $\boxed{\text{2nd}}$ then the appropriate key. $\boxed{\text{2nd}}$ operates similarly to the SHIFT key on a typewriter or computer keyboard. Notice when you press $\boxed{\text{2nd}}$, the entry cursor changes in appearance—a blinking highlighted up arrow appears in the center of the rectangle. This is called the **2nd cursor**. For example, suppose you want to find the square root of 5. (Notice that the square root function is accessed via the same key as is the $\boxed{x^2}$ function.) To access the square root function, press $\boxed{\text{2nd}} \boxed{\sqrt{\ }}$. To complete the calculation of the square root of 5, press

$$5 \boxed{\text{ENTER}}$$

Note that the TI-84 will automatically add an open parenthesis, (, to many functions such as the square root function. In this example, it is not necessary to press $\boxed{\ )\ }$. If a closing parenthesis is missing, the TI-84 will assume that it goes at the end of the expression.

You also can use the calculator's keypad to key in the capital letters of the alphabet, plus the special symbols θ, ' " ', '**bracket facing upward**' (space), and '?'. The letters and symbols are shown in green above the keys. To access them, do the following:

1. Press

$$\boxed{\text{ALPHA}}$$

This green key is located near the upper left-hand corner of the keypad.

2. Press the appropriate letter or symbol.

Note: *A short-cut for entering the variable X is to press* $\boxed{\text{X,T,}\theta\text{,}n}$ *rather than* $\boxed{\text{ALPHA}}$ **X**.

2.1.5 Setting the Contrast of the Screen's Display

The brightness and contrast of the display depend on room lighting, battery freshness, viewing angle, and adjustment of the display contrast. You can adjust the display contrast at any time to suit your viewing angle and lighting conditions. The contrast setting is retained in memory when the calculator is turned off. To adjust the contrast, do the following:

1. To increase the contrast,

   press $\boxed{\text{2nd}}$ and then press *and hold* $\boxed{\blacktriangle}$.

2. To decrease the contrast,

   press $\boxed{\text{2nd}}$ and then press *and hold* $\boxed{\blacktriangledown}$.

Notice that as you change the contrast setting up or down, two things happen:

1. The display contrast changes.

2. A number in the upper right-hand corner of the screen changes to reflect the current contrast setting. This number moves between 0 (the lightest contrast) and 9 (the darkest contrast).

Observe also that if you adjust the contrast setting to 0, the display might appear to go completely blank. To correct this, simply press [2nd] and then press and hold [▲] until the display appears.

Note: When the batteries are low, the display begins to dim, especially during calculations. You will need to adjust the contrast to a higher setting to compensate for this. However, if you need to adjust it as high as 8 or 9, you should replace the batteries soon.

2.1.6 Display Data on the Viewing Screen

The calculator displays both text and graphics. For text, the viewing screen can show up to eight lines of 16 characters per line each. When all eight lines are filled, the text scrolls off the top of the screen.

For simple functions, the calculator shows the results immediately. However, when the calculator is involved in a relatively lengthy calculation or graphing function, a small moving line appears in the upper right-hand corner of the screen to signal that the calculator is busy.

Displaying Cursors. The calculator has several types of cursors, as shown in Table 2.1. In most cases, the appearance of the cursor indicates what will happen when you press the next key.

Table 2.1

Cursor	Appearance	Meaning
Entry cursor	Solid blinking rectangle	The next keystroke is entered at the cursor, overwriting any character already at that position.
Insert cursor	Blinking underline cursor	The next keystroke is inserted at the cursor.
2nd cursor	Highlighted blinking ↑	The next keystroke is a second function.
Alpha cursor	Highlighted blinking **A**	The next keystroke is an alpha character.
Free-moving cursor	Large + sign with blinking center	Moving the cursor updates the x- and y- coordinate values.
Zoom In or Out cursor	Small + sign with blinking center	Move and enter at a point to adjust the viewing window.
Trace cursor	Blinking × with highlighted blinking box center	Move among all functions that are defined or selected.
Zoom Box cursor	Small + sign with blinking center	Move and enter points for a box outlining the viewing window.

Displaying Calculations. One advantage of the TI-84, in contrast to a typical scientific calculator, is that you can see the complete expression *and* its solution simultaneously on the screen. For example, enter $1000(1.06)^{10}$ by pressing

$$1000 \boxed{\times} 1 \boxed{\cdot} 06 \boxed{\wedge} 10$$

(See Fig. 2.1.) Notice that the entire expression is shown on the first line beginning at the left margin. Press [ENTER] to have the calculator evaluate the expression. After the evaluation, the result is shown on the right-hand side of the second line of the display, while the cursor is positioned on the left-hand side of the third line, ready for you to enter the next expression. Note that if an expression requires more than one line, it will flow automatically to the next line and the result and cursor will be moved down one line each.

Using Concatenation. The calculator supports the combining of two or more commands. This is done using : to separate commands. For example, to store the number 20 in *N* and then evaluate 1000×1.06^N, on the TI-84 press

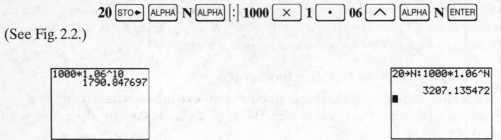

(See Fig. 2.2.)

```
1000*1.06^10
       1790.847697
```

Figure 2.1 $100(1.06)^{10}$.

```
20→N:1000*1.06^N
           3207.135472
■
```

Figure 2.2 Using concatenation.

2.1.7 Accessing Advanced Functions via Menus

Through menus you can access functions and operations that you cannot access directly from the keyboard. When you press a menu key, a screen displaying the selections available for that menu item temporarily replaces the screen on which you were working. After you select an item from a menu, the screen on which you were working is redisplayed. The four black menu keys are MATH, APPS, PRGM, and VARS.

The VARS key is used to access variables built into the graphing calculator. It also gives access to the functions entered in the Y = edit screen. (See Section 2.2.2 to learn about the Y = screen.)

For example, the MATH menu, which is typical of all the numbered menus, is shown in Fig. 2.3. To display it, press

MATH

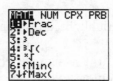

Figure 2.3 The MATH menu.

This menu offers you four more menus from which to choose. These menus are listed across the top of the screen: [MATH], [NUM], [CPX], and [PRB]. To access them, press ▶. Notice that as the cursor moves across the list of categories, the selected category is highlighted. Further, as each category is highlighted, a list of options appears beneath the category name. Options in menus are numbered in the left-hand column, with each number followed by a colon. For example, the NUM menu has nine options and the PRB menu has seven options.

Sometimes more options are available that can be viewed simultaneously on the screen. For example, press MATH. This menu has 10 options from which to choose. Notice, however, that only seven are displayed, and those seven fill the viewing screen. To learn whether a menu has additional options, notice Option 7, whose number is followed by an arrow instead of a colon. The arrow indicates there are more options. To see them, do the following:

1. Press ▼ to reach the bottom of the screen.

2. Then continue to press that key to cause the screen to scroll upward and reveal additional options.

In this case, scrolling enables you to see the last three options of the MATH [Math] menu.

You can select the option you want in one of two ways:

1. Press the number that corresponds to the desired option. This is the easiest way.

2. Move the cursor to the desired option and press

ENTER

Keying Sequence Notation for Numbered Menus. For numbered menus like the MATH menu, we have adopted a special keying sequence notation. For instance, to compute 7!, do the following:

1. Clear the screen (if necessary) by pressing

CLEAR

2. Press

7 MATH ▶ ▶ ▶ [4:!] ENTER

(See Fig. 2.4.)

The results are shown in Fig. 2.4. You can see from the [PRB] menu, shown in Fig. 2.5, that option 4 is the factorial function (!). To indicate that you should have selected that fourth option, we donated the keystroke by [4:!].

Figure 2.4 Keying sequence notation for numbered menus.

Figure 2.5 The PRB menu.

In another example, to compute $\sqrt[3]{7}$, we would instruct you to press

MATH $[4:\sqrt[3]{\ }(]$ **7** ENTER

where $[4:\sqrt[3]{\ }(]$ means you should select option 4 (cube root) from the MATH menu (see Fig. 2.6).

2.1.8 Changing Modes

A **mode** is one of a number of optional systems of operation. For example, you can choose to operate in Normal, Scientific, or Engineering mode with regard to how numeric results are displayed on the screen. To view the Mode screen, press

MODE

The first column of options are the defaults. On the TI-84 they are: Normal, Float, Radian, Func (Function), Connected, Sequential, Real, and Full. The TI-84 also has a clock at the bottom of the screen that can be easily set. The following are descriptions of all of the modes (see Fig. 2.7):

Figure 2.6 Option 4: the cube root option.

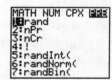

Figure 2.7 The MODE menu.

- Normal, Sci (Science), Eng (Engineering)
  Determines how a numeric result will be formatted. You can enter a number in any format. **Normal notation** is how we usually express numbers, with digits to the left and right of the decimal point, as in 12345.67. **Scientific notation** expresses numbers in two parts. The significant digits are displayed with one digit to the left of the decimal point. The appropriate power of 10 is displayed to the right of E, as in 1.234567E4. **Engineering notation** is similar to scientific notation, except that one, two, or three digits before the decimal point may be displayed and the power-of-10 exponent is a multiple of three, as in 13.34567E3.

- Float, 0123456789
  Represent the Floating (Float) or Fixed Decimal Point (0123456789) modes.

- Radian, Degree
  Represent the Radian and Degree angle modes. **Radian mode** means that angle arguments in trigonometric functions or polar-rectangular conversions are interpreted as radians and results are displayed in radians. **Degree mode** means that angle arguments in these functions or conversions are interpreted as degrees and results are displayed in degrees.

- Func (Function), Par (Parametric), Pol (Polar), Seq (Sequential)
  Stand for the Function, Parametric, Polar, and Sequential graphing modes. **Function graphing** plots a function where y is expressed in terms of x. See Section 2.2 for more information about graphing functions. **Parametric graphing** plots a relation in which x and y are each expressed in terms of a third variable, t. See Section 2.3 for more information about graphing parametric equations. Section 2.4 contains more information about polar equations, while Section 2.5 gives more information about sequences where the nth term is defined explicitly in terms of n or where the nth term is defined recursively.

- Connected, Dot
  Represent the Connected Line and Dot graph modes. A **connected line** graph draws a line between the points calculated on the graph of a function in the Y = edit screen. A **dot graph** plots only the calculated points in the graph.

- Sequential, Simul (Simultaneous)
  Stand for the Sequential and Simultaneous plotting modes. **Sequential plotting** means that if more than one function is selected, one function is evaluated and plotted completely before the next function is evaluated and plotted. **Simultaneous plotting** means that if more than one function is selected, all functions are evaluated and plotted for a single point before the functions are evaluated and plotted for the next point.

- Real, a + bi, re$^{\wedge}\theta i$
  Determines whether a complex result is displayed. In the **Real** mode, a complex result is not displayed unless complex numbers are entered as input. In the **a + bi** mode, or regular complex mode, complex numbers are displayed in the form a + bi, where a is the real part and b is the imaginary part of the number. In the **re$^{\wedge}\theta i$** mode, or complex mode, complex numbers are displayed in the form re$^{\wedge}\theta i$, where r is the argument and θ is the angle of the complex number.

- Full (Full Screen), Horiz (Horizontal), G-T (Graph-Table)
  Stand for a Full Screen, Horizontal, or Graph-Table display. In the **Full Screen** mode, the entire screen consists of the graph that is plotted. In the **Horizontal** mode, the upper half of the screen shows graphs while the lower half shows calculations, tables, menus, or other information that is normally displayed on the Home screen. In the **Graph-Table** mode, the left side of the screen shows graphs while the right side shows the table screen (see Figs. 2.8, 2.9, and 2.10).

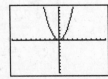

Figure 2.8 A Full Screen display.

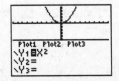

Figure 2.9 A Horizontal display.

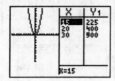

Figure 2.10 A Graph-Table display.

To change a mode, do the following:

1. Press

MODE

2. Move the cursor to the row and column that contain the mode you want to change.

3. Press

ENTER

4. Follow the same sequence if you want to change other modes.

5. When you have changed all the modes you want at that time, return to the Home screen by pressing

CLEAR or 2nd QUIT

For example, to change the Connected to the Dot mode, do the following:

1. Press

MODE

2. Press the cursor-movement keys until you reach Dot.

3. Press

ENTER CLEAR

New selections are saved in the calculator's memory, even when the computer is turned off, until you change them again.

2.1.9 Recalling a Previous Entry

After an expression has been evaluated, the calculator stores it in a special storage area called Last Entry. You can recall that expression by pressing

2nd ENTRY

You can recall it even if you have begun entering the next expression; the recalled expression replaces the newer one on the viewing screen.

As an example, perform the following steps:

1. Press

7 × 5 ENTER

The expression is calculated and the screen shows the result: 35.

2. Press

2 × 5

Do **not** press ENTER.

3. Press

2nd ENTRY

The expression 2×5 is replaced by the first one—7×5—which was saved in Last Entry (see Fig. 2.11).

```
          3207.135472
7!
              5040
³√(7)
        1.912931183
7*5
                35
7*5
```

Figure 2.11 The Last Entry Storage area.

In Example 1, we show you how you can use Last Entry.

The calculator stores as many of the most recent calculations in memory as is possible (up to a total of 128 bytes), even when it is turned off. To further see how this feature works, do the following:

1. Calculate the Last Entry expression by pressing

ENTER

2. Press

2nd [ENTRY] 2nd [ENTRY] 2nd [ENTRY] 2nd [ENTRY]

Notice that after each time you press 2nd [ENTRY], a preceding calculation appears on the screen. Before continuing to Example 1, press CLEAR until the Home screen is blank.

Example 1 Last Entry

Problem Determine when an investment earning interest at 8.5% compounded monthly will double in value. The applicable compound interest equation is

$$2 5 (1 1 0.085/12)^N.$$

Solution We want to solve this equation for N. We start by estimating $N = 100$. Press

(1 + . 085 ÷ 12) ^ 100 ENTER

The result is shown in Fig. 2.12. From this result, we see that our estimate of 100 was too high, so we try again with another, smaller estimate, say $N = 99$. This time, we use the LAST ENTRY feature, as follows:

1. Press

2nd [ENTRY]

The original equation is retrieved from Last Entry memory and appears on your screen. Notice that the cursor is at the end of the equation (see Fig. 2.13).

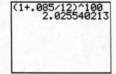

Figure 2.12 The compound interest equation entered.

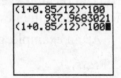

Figure 2.13 Using the LAST ENTRY feature.

2. Move the cursor left three spaces.
The cursor is positioned over the 1 in 100.

3. Type 99.

4. To erase the last 0, press

DEL

5. Press

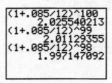

Continue estimating in this manner until your answer is as accurate as you want; for example, make your next estimate $N = 98$ and see the result in Fig. 2.14.

```
(1+.085/12)^100
         2.025540213
(1+.085/12)^99
         2.01129355
(1+.085/12)^98
         1.997147092
```

Figure 2.14 Solution for N of $2 = (1 + 0.085/12)^N$.

2.1.10 Recalling the Last Answer

You also can recall the last answer obtained from a calculation. This last answer is then stored in memory as a variable (ANS) that can be used in computations. To recall an answer, press

2nd |ANS|

The following example shows how to use this feature:

1. Press

7 × 5 ENTER

The expression is calculated and the screen shows the result: 35.

2. Press

4 +

4 + appears on the Home screen.

3. Press

2nd |ANS|

ANS appears to the immediate right of 4 +. The calculator then waits for you to either accept or reject insertion of the last answer.

4. a. To accept the stored answer (variable ANS), press

ENTER

The last saved answer—35—is retrieved from memory and added to 4. 4 + ANS appears at the left-hand margin and the result of adding 4 to the saved answer of 35, that is, 39, appears at the right-hand margin one line down.

  b. To reject the stored answer,

   1. Press

4 + 2nd |ANS|

   2. Move the cursor so it is positioned over the A and

   3. Press

DEL

ANS is erased, but 4 + remains on the screen.

  c. To reject the stored answer and erase the current expression, press

Graphing on the TI-84 Plus Silver Edition

2.2.1 Introducing the Graphing Keys

The keys most closely related to graphing are the graphing keys located directly beneath the viewing screen. We summarize each of these next and follow with a more-detailed discussion of them:

- $\boxed{\text{Y=}}$

  Displays an edit screen on which you enter, edit, and display the functions you want to graph.

- $\boxed{\text{WINDOW}}$

  Displays an edit screen on which you define the viewing window for a graph.

- $\boxed{\text{ZOOM}}$

  Displays a menu of options that enables you, among other actions, to zoom in on a portion of the graph and to otherwise change the appearance of the viewing window.

- $\boxed{\text{TRACE}}$

  Displays the last graph generated and the **Trace cursor**, a blinking $\times$ with a blinking box in its center, that you use to trace the path of the graphed function.

- $\boxed{\text{GRAPH}}$

  Displays the graph of the currently selected functions in the chosen viewing window.

2.2.2 Y=: Entering a Function

Entering functions involves the following steps. It's usually best to clear any old equations appearing on the screen before entering new equations. Clear previous equations entered on the Y = edit screen as follows:

1. Position the cursor on the equation to be deleted.

2. a. Press

   $\boxed{\text{CLEAR}}$

   or

   b. Type the new equation over the old one.

To illustrate, we use an example with two functions (see Fig. 2.15).

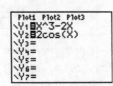

Figure 2.15 Entering functions.

1. Ensure the calculator is in Function mode by pressing

   $\boxed{\text{MODE}}$

   to display the MODE menu and press $\boxed{\blacktriangledown}$ three times and select the Func graphing mode.

2. Return to the Home screen by pressing

   $\boxed{\text{CLEAR}}$

3. Press

   $\boxed{\text{Y=}}$

The screen can display labels for up to 10 functions, Y_1 through Y_0 (10). After each label is a field in which you enter the function. The entry cursor is positioned at the first field.

4. Enter the function $f(x) = x^3 - 2x$ by pressing

$$\boxed{\text{X,T,}\theta,n} \quad \boxed{\wedge} \quad 3 \quad \boxed{-} \quad 2 \quad \boxed{\text{X,T,}\theta,n} \quad \boxed{\text{ENTER}}$$

Note: *Recall that pressing* $\boxed{\text{X,T,}\theta,n}$ *is a short-cut for entering the variable X. The function is entered in the Y_1 field and the cursor moves to the field next to Y_2. The = sign next to Y_1 is highlighted, indicating the function has been selected for graphing.*

5. Enter the function $g(x) = 2 \cos x$ by pressing

$$2 \quad \boxed{\text{COS}} \quad \boxed{\text{X,T,}\theta,n} \quad \boxed{\text{ENTER}}$$

The function is entered in the Y_2 field and the cursor moves to the field next to Y_3. Here too, the = sign next to Y_2 is highlighted, indicating this function also has been selected for graphing.

Note: *These functions are used in demonstrating principles in later sections.*

Selecting functions for graphing. As indicated in these steps, highlighting the = sign before the function selects that function for graphing. You may select as many of the functions you enter as you want. To deselect a function, that is, to have it not graphed, do the following:

1. Position the entry cursor over the = sign before the applicable function.
2. Press

$$\boxed{\text{ENTER}}$$

The highlighting is erased and the function is no longer selected for graphing.

2.2.3 WINDOW: Defining the Viewing Window

The WINDOW menu enables you to choose the coordinates of the viewing window that define the portion of the coordinate plane that appears in the display.

Using the Window edit screen. The values of the Window edit screen variables determine the following:

* The size of the viewing window
* The scale units for each axis

You can view and change these values easily. Do this as follows:

1. Press $\boxed{\text{WINDOW}}$.

The Window edit screen appears as shown in Fig. 2.16, which displays the default values for this feature. The entry cursor is initially positioned at the value of the first variable.

Figure 2.16 The default values for
the Window edit screen.

2. For each value you want to change,
   a. move the cursor to the current value,
   b. clear the current value by pressing

   $$\boxed{\text{CLEAR}}$$

   c. and then type in the new value.
3. After changing the values, leave the screen by pressing

$$\boxed{\text{2nd}} \quad \boxed{\text{QUIT}}$$

The variables are defined as follows:

- $x$min, $x$max, $y$min, and $y$max
  Tell the minimum and maximum x- and y-coordinates for the desired viewing window. In Fig. 2.16, these values define the Standard window of $[-10, 10]$ by $[-10, 10]$.

- $x$scl and $y$scl
  Give the distance between consecutive tick marks on the coordinate axes; in Fig. 2.15, the distance is a value of 1.

Expression, such as $\pi/2$, $-1 + \sqrt{3}$, and x^2, can be entered directly as values for Window variables.

2.2.4   FORMAT: Defining a Graph's Appearance

Using the FORMAT menu, you can determine how information on the screen is presented, for example, whether the coordinates at the bottom of the screen are displayed in Rectangular or Polar mode.

Using the FORMAT menu. The FORMAT menu offers six options from which you can choose to affect the way data are displayed in the window. To access this menu, press:

The six options of the FORMAT menu are displayed.

3. Move the cursor to highlight the option you want to select.

4. Select an option by pressing

ENTER

5.   Leave the menu by pressing

CLEAR

The options in the FORMAT menu are defined as follows:

- RectGC (Rectangular)/PolarGC (Polar)
  Determine whether the free-moving or Trace cursors display Rectangular or Polar coordinates at the bottom of the screen.

- CoordOn/CoordOff
  Determine whether coordinates are displayed at the bottom of the screen.

- GridOff/GridOn
  Activate and deactivate the grid of points that appear on a graph. The grid points correspond to the axis tick marks.

- AxesOn/AxesOff
  Determine whether the x- and y-axes will appear on the graph.

- LabelOff/LabelOn
  Tell whether the x- and y-axes will be labeled.

- ExprOn/ExprOff
  Determine whether the Y = expression is displayed when the trace cursor is active.

2.2.5 GRAPH: Displaying and Exploring the Graph

To plot and display a graph in the current viewing window with default values, press

$$\boxed{\text{GRAPH}}$$

to graph the functions entered in Section 2.2.2 (Fig. 2.17). When the plotting is completed, you can explore the graph using the **free-moving cursor**, a plus sign (+) with a blinking center. Note that when you first press $\boxed{\text{GRAPH}}$, this cursor isn't visible. To see it, press any of the cursor-movement keys and the cursor will appear near the origin of the *x*- and *y*-axes. Along the bottom of the viewing screen are displayed the coordinates of the cursor's current position.

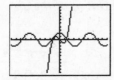

Figure 2.17 Graphing functions.

If the coordinates are not displayed, you can turn them on as follows. Press a cursor-movement key.

a. If the CoordOn option in the FORMAT menu is selected, pressing a cursor-movement key causes the coordinates to reappear on the screen. Note that which key you press determines which coordinate values are shown. To erase the coordinate display from the screen, press

$$\boxed{\text{CLEAR}}$$

b. If the CoordOff option in the FORMAT menu is selected, pressing a cursor-movement key will not cause the coordinates to reappear on the screen. To see the coordinates, you must select CoordOn.

In Rectangular mode (RectGC in the FORMAT menu), the *x*- and *y*-coordinates are displayed; in Polar mode (PolarGC in the FORMAT menu), the *r*- and *θ*-coordinates are displayed. Press any cursor-movement key and notice how the coordinates change as the cursor changes position. The free-moving cursor can be used to identify the coordinates of any location on the graph and operates in the Full, Horizontal, and Graph-Table modes (see Figs. 2.18, 2.19, and 2.20, respectively).

This cursor moves from dot to dot on the screen, so be aware that when you move it to a dot that appears to be "on" a function, it might be near, but not on, that function. The coordinate value is accurate to within the width of the dot. To move the cursor *exactly* along a function, use the TRACE feature.

Note: *Coordinate values at the bottom of the viewing screen always appear in floating decimal-point format. The numeric display settings in MODE do not affect coordinate display.*

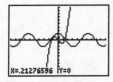

Figure 2.18 The free-moving cursor in the Full Screen mode.

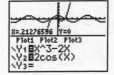

Figure 2.19 The free-moving cursor in the Horizontal Screen mode.

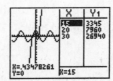

Figure 2.20 The free-moving cursor in the Graph-Table mode.

2.2.6 TRACE: Moving the Cursor along a Function's Graph

The TRACE feature enables you to trace the graph of functions. As you do this, the coordinates at the bottom of the viewing screen change to reflect the changing position of the cursor. (If the cursor moves off the top or bottom of the screen, the values continue to change.) Note that in the Rectangular coordinate system, the y-value is the calculated function value $f(x)$.

Trace the functions graphed in Section 2.2.4 as follows:

1. Press

$$\boxed{\text{TRACE}}$$

The Trace cursor appears near the origin of the axes.

2. a. To trace a graph, press

$$\boxed{\blacktriangleright} \text{ or } \boxed{\blacktriangleleft}$$

   b. To move among all functions that are defined *and* selected (that is, active), press

$$\boxed{\blacktriangle} \text{ or } \boxed{\blacktriangledown}$$

   If ExprOn is selected from the FORMAT menu, then the function being traced will be displayed at the top of the screen. Otherwise, a number in the upper right-hand corner tells you which function is being traced.

   c. To pan in order to view graphs that disappear off the left or right of the screen, press and hold

$$\boxed{\blacktriangleright} \text{ or } \boxed{\blacktriangleleft}$$

3. To quit the feature and leave the graph display, press

$$\boxed{\text{CLEAR}} \boxed{\text{CLEAR}} \text{ or } \boxed{\text{2nd}} \boxed{\text{QUIT}}$$

4. To view the graph after quitting the feature, press

$$\boxed{\text{GRAPH}} \text{ or } \boxed{\text{GRAPH}}$$

To view at any time the original functions entered for this graph, press

$$\boxed{\text{Y=}}$$

Figures 2.21 and 2.22 show tracing the Y_1 and Y_2 graphs, respectively. Note that the figures are graphed on $[-2, 4]$ by $[-2, 3]$ window. The values for $x$min, $x$max, $y$min, and $y$max were changed in the WINDOW edit screen.

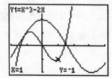

Figure 2.21 Using the TRACE feature.   **Figure 2.22** Tracing along a function's graph.

Note: The calculator stores in memory the set of functions and the graph involved with this problem, provided you have not entered a new set of variables, even after you turn off the calculator. Entering new data replaces the old that is stored in memory.

2.2.7 ZOOM: Magnifying and Shrinking Parts of a Graph

The ZOOM feature enables you, among other capabilities, to adjust that portion of the viewing window that you see, for example, by magnifying a portion (zoom in) or retreating (zoom out) to give you a more global view. To access the feature, press

$$\boxed{\text{ZOOM}}$$

The ZOOM feature consists of two menus: ZOOM and MEMORY. Figure 2.23 shows the ZOOM menu and Figure 2.24 shows the MEMORY menu. Several of the options shown on these menus are discussed in the next several subsections.

Figure 2.23 The ZOOM menu.

Figure 2.24 The MEMORY menu.

When the calculator executes a Zoom option, it updates the values of the Window variables to reflect the new viewing window. The modified values depend on the exact cursor position when you executed the option. To see these new values, press

WINDOW

To return to the graph without having to replot it, press

GRAPH

To practice the following features, use the functions graphed in Section 2.2.5.

The Zoom Box Option. This option lets you adjust the viewing window by drawing a box anywhere on the screen display to define the size of the desired window. To draw the box, do the following:

1. Press

ZOOM [1:ZBox]

*You are returned to the graph. The **Zoom In/Out cursor**, a cross with a blinking center, is in the middle of the screen at the origin of the axes.*

2. Move the cursor to the place where you want one corner of the new viewing window to be (see Fig. 2.25).

3. Press ENTER

*The cursor changes to the **Zoom Box cursor**, a box with a blinking center.*

4. Move the cursor to the diagonally opposite corner of the desired viewing window (see Fig. 2.26).

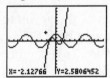

Figure 2.25 Using the Zoom Box option.

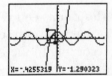

Figure 2.26 Drawing a box to define the new viewing window.

The outline of the new viewing window is drawn as you move the cursor.

5. To accept the new cursor location, press ENTER.

The graph is replotted using the box outline as the new viewing window (see Fig. 2.27).

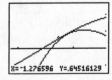

Figure 2.27 A new viewing window.

6. To leave the graph display, press

CLEAR CLEAR or 2nd [QUIT]

You can continue to draw boxes to zoom in on even more specific portions of the graph.

The Zoom-In Option. This option allows you to zoom in on (magnify) a portion of the graph. Using this option adjusts the viewing window in both the *x*- and *y*-directions according to the zoom factors set in the SET FACTORS menu (see later in this section for details on setting zoom factors). To use this option, do the following:

1. Press

ZOOM [2:Zoom in]

You are returned to the graph. The Zoom In/Out cursor is in the middle of the screen at the origin of the graphs.

2. Place the cursor approximately in the center of the area you want to magnify.
3. Press ENTER.

The calculator adjusts the viewing window by the zoom factors, replots the selected functions with the cursor in the center of the new window, and updates the values of the Window variables.

4. To zoom-in more,
   a. centered at the same point, press ENTER.
   b. centered at new point,
      • move the cursor to the point you want as the center of the new viewing window, and
      • press ENTER.
5. Exit the screen by pressing 2nd QUIT.

You also can select another screen by pressing the appropriate key.

For example, Figs. 2.28 and 2.29 show the before and after of using the feature. In Fig. 2.28, the cursor is placed at an intersection of the two graphs; in Fig. 2.29, that intersection with the cursor on it has become the center of a new viewing window.

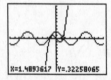

Figure 2.28 Before using the ZOOM-In feature.   **Figure 2.29** After using the ZOOM-In feature.

The Zoom-Out Option. Zoom-out displays a greater portion of the graph to present a more global view of it. Using this option adjusts the viewing window in both the x- and y-directions according to the zoom factors set in the SET FACTORS menu (see the next subsection for details on setting zoom factors). To use this option, do the following:

1. Press

ZOOM [3:Zoom Out]

You are returned to the graph. The Zoom In/Out cursor is in the middle of the screen at the origin of the graphs.

2. Place the cursor at the point you want as the center of the new viewing window.
3. Press

The calculator adjusts the viewing window by the zoom factors, replots the selected functions with the cursor in the center of the new window, and updates the values of the Window variables.

4. To zoom-out more,
   a. centered at the same point, press

ENTER

   b. centered at new point,
      • move the cursor to the point you want as the center of the new viewing window, and
      • press

5.   Exit the screen by pressing

[2nd] |QUIT|

You also can select another screen by pressing the appropriate key.

The Set Factors Option. Zoom factors determine the scale of the magnification for the Zoom-In and Zoom-Out options. These factors are positive numbers (not necessarily integers) greater than or equal to one.

Before using Zoom In or Zoom Out, you can review or change the current values. To use this feature, do the following:

1. Press

|ZOOM|

and select

[Memory] [4:Set Factors...]

The Zoom Factors editing screen appears, as shown in Fig. 2.30. In that figure, the default factors of 4 in the x-direction (xFact) and y-direction (yFact) are shown.

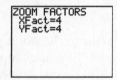

Figure 2.30 The Zoom Factors edit screen.

2. To change the factors.
    a. enter a new value in the *x*Fact field,

    or

    b. use [▼] to reach *y*Fact and enter a new value.

The new value overwrites the old.

3. Exit the feature by pressing

[2nd] |QUIT|

You also can select another screen by pressing the appropriate key.

Other ZOOM Features. Several of the ZOOM features either reset the values of the Window variables to predefined values or use factors to adjust those values. Two of the MEMORY features save and recall Window variables.

• ZDecimal
  Sets the values of the Window variables to the following values and replots the functions; for example:

xmin $= -4.7$ ymin $= -3.1$

xmax $= 4.7$ ymax $= 3.1$

xscl $= 1$ yscl $= 1$

  In the window with these coordinates, the *x*-coordinate changes in units of 0.1 when you use either the Trace or free-moving cursor. The *y*-coordinate also changes in units of 0.1 as the free-moving cursor moves but not when you trace. This latter situation is because the *y*-coordinate is determined by the function being traced.

• ZSquare
  Replots the selected functions as soon as the option is selected. It redefines the viewing window using values that are based on the current values of the Window variables but adjusted to equalize the width of the dots on the *x*- and *y*-axes. The center of the current graph becomes the center of the new graph. This feature makes the graph of a circle look like a circle (see Example 2).

- ZStandard
  Updates the values of the Window variables to the standard default values and then replots the graph. The standard default values of the Window variables are as follows:

xmin = −10	ymin = −10
xmax = 10	ymax = 10
xscl = 1	yscl = 1

- ZTrig
  Updates the values of the Window variables using present values appropriate for trigonometric functions and then replots the graph. The values of the trig Window variables in Radian mode are as follows:

xmin = −6.152285...	ymin = −4
xmax = 6.1522856...	ymax = 4
xscl = 1.5707963...	yscl = 1

Note: The display shows the numeric values of -2π ($-6.152286...$), 2π ($6.1522856...$), and $\pi/2$ ($1.570796327...$)

- ZInteger
  Enables you to move the cursor to the point you want as the center of the new viewing window. Press ENTER to have the functions replotted, with the new viewing window redefined so that the midpoint of each dot on the *x*- and *y*-axes is an integer. *x*scl and *y*scl are equal to 10.

- ZoomStat
  Updates the values of the Window variables in order to display all statistical data points.

- ZoomFit
  Replots the selected functions as soon as the option is selected. The Ymin and Ymax variables are updated to include the minimum and maximum *y*-values of the selected functions between the current Xmin and Xmax values. The Xmin and Xmax values are not changed.

The following are the Memory features:

- ZPrevious
  Toggles you back and forth between the graph currently on the screen and the previous graph that was on the screen.

- ZoomSto
  Saves the values of the current window variables for later recall by the ZoomRcl option. After the values are saved, you are returned automatically to the Graph screen.

- ZoomRcl
  Recalls the values of the Window variables that were saved with the ZoomSto option and then draws the current functions in the new window.

Example 2 Graphing a Circle

Problem Graph a circle of radius 10, centered around the origin $x^2 + y^2 = 10$.

Solution To graph a circle, you must enter separate formulas for the upper and lower portions of the circle. Use the Connected mode and do as follows:

1. Press [Y=] and enter the expressions to define two functions.

   a. The top half of the circle is defined by $Y_1 = \sqrt{100 - X^2}$, so press

   [2nd] [√] **100** [−] [X,T,θ,*n*] [x^2] [ )] [ENTER]

   b. The bottom half of the circle is defined by $Y_2 = -Y_1$, so press

   [CLEAR] [(−)] [VARS] [Y-VARS] [1:Function...] [1:Y₁] [ENTER]

2. Press

$$\boxed{\text{ZOOM}}\ [\text{6:ZStandard}]$$

This is a quick way to reset the values of the Window variables to the standard default values. As this option also graphs the functions, you don't need to press $\boxed{\text{GRAPH}}$. Notice that the graph appears to be an ellipse (see Fig. 2.29).

3. To adjust the display so that each "dot" has an equal width and height, press

$$\boxed{\text{ZOOM}}\ [\text{5:ZSquare}]$$

The functions are replotted and now appear as a circle on the display (see Fig. 2.32).

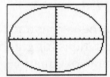

Figure 2.31 Graph of $x^2 + y^2 = 10$.

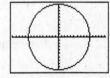

Figure 2.32 Graph of a circle.

4. To see the effect of the ZSquare option on the values of the Window variables, press

$$\boxed{\text{WINDOW}}$$

and notice how the $x$min, $x$max, $y$min, and $y$max values change.

2.3 Graphing Parametric Equations

2.3.1 Defining and Displaying a Parametric Graph

Parametric equations consist of an x-component and a y-component, each expressed in terms of the same independent variable, t. You can define and graph up to six *pairs* of parametric equations simultaneously. The steps for defining a parametric graph are similar to those for defining a function graph. To define a parametric graph, do the following:

1. Press

$$\boxed{\text{MODE}}$$

and select Parametric and Connected modes.

Notes: You must set the calculator in Parametric mode before you enter the values of the Window variables or enter the components of parametric equations.

2. To return to the Home screen, press

$$\boxed{\text{CLEAR}}$$

3. Press

$$\boxed{\text{Y=}}$$

The Y = edit screen displays labels for up to six pairs of x-y parametric equations. After each label is a field in which you enter the function. The entry cursor is positioned at the first field.

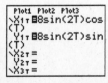

Figure 2.33 Enter parametric equations.

4. Enter the two equations in the same manner as for functions, as follows (see Fig. 2.33):

   a. 8 sin 2*T* cos *T*; press

   CLEAR **8** SIN **2** X,T,θ,*n*) COS X,T,θ,*n*) ENTER

   b. 8 sin 2*T* sin *T*; press

   CLEAR **8** SIN **2** X,T,θ,*n*) SIN X,T,θ,*n*) ENTER

In this case, note the following:

- You must define both the *x*- and *y*-components in a pair.
- The independent variable in each component must be *t*. To enter the variable, you can press X,T,θ,*n* rather than ALPHA **T** as a short-cut.

The procedures for editing and clearing parametric equations and for exiting the screen are the same as for function graphing. Selecting equations for graphing, also, is the same as for function graphing. You can select up to six pairs of equations at a time and only those selected are graphed. Note that when you enter, edit, or select either component of an equation, the *pair* of equations is selected.

5. To display the current values of the Window variables, press

   WINDOW

The standard values in Radian mode are shown in Table 2.2.

6. As needed, change the values on your screen to match those in Table 2.2.

Table 2.2

Setting	Meaning
WINDOW	
*t*min = 0	The smallest *t*-value to be evaluated
*t*max = 2π	The largest *t*-value to be evaluated
*t*step = π/24	The increment between *t*-values
*x*min = −10	The smallest *x*-value to be displayed
*x*max = 10	The largest *x*-value to be displayed
*x*scl = 1	The spacing between *x* tick marks
*y*min = −10	The smallest *y*-value to be displayed
*y*max = 10	The largest *y*-value to be displayed
*y*scl = 1	The spacing between *y* tick marks

Note: The display shows the numeric value of 2π (6.283185307...) for tmax and π/24 (.1308996...) for tstep.
Notice the three new variables: tmin, tmax, and tstep.

7. To graph the equations, press

   GRAPH

   (See Fig. 2.34.)

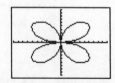

Figure 2.34 Graphing parametric equations.

Pressing $\boxed{\text{GRAPH}}$ causes the calculator to plot the selected parametric equations. It evaluates both the x- and y-components for each value of t (taken from $t$min to $t$max in intervals of $t$step) and then plots each point defined by x and y. The values of the Window variables define the viewing window. As the graph is plotted, the calculator updates the x- and y-coordinates and the values of the parameter t.

2.3.2 Exploring a Parametric Graph

As in function graphing, you have three tools for exploring a graph:

- Using the free-moving cursor
- Tracing an equation
- Zooming

The free-moving cursor works in parametric graphing in the same manner as it does in function graphing: As the cursor moves, the displayed coordinate values of x and y in Rectangular (RectGC) mode—r and θ in Polar (PolarGC) mode—are updated.

Using the TRACE feature, you can move the cursor along the graph one $t$step at a time. When you begin a trace, the cursor is on the first selected equation at the initial t-value, and the coordinate values of x, y, and t are displayed at the bottom of the screen. The parametric functions are displayed at the top of the screen. To erase the functions from the top of the screen, select ExprOff from the FUNCTION menu. As you trace the graph, the displayed values of x, y, and t are updated, where the x- and y-values are calculated from t.

If the cursor moves off the top or bottom of the screen, the coordinate values continue to change and be displayed. However, panning is not possible on parametric curves. To see section of the equations not displayed on the graph, you must change the values of the Window variables.

The ZOOM features work in parametric graphing as they do in function graphing. Only the values of the x Window variables ($x$min, $x$max, and $x$scl) and y Window variables ($y$min, $y$max, and $y$scl) are affected. The values of the t Window variables ($t$min, $t$max, and $t$step) are affected only when you select [ZStandard], in which case, they become $t$min $= 0$, $t$max $= 2\pi$, and $t$step $= \pi/24$. You might want to change the values of the t Window variables to ensure sufficient points are plotted.

2.3.3 Applying Parametric Graphing

Example 3 Simulating Motion

Problem Graph the position of a ball kicked from ground level at an angle of 60° with an initial velocity of 40 ft/sec. (Ignore air resistance.) What is the maximum height, and when is it reached? How far away and when does the ball strike the ground?

Solution If v_0 is the initial velocity and θ is the angle, then the horizontal component of the position of the ball as a function of time is described by

$$X(T) = Tv_0 \cos \theta.$$

The vertical component of the position of the ball as a function of time is described by

$$Y(T) = -16T^2 + Tv_0 \sin \theta.$$

To graph the equations, do as follows:

1. Press $\boxed{\text{MODE}}$ and select Degree, Parametric, and Connected modes.
2. Press $\boxed{\text{Y=}}$ and enter the following expressions to define the parametric equation in terms of t:

   a. $X_{1T} = 40T \cos 60$; press

   $\boxed{\text{CLEAR}}$ **40** $\boxed{\text{X,T,}\theta\text{,n}}$ $\boxed{\text{COS}}$ **60** $\boxed{\text{ENTER}}$

   b. $Y_{1T} = 40T \sin 60 - 16T^2$; press

   $\boxed{\text{CLEAR}}$ **40** $\boxed{\text{X,T,}\theta\text{,n}}$ $\boxed{\text{SIN}}$ **60** $\boxed{)}$ $\boxed{-}$ **16** $\boxed{\text{X,T,}\theta\text{,n}}$ $\boxed{x^2}$ $\boxed{\text{ENTER}}$

3. Set the values of the Window variables appropriately for this problem by pressing $\boxed{\text{WINDOW}}$ and entering the following values as needed:

tmin = 0	xmin = −5	ymin = −5
tmax = 2.5	xmax = 50	ymax = 20
tstep = .02	xscl = 5	yscl = 5

Note: recall for negative numbers, press $\boxed{\text{(−)}}$ not $\boxed{\text{−}}$.

4. To graph the equations, press $\boxed{\text{GRAPH}}$.

5. To explore the graph, press $\boxed{\text{TRACE}}$.

As the cursor moves along the ball's path, observe the changing x-, y-, and t-values at the bottom of the screen. Notice you have a "stop action" picture at each 0.02 sec. See Fig. 2.35.

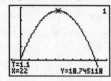

Figure 2.35 Simulating motion.

2.4 Graphing Polar Equations

You can enter up to six equations for graphing.

Example 4 Graphing a Spiral

Problem Graph the spiral of Archimedes, that is, the curve defined by the polar equation $r = a\theta$.

Solution A polar equation $r = f(\theta)$ can be graphed using the calculator's polar graphing features. Thus the spiral of Archimedes (with $a = 0.5$) can be expressed as follows:

1. Press

$$\boxed{\text{MODE}}$$

   a. Select Polar mode.

   b. Choose the default settings, including Normal, Radian, and Connected, for the other modes.

2. Press $\boxed{\text{Y=}}$ and enter the polar equation in terms of θ:

$$r_1 = .5\theta$$

by pressing

$$\boxed{\text{CLEAR}} \quad \boxed{\text{.}} \quad \textbf{5} \quad \boxed{\text{X,T,}\theta\text{,}n} \quad \boxed{\text{ENTER}}$$

3. To graph the equations in the Standard default viewing window, press

$$\boxed{\text{ZOOM}} \ [6\text{:ZStandard}]$$

The graph shows only the first loop of the spiral because the standard default values for the Window variables define θmax as 2π.

4. To explore the behavior of the graph further, press $\boxed{\text{WINDOW}}$ and change θmax to 25.

5. To display the new graph as shown in Fig. 2.36, press

$$\boxed{\text{GRAPH}}$$

6. Press

$$\boxed{\text{ZOOM}} \ [5\text{:ZSquare}]$$

and notice what happens (see Fig. 2.37).

Compare Figs. 2.36 and 2.37.

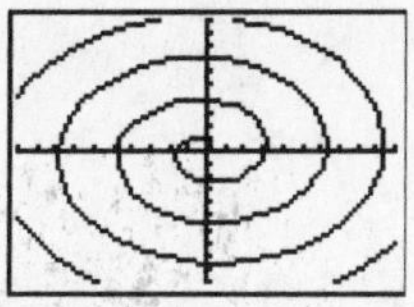

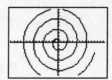

Figure 2.36 Graphing a spiral.

Figure 2.37 The spiral of Archimedes.

Example 5 Graphing a Leafed Rose

Problem Graph a leafed rose defined by the polar equation $r = a \sin(n\theta)$.

Solution Graph a four-leafed rose with $a = 7$ and $n = 2$ as follows:

1. Press

   MODE

   a. Select Polar mode.

   b. Choose the defaults for the the other modes.

2. Press [Y=] and enter the expression

$$r_1 = 7 \sin(2\theta)$$

   by pressing

   CLEAR **7** [SIN] **2** [X,T,θ,n]

3. To graph the rose in the Standard default viewing window, press

   ZOOM [6:ZStandard]

4. Press

   ZOOM [5:ZSquare]

   and observe what happens.

The graph should look like that in Fig. 2.38.

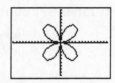

Figure 2.38 Graph of a four-leafed rose.

2.5 Graphing a Sequence

The calculator can graph sequences defined recursively or with an nth-term formula. For example, the sequence $\{1/2, 1/4, 1/8, 1/16...\}$ can be defined by the nth-term formula $a_n = 1/2^n$ or by the recursive formula $a_n = (1/2)a_{n-1}, a_1 = 1/2$.

Example 6 Graphing an *n*th-term Formula Sequence

Problem Graph a sequence defined by $a_n = 1/2^n$.

Solution To graph this sequence, use the following steps

1. Press [MODE] and select the Seq and Dot modes.

2. Press $\boxed{\text{Y=}}$ and enter the expression

$$a_n = 1/2^n$$

by pressing

$$\boxed{\text{CLEAR}}\ \mathbf{1}\ \boxed{\div}\ \mathbf{2}\ \boxed{\wedge}\ \boxed{\text{X,T,}\theta\text{,}n}\ \boxed{\text{ENTER}}$$

(See Fig. 2.39.)

Figure 2.39 Entering the nth-term formula.

3. Press $\boxed{\text{WINDOW}}$ and enter the following values for the Window variables:

nMin$=1$	PlotStart$=1$	$x$min$=0$	$y$min$=0$
nMax$=10$	PlotStep$=1$	$x$max$=10$	$y$max$=1$
		$x$scl$=1$	$y$scl$=1$

4. Press $\boxed{\text{GRAPH}}$.
Your graph should look like that in Fig. 2.40.

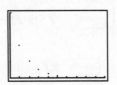

Figure 2.40 Graph of a sequence defined by $a_n = 1/2^n$.

Example 7 Graphing a Recursive Sequence

Problem Graph the recursive sequence defined by $a_n = (1/2)a_{n-1}, a_1 = 1/2$.
Solution To graph this sequence, do the following:

1. Press $\boxed{\text{MODE}}$ and select the Seq and Dot modes.

2. Press $\boxed{\text{Y=}}$ and enter the expression

$$a_n = (1/2)a_{n-1}$$

by pressing
$$\boxed{\text{CLEAR}}\ \boxed{(}\ \mathbf{1}\ \boxed{\div}\ \mathbf{2}\ \boxed{)}\ \boxed{\text{2nd}}\ \boxed{u}\ \boxed{(}\ \boxed{\text{X,T,}\theta\text{,}n}\ \boxed{-}\ \mathbf{1}\ \boxed{)}\ \boxed{\text{ENTER}}$$
and then enter the condition

$$a_1 = 1/2$$

for u(nMin) by pressing
$$\mathbf{1}\ \boxed{\div}\ \mathbf{2}\ \boxed{\text{ENTER}}$$

3. Enter the following values for the WINDOW variables:

nMin$=1$	PlotStart$=1$	$x$min$=0$	$y$min$=0$
nMax$=10$	PlotStep$=1$	$x$max$=10$	$y$max$=1$
		$x$scl$=1$	$y$scl$=1$

4. Press GRAPH.
Your graph should look like that in Fig. 2.41.

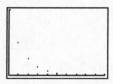

Figure 2.41 Graph of the recursive sequence
defined by $a_n = 1/2a_{n-1} \, a_1$.

2.6 Representing Functions Numerically Using Tables

The TI-84 can represent functions numerically by making a table of selected values for the independent and dependent variables. To create such a table, you enter the function in Y_1 and then designate the initial value and the increment for the independent variable.

Example 8 Describing a Function in a Table; Building the Table Automatically

Problem Describe the function $f(x) = 1/2^x$ in a table and use the automatic feature to build the table.

Solution To solve this problem, do the following:

1. Press MODE and select Function mode.

2. Press Y= and enter the function

$$Y_1 = 1/2^X$$

by pressing

CLEAR **1** ÷ **2** ∧ X,T,θ,n ENTER

3. Access the TABLE SETUP menu by pressing

2nd TBLSET

4. To make the independent variable (X) begin at 0 and increase by 1, press

0 ENTER **1**

Note: [Indpnt: Auto] *is highlighted, indicating the table will be generated automatically. See Fig. 2.42.*

Figure 2.42 The TABLE SETUP menu.

TblStart is the initial value of the independent variable and ΔTbl is the amount by which that variable increases in each row of the table. In Auto mode, the rows of the table are filled in automatically. The table begins with the initial values of X and Y_1 and increments X by ΔTbl. The corresponding value of Y_1 is calculated with each new row.

5. To build the table, press

2nd TABLE

The result should be the table shown in Fig. 2.43.

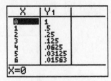

Figure 2.43 Describing a function in a table.

6. To leave the table, press

$$\boxed{\text{2nd}} \;\; \boxed{\text{QUIT}}$$

You can use the cursor-movement keys to scroll through more of the table that lies beyond the bottom and top of the screen.

Example 9 Describing a Function in a Table; Building the Table Manually

Problem Describe the function $f(x) = \sin(x)$ in a table and build the table manually using the Ask mode.

Solution To solve this problem, do the following:

1. Press

$$\boxed{\text{MODE}}$$

   and select the Degree and Function modes.

2. Press $\boxed{\text{Y=}}$ and enter the function

$$Y_1 = \sin X$$

   by pressing

$$\boxed{\text{CLEAR}} \;\; \boxed{\text{SIN}} \;\; \boxed{\text{X,T,}\theta,n} \;\; \boxed{\text{ENTER}}$$

3. Access the TABLE SETUP menu by pressing

$$\boxed{\text{2nd}} \;\; \boxed{\text{TBLSET}}$$

   and select the manual option [Indpnt: Ask].

   In Ask mode, you must enter the values of the independent variable to be used in each row of the table.

4. Enter the independent variables—15, 20, 30—to be used on each row of the table as follows:

$$\boxed{\text{2nd}} \;\; \boxed{\text{TABLE}} \;\; \mathbf{15} \;\; \boxed{\text{ENTER}} \;\; \mathbf{20} \;\; \boxed{\text{ENTER}} \;\; \mathbf{30} \;\; \boxed{\text{ENTER}}$$

   (See Fig. 2.44.)

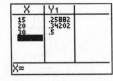

Figure 2.44 Entering the independent variable.

5. To leave the table, press

$$\boxed{\text{2nd}} \;\; \boxed{\text{QUIT}}$$

2.7 Finding Approximations to Solutions

The TI-84 includes powerful tools for finding accurate approximations to solutions of equations. Two of these are the Zero and Intersect options found in the CALCULATE (CALC) menu. The Zero option finds real zeros of a function; the Intersect option finds the points of intersection of two functions.

Example 10 Finding the Real Zero of an Equation

Problem Find the zero of the equation $Y_1 = X^3 - 2X$.

1. Press MODE and select the default modes.

2. Press Y= and enter the function

$$Y_1 = X^3 - 2X$$

by pressing

CLEAR X,T,θ,n ∧ 3 − 2 X,T,θ,n ENTER

3. Graph the equation in the Standard viewing window by pressing

ZOOM [6:ZStandard]

4. Select the Zero option in the CALCULATE menu by pressing

2nd CALC [2:zero]

The graph of the equation appears on the screen, with a request for a Left Bound? in the lower left-hand corner.

5. Press ▶ to move the cursor to just below the largest root (see Fig. 2.45).

6. To accept the Left Bound, press

ENTER

A prompt for the Right Bound replaces the Left Bound prompt in the lower left-hand corner.

7. Use the right cursor-movement key to move the cursor to just above the largest root (see Fig. 2.46).

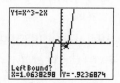

Figure 2.45 Finding the zero of $f(x) = x^3 - 2x$.

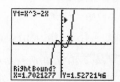

Figure 2.46 The Right Bound.

8. To accept the Right Bound, press ENTER.

A prompt for a Guess? for the root replaces the Right Bound prompt in the lower left-hand corner.

9. Press ◀ to move the cursor until it is close to the zero (see Fig. 2.47).

10. To accept the zero, press ENTER.

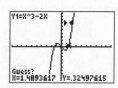

Figure 2.47 The cursor is close to the zero.

The calculator returns an accurate approximation of the zero. Compare this value with $\sqrt{2}$.

Example 11 Finding the Intersection of Two Curves

Problem Find the intersection of the equations $Y_1 = X^3 - 2X$ and $Y_2 = 2\cos X$.

Solution Do the following:

1. Press $\boxed{\text{MODE}}$ and select the default modes.

2. Press $\boxed{\text{Y=}}$ and enter the functions

   a. $Y_1 = X^3 - 2X$; press

   $$\boxed{\text{X,T,}\theta\text{,}n} \quad \boxed{\wedge} \quad 3 \quad \boxed{-} \quad 2 \boxed{\text{X,T,}\theta\text{,}n} \quad \boxed{\text{ENTER}}$$

   b. $Y_2 = 2\cos X$; press

   $$2 \boxed{\text{COS}} \quad \boxed{\text{X,T,}\theta\text{,}n} \quad \boxed{\text{ENTER}}$$

3. Graph the equation in the Standard viewing window by pressing

   $$\boxed{\text{ZOOM}} \text{ [6:ZStandard]}$$

4. Select the Intersect option in the CALCULATE menu by pressing

   $$\boxed{\text{2nd}} \quad \boxed{\text{CALC}} \text{ [5:intersect]}$$

The graph of the equation appears on the screen, with a prompt for the first curve in the intersection (First curve?) in the lower left-hand corner.

5. The cursor is already on the graph of Y_1, so press

   $$\boxed{\text{ENTER}}$$

   to accept the graph marked by the cursor.

The cursor moves to the graph of Y_2. A prompt for the second curve (Second curve?) replaces the first curve prompt in the lower left-hand corner.

6. As the cursor is already on the graph of Y_2, press $\boxed{\text{ENTER}}$.

A prompt for an initial guess (Guess?) replaces the second curve prompt in the lower left-hand corner (see Fig. 2.48).

7. Move the cursor close to the intersection in the first quadrant and press $\boxed{\text{ENTER}}$.

The calculator returns a very accurate approximation of the x- and y-coordinates for the intersection of the two curves (see Fig. 2.49).

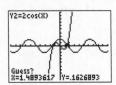

Figure 2.48 An initial guess.

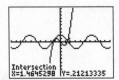

Figure 2.49 An approximation of the intersection of two curves.

2.8 Graphing Piecewise Functions

Piecewise functions like

$$f(x) = \begin{cases} 2x - 1 & \text{if } x \leq 1 \\ x^2 - 2x + 2 & \text{if } x > 1 \end{cases}$$

can be graphed on the calculator using the boolean functions in the TEST menu. To graph this function, do as follows:

1. Press

   and select the default modes, including Func.

2. Press $\boxed{\text{Y=}}$ and enter the expressions

a. $Y_1 = (2X - 1)/(X \leq 1)$; press

$$\boxed{\text{CLEAR}} \quad \boxed{(} \quad \mathbf{2} \boxed{\text{X,T,}\theta,n} \boxed{-} \mathbf{1} \boxed{)} \quad \boxed{\div}$$

$$\boxed{(} \quad \boxed{\text{X,T,}\theta,n} \quad \boxed{\text{2nd}} \quad \boxed{\text{TEST}} \; [6:\leq] \; \mathbf{1} \boxed{)} \quad \boxed{\text{ENTER}}$$

b. $Y_2 = (X^2 - 2X + 2)/(X > 1)$; press

$$\boxed{\text{CLEAR}} \quad \boxed{(} \quad \boxed{\text{X,T,}\theta,n} \boxed{x^2} \quad \boxed{-} \mathbf{2} \boxed{\text{X,T,}\theta,n} \boxed{+} \mathbf{2} \boxed{)} \quad \boxed{\div}$$

$$\boxed{(} \quad \boxed{\text{X,T,}\theta,n} \quad \boxed{\text{2nd}} \quad \boxed{\text{TEST}} \; [3:>] \; \mathbf{1} \boxed{)} \quad \boxed{\text{ENTER}}$$

3. Graph the equations in a $[-2, 2]$ by $[-2, 2]$ viewing window.

The graph should look like that in Fig. 2.50.

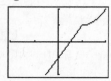

Figure 2.50 Graph of a piecewise function.

The boolean expression $x \leq 1$ returns the value 1 when x is less than or equal to 1, and it returns the value 0 when x is greater than 1. So the function Y_1 is equal to $2x - 1$ when x is less than or equal to 1 and is undefined when x is greater than 1. Because the boolean expression $x > 1$ has the value 1 when it is true and 0 when it is false, Y_2 is equal to $x^2 - 2x + 2$ when $x > 1$ and Y_2 is undefined when $x \leq 1$.

2.9 Working with Graphical Databases

The equations, viewing window, and modes used to create a graph such as that in Section 2.8 can be saved as a graphical database and then retrieved later. After you have selected the desired modes, entered the equations, and created an appropriate viewing window, save the data as follows:

1. Select the StoreGDB option in DRAW [Sto] menu by pressing

$$\boxed{\text{2nd}} \quad \boxed{\text{DRAW}} \quad \boxed{\blacktriangleright} \quad \boxed{\blacktriangleright} \; [3:\text{StoreGDB}]$$

The calculator displays the message 'StoreGDB.'

2. Enter the GRAPHICAL DATABASE menu and select the GDB3 option in the VARS menu by pressing

$$\boxed{\text{VARS}} \; [3:\text{GDB...}] \; [1:\text{GDB1}] \boxed{\text{ENTER}}$$

The calculator returns a DONE message indicating the entered data is saved as Graphical Database 1.

3. Quit the feature by pressing

$$\boxed{\text{CLEAR}}$$

To see how graphical databases work, do the following:

1. Press

$$\boxed{\text{Y=}}$$

and clear the equations in Y_1 and Y_2.

2. Return to the Home screen by pressing

$$\boxed{\text{2nd}} \quad \boxed{\text{QUIT}}$$

3. Retrieve the equations from Graphical Database 1 as follows:

   a. Select the RecallGDB option from the DRAW [Sto] menu by pressing

   [2nd] [DRAW] [▶] [▶] [4:RecallGDB]

   The calculator displays the message 'RecallGDB.'

   b. Enter the GRAPHICAL DATABASE menu and select the GDBI option in the VARS menu by pressing

   [VARS] [3:GDB] [1:GDB1] [ENTER]

The calculator returns a DONE message.

4. Quit the feature by pressing

   [CLEAR]

5. To see the original graph saved, press

   [GRAPH]

You can save the data for up to six graphs in six different graphical databases.

2.10 Drawing Pictures

Several tools in the calculator are useful for drawing pictures and diagrams. These features are found in the DRAW menu.

Example 12 Drawing with DRAW Menu Tools

Problem Duplicate the picture found in Fig. 2.51.
Solution To draw the figure, do the following:

1. Select Func mode, press [Y=] and clear the equations from the edit screen.

2. Select the Decimal viewing window by pressing

   [ZOOM] [4:ZDecimal]

The Graph screen appears and the free-moving cursor is at the origin.

3. Draw a circle as follows:

   a. Select the Circle option from the DRAW menu by pressing

   [2nd] [DRAW] [9:Circle(]

   b. Move the cursor to the point $(1, 1)$ and press ENTER.

   c. Move the cursor to the point $(3, 1)$ and press ENTER.

   A circle with center (1, 1) and radius 2 is drawn on the graph.

4. Draw a diameter of the circle as follows:

   a. Press

   [2nd] [DRAW] [2:Line(]

   b. Move the cursor to the point $(-1, 1)$ and press [ENTER].

   c. Use the cursor-movement keys to drag a line across the circle to the point $(3, 1)$ and press [ENTER].

5. Label the endpoints of the diameter as follows:

   a. Select the Text option by pressing

   [2nd] [DRAW] [0:Text]

   b. Move the cursor text to the left endpoint of the diameter and press

   [ALPHA] **A**

c. Move the cursor next to the right endpoint of the diameter and press

$\boxed{\text{ALPHA}}$ **B**

The graph should resemble that in Fig. 2.51.

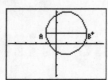

Figure 2.51 Drawing with DRAW
menu tools.

6. Save the picture by pressing

$\boxed{\text{2nd}}$ $\boxed{\text{QUIT}}$ $\boxed{\text{2nd}}$ $\boxed{\text{DRAW}}$ $\boxed{\blacktriangleright}$ $\boxed{\blacktriangleright}$ [1:StorePic] $\boxed{\text{VARS}}$ [4:Picture] [1:Pic1] $\boxed{\text{ENTER}}$

7. Quit the feature and clear the picture by pressing

$\boxed{\text{2nd}}$ $\boxed{\text{QUIT}}$ $\boxed{\text{2nd}}$ $\boxed{\text{DRAW}}$ [1:ClrDraw] $\boxed{\text{ENTER}}$

Press $\boxed{\text{GRAPH}}$ to verify the picture has been erased.

8. To recall the picture, press

$\boxed{\text{2nd}}$ $\boxed{\text{QUIT}}$ $\boxed{\text{2nd}}$ $\boxed{\text{DRAW}}$ $\boxed{\blacktriangleright}$ $\boxed{\blacktriangleright}$ [2:RecallPic] $\boxed{\text{VARS}}$ [4:Picture] [1:Pic1] $\boxed{\text{ENTER}}$

2.11 Working with Increments and Screen Coordinates

When you selected $\boxed{\text{ZOOM}}$ [4:ZDecimal] to set the viewing window in Example 12, the free-moving cursor coordinates each changed by 0.1 units as the cursor moved one pixel horizontally or vertically. This means the relative dimensions of the pixels are 0.1. The relative width of the pixel is stored in the variable Δx and the relative height is stored in the variable Δy. The value of Δx is determined by the formula $(x\text{max} - x\text{min})/94$ and $\Delta y = (y\text{max} - y\text{min})/62$.

You can store values in Δx and Δy directly. Doing so changes the viewing window by altering the values of $x$max and $y$max. To see how this works, observe Δx and Δy in the Standard viewing window by pressing $\boxed{\text{ZOOM}}$ [6:Standard]. Move the cursor one pixel horizontally to see how the x-coordinate changes—this is Δx. Then move the cursor one pixel vertically and notice how the y-coordinate changes—this is Δy.

Next, store 1 in both Δx and Δy as follows:

1. Press

1 $\boxed{\text{STO}\blacktriangleright}$ $\boxed{\text{VARS}}$ [1:Window] [9:ΔY] $\boxed{\text{ENTER}}$ **1** $\boxed{\text{STO}\blacktriangleright}$ $\boxed{\text{VARS}}$ [1:Window] [8:ΔX] $\boxed{\text{ENTER}}$

2. Press $\boxed{\text{GRAPH}}$ and move the cursor.

The screen coordinates change by 1 each time the cursor moves one pixel.

3. To see how the values of the Window variables have changed, press

$\boxed{\text{WINDOW}}$

CHAPTER

3

Graphing with the TI-86

This chapter introduces some basic calculator operations, function graphing features, and an equation solving feature. The following aspects of working with the TI-86 is covered:

- Section 1—the keypad and major features and functions
- Section 2—graphing
- Section 3—applying graphing and SOLVER techniques
- Section 4—applications in graphing functions
- Section 5—graphing parametric equations
- Section 6—graphing polar equations
- Section 7—graphing piecewise functions
- Section 8—other features

To learn more about these features and the many other capabilities of the calculator, consult your TI-86 User's Guide.

3.1 Getting Started on the TI-86

The front of the calculator can be divided into two sections: the viewing screen in the upper third and the key in the lower two-thirds. We discuss both of these in the following sections.

3.1.1 Turning the TI-86 On and Off

To turn on the calculator:

Press ⎡ ON ⎤, which is located in the far lower left-hand corner of the keypad.

To turn off the calculator:

Press ⎡ 2nd ⎤ ⎡ ON ⎤.

⎡ 2nd ⎤ is the orange key in the upper left-hand corner of the keypad. (See Section 3.1.3 for more information and ⎡ 2nd ⎤.) In this manual we will give keystrokes by their function on the keypad, not by the name of the button. For example, we write the keystrokes for turning off the calculator as ⎡ 2nd ⎤ ⎡OFF⎤, not ⎡ 2nd ⎤ ⎡ ON ⎤. Note that the word OFF is in yellow above the ⎡ ON ⎤ button.

When you first turn on the calculator, you see the **Home screen**, which is the calculator's primary viewing screen, and the **entry cursor**, a blinking rectangle (▮) that is the calculator's basic cursor for entering data. On the Home screen, you see the results of the data and instructions you entered at the keyboard.

Note: The TI-86 include a power-saver feature that results in the calculator's turning itself off after approximately three to four minutes of nonuse. To reactivate the calculator when it has powered-off on its own, press ⎡ ON ⎤. When the calculator turns itself off under the power-saver feature, any data on the screen at the time of power-off reappears just as it was before the calculator shut down. If you were in another screen or in a menu, you are returned to your original location.

3.1.2 Exploring the Keypad

The keypad is divided into parts according to the position and color of the keys.
    The keys are grouped according to position as follows:

- Row 1—the **Menu keys**. Used to access the calculator's interactive graphing features.
- Rows 2 and 3 (the first three keys of each row)—the **Editing keys**. Used to edit expressions and values.
- Rows 4—the **Advanced Function keys** (left four keys). Used to access advanced functions through various full-screen menus.
- Row 5–10—the **Scientific Calculator keys**. Used to access the capabilities of a standard scientific calculator.

The keys are grouped according to color as follows:

- Cursor-movement keys (gray)
  Notice the triangles on these four keys. Each triangle points in the direction in which the cursor moves when the key is pressed.
- Number pad (gray)
  The numbers 0–9 are set out in gray, as is the negative sign $\boxed{(-)}$ and the decimal point $\boxed{\cdot}$.
- $\boxed{\text{ENTER}}$
  Causes the calculator to calculate the function you entered. In some cases, it also is used to accept certain variable information and performs other duties.
- All other keys (except $\boxed{\text{2nd}}$ [orange] and $\boxed{\text{ALPHA}}$ [light blue], which we discuss in the next subsections) are black and represent the various features and functions available on the TI-86.

3.1.3 Accessing the Calculator's Features and Functions

The TI-86 offers numerous features and functions, so many that if each were assigned a separate key, the size of the keypad would more than double. Therefore to keep the size of the keypad manageable, most of the keys perform double or triple duty. This capability resembles that of a typewriter or computer keyboard on which each key can be used to access more than one character, number, or function.
    The first level of features or functions is represented by the names or symbols printed on the keys. As on a typewriter, to access one of these, simply press the key. For example, to enter the number 5, press 5. Or to calculate the square of 5, enter the following key sequence:

$$5 \boxed{x^2} \boxed{\text{ENTER}}$$

The second level of features or functions is represented by names or symbols printed in yellow directly above the first. To access this level, press $\boxed{\text{2nd}}$, then the appropriate key. $\boxed{\text{2nd}}$ operates similarly to the SHIFT key on a typewriter or computer keyboard. Notice that when you press $\boxed{\text{2nd}}$, the entry cursor changes in appearance—a blinking highlighted up arrow appears in the center of the rectangle. This is called the **2nd cursor**. For example, suppose you want to find the square root of 5. (Notice that the square root function is accessed via the same key as is the $\boxed{x^2}$ function.) To access the square root function, press $\boxed{\text{2nd}} \, [\sqrt{\ }]$. To complete the calculation of the square root of 5, press

$$5 \boxed{\text{ENTER}}$$

You also can use the calculator's keypad to key in the letters of the alphabet, the special symbols '=' and '_' (space), and the variable letter x. The letters and symbols are shown in blue above the keys. To access them, do the following:

1. Press ALPHA.
   This blue key is located near the upper left-hand corner of the keypad.

2. Press the appropriate letter of symbol.

Note: A short-cut for entering the variable x is to press x-VAR *rather than* 2nd ALPHA **X**.

Accessing and Selecting Advanced Functions via Menus. Through menus you can access advanced functions and operations that you cannot access directly from the keyboard. You reach the menus through the advanced function keys, which include GRAPH, TABLE, PRGM, 2nd STAT, and 2nd MATH. When you press an advanced function key, a row of first-level options appears at the bottom of the screen. Look at the GRAPH menu, which is typical of all the numbered menus. Press GRAPH to reveal the first-level options:

- y(x)=
- WIND
- ZOOM
- TRACE
- GRAPH

The screen can display up to five options. But sometimes there are additional ones; for example, the GRAPH feature has 13 in all. If there are more, a ▶ appears in the far right-hand side at the bottom of the display; see, for example, the ▶ that appears to the right of the GRAPH option. To see the additional options, press

MODE

Press MORE two more times to return to the original five options.

To select a first-level, press the F-numbered key that appears directly below the screen. For example, to select the ZOOM feature, press

[F3:ZOOM]

As you can see, pressing F3 brought up a second level of additional choices that appears in a row *below* the first-level options (see Fig. 3.1), as follows:

- BOX
- ZIN
- ZOUT
- ZSTD
- ZPREV

Figure 3.1 The two levels of Zoom options.

To select one of these options, press

[F-numbered key]

Suppose, however, you want to select a feature such as TRACE that is on the top row. To access this level, press

2nd [M-numbered key]

In summary,

1. to select an item from the *bottom* row of options, press [F#].
2. to select an item from the *top* row of options, press [2nd] [M#].

Keying Sequence Notation for [F#] and [M#] Menus. For menus like the GRAPH menu, we adopt a special keying sequence notation in these instructions. For example, to access the Zoom-in option, you first enter the GRAPH menu, then the ZOOM menu, and finally reach the Zoom-in option. To show you have to enter the key sequence that produces these results, we would write

[GRAPH] [F3:ZOOM] [F2:ZIN]

3.1.4 Entering Commands and Functions

All commands and functions can be found either in two or more menus or directly on the keys. Also, all commands, functions, variables, and program names can be typed directly on the screen letter by letter using [ALPHA].

- [ALPHA] alone enters uppercase letters.
- [2nd] [ALPHA] enters lowercase letters.
- [ALPHA] [ALPHA] triggers the "cap lock" (called ALPHA-lock) feature.

Using the CATALOG/VARIABLES menu. The CATALOG/VARIABLES menu contains all functions, commands, and variables. The first menu item, [F1:CATLG], contains all of the functions and commands in alphabetical order. To access this menu, press

[2nd] [CATLG-VARS] [F1:CATLG]

You can reach the command or function you want in two ways:

1. a. Press

[▲] and [▼]

to scroll through the list until you reach the item you want.

b. Press

[ENTER]

2. a. Press the letter on the keypad that corresponds to the first letter of the command you want to reach (in this case, there is no need to press [ALPHA] first).

b. Press

[▲] and [▼]

cursor-movement keys to reach the item you want.

c. Press

[ENTER]

Accessing Variables. All variables can be found in the other menu items of the CATALOG/ VARIABLES menu. Variable names may be up to eight characters in either uppercase and/or lowercase. Note, these names are case-sensitive, which means, for example, that the variables *HITHERE, hithere*, and *Hithere* are three different variables.

Using Concatenation. The TI-86 supports the combining of two or more commands. This is done using a ":" to separate commands. For example, to store the number 20 in *N* and then evaluate

$$100 \cdot 1.06^{N}$$

Press

20 $\boxed{\text{STO►}}$ **N** $\boxed{\text{2nd}}$ $\boxed{\text{[:]}}$ $\boxed{\text{ALPHA}}$ **1000** $\boxed{\times}$ **1** $\boxed{•}$ **06** $\boxed{\wedge}$ $\boxed{\text{ALPHA}}$ **N** $\boxed{\text{ENTER}}$

(see Fig. 3.2).

Figure 3.2 Using concatenation.

3.1.5 Setting the Contrast of the Screen's Display

The brightness and contrast of the display depend on room lighting, battery freshness, viewing angle, and adjustment of the display contrast. You can adjust the display contrast at any time to suit your viewing angle and lighting conditions. The contrast setting is retained in memory when the calculator is turned off. To adjust the contrast, do the following:

1. To increase the contrast,
   - press $\boxed{\text{2nd}}$ and then
   - press *and hold* $\boxed{\blacktriangle}$.

2. To decrease the contrast,
   - press $\boxed{\text{2nd}}$ and then
   - press *and hold* $\boxed{\blacktriangledown}$.

Notice that as you change the contrast setting up or down, two things happen:

1. The display contrast changes.

2. A number in the upper right-hand corner of the screen changes to reflect the current contrast setting. This number moves between 0 (the lightest contrast) and 9 (the darkest contrast).

Observe also that if you adjust the contrast setting to 0, the display might appear to go completely blank. To correct this, simply press $\boxed{\text{2nd}}$ and then press and hold $\boxed{\blacktriangle}$ until the display reappears.

Note: When the batteries are low, the display begins to dim, especially during calculations. You will need to adjust the contrast to a higher setting to compensate for this. However, if you need to adjust it as high as 8 or 9, you should replace the batteries soon.

3.1.6 Resetting the Calculator

Resetting the calculator erases all previously entered data and programs. Before beginning the sample problems in these instructions, reset the calculator.

To reset the calculator, do the following:

1. Turn the calculator on by pressing $\boxed{\text{ON}}$.

2. Press $\boxed{\text{2nd}}$ $\boxed{\text{MEM}}$.

The MEM (memory) first-level menu is displayed (see Fig. 3.3).

Figure 3.3 The MEM (memory) first-level menu.

3. Press

[F3:RESET]

The second-level menu appears below the first-level menu (see Fig. 3.4).

4. Press

[F1:ALL]

The prompt "Are you sure?" appears on the screen.

5. Press

[F4:YES]

The screen goes blank.

Clearing the memory causes the screen display to disappear (this is the default setting for the screen display), so you next need to increase the contrast of the screen display in order to see the display.

6. Increase the screen display by pressing

   a. [2nd] and

   b. pressing and *holding* [▲].

The screen displays the message "Mem cleared Defaults set" (see Fig. 3.5).

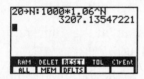

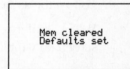

Figure 3.4 The MEM first-level and second-level menus.

Figure 3.5 Resetting the calculator.

7. To return to Home screen, press

[CLEAR]

3.1.7 Displaying Data on the Screen

The TI-86 displays both text and graphics. For text, the viewing screen can show up to eight lines of 21 characters per line each. When all eight lines are filled, the text scrolls off the top of the screen.

For simple functions, the TI-86 shows the results immediately. However, when the calculator is involved in a relatively lengthy calculation or graphing function, a small moving line appears in the upper right-hand corner of the screen to signal that the calculator is busy.

One advantage of the TI-86, in contrast to a typical scientific calculator, is that you can see the complete expression *and* its solution simultaneously on the screen. For example, enter $1000(1.06)^{10}$ by pressing

1000 [×] **1** [·] **06** [^] **10**

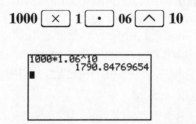

Figure 3.6 The expression $1000(1.06)^{10}$ and its solution.

Notice that the entire expression is shown on the first line beginning at the left margin. Press [ENTER] to have the expression evaluated. After the evaluation, the result is shown on the right-hand side of the second line of the display, while the cursor is positioned on the left-hand side of the third line, ready for you to enter the next expression (see Fig. 3.6). Note that if an expression requires more than one line, it will flow automatically to the next line and the result and cursor will be moved down one line each.

3.1.8 Changing Modes

A **mode** is one of a number of optional systems of operation. For example, you can choose to operate in normal, scientific, or engineering mode with regard to how numeric results are displayed on the screen. To view the Mode screen, press

$$\boxed{\text{2nd}} \; \boxed{\text{MODE}}$$

The first column of options are the defaults: Normal, Float, Radian, RectC (Rectangular), Func (Function), Dec, RectV, and dxDerl.

To change a mode, do the following:

1. Press

$$\boxed{\text{2nd}} \; \boxed{\text{MODE}}$$

2. Move the cursor to the row and column that contain the mode you want to change.

3. Press $\boxed{\text{ENTER}}$.

4. Follow the same sequence if you want to change other modes.

5. When you have changed all the modes you want at that time, return to the previous screen on which you were working by pressing $\boxed{\text{CLEAR}}$.

For example, to change the Function mode to the Parametric mode, do the following:

1. Press

$$\boxed{\text{2nd}} \; \boxed{\text{MODE}}$$

2. Press the cursor-movement keys until you reach Param.

3. Press

$$\boxed{\text{ENTER}} \; \boxed{\text{CLEAR}}$$

New selections are saved in the calculator's memory, even when the computer is turned off, until you change them again.

3.1.9 Entering Expressions

You enter expressions as you would write them on a single line. In Example 1, we demonstrate how to enter an expression.

An expression to be evaluated may contain variable names. You also can enter an expression that evaluates a number directly in an edit screen such as WIND. For example, you could enter $2A - \cos 2.2$ directly in the xMin field of WIND (assuming A is defined).

Further, you can store an unevaluated expression as an equation variable. For example, in Function mode, this is done using the $\boxed{\text{STO▸}}$ feature as follows:

1. Enter the value to be stored.

2. Press

The symbol → is copied to the cursor location and the keypad is set in ALPHA-lock (recall that ALPHA-lock means all subsequent key presses of letters will be uppercase).

3. Enter the name of the variable to which the value is assigned.

4. Take the keypad out of ALPHA-lock by pressing

[ALPHA]

5. Press

[ENTER]

Example 1 Entering an Expression

Problem Determine the future value of annuity.

Solution You invest $25 at the beginning of each month at 6% annual interest, compounded monthly. We want to find out how much money you would have at the end of 3 years. We use the following future value formula:

$$PMT = \frac{(1+I)^{N+1} - (1+I)}{I}$$

To solve this problem, do the following:

1. Place the calculator in Function mode by pressing

[2nd] [MODE]

and selecting Func, then press [CLEAR] to exit to the Home screen, followed by [CLEAR] to erase the Home screen.

2. Store the value $25 for the payment amount in the variable *PMT* by pressing

25 [STO▶]

The symbol → is copied to the cursor location and the keypad is set in ALPHA-lock.

3. Press

PMT [ALPHA]

(see Fig. 3.7).

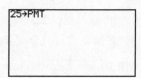

Figure 3.7 Store 25 in *PMT*.

4. To begin another command on the same line (concatenation), press

[2nd] [:]

5. Store the expression for the number of periods (years × 12) in the variable *N* by pressing

3 [×] **12** [STO▶] **N** [ALPHA]

6. Begin a new command and store the interest per period (rate ÷ 12) in the variable *I* by pressing

(see Fig. 3.8).

Figure 3.8 Store expressions in *N* and in *I*.

7. Enter the expression to define the future value formula by pressing

The values of the variables are stored and the expression is evaluated. The 12-digit result of the expression is shown on the right-hand side of the next line (see Fig. 3.9).

Figure 3.9 The evaluated expression.

8. Access the Mode screen by pressing 〔2nd〕 〔MODE〕 and change the display mode to two fixed decimal places by pressing

(Two decimal places are appropriate since we are working in dollars.) (See Fig. 3.10).

Figure 3.10 Changing the display mode to two decimal places.

9. To reevaluate the last answer, press

〔2nd〕 〔QUIT〕 〔ENTER〕

The new result is displayed with two decimal places.

If you save $25 per month for 36 months invested at 6% annual interest, compounded monthly, you will have $988.32 at the end of 3 years (see Fig. 3.11). (Do not clear these equations from the calculator as you will need them for other examples in these instructions.)

Figure 3.11 The new result displayed with two decimal places.

3.1.10 Recalling and Editing Expressions

The TI-86 offers two tools that help you quickly recall and edit the last entered command and its result: Last Entry and Last Answer.

Example 1 (continued)

If you continue to invest $25 per month for another year, how much will you have at the end of the additional year? To find out, follow these steps:

1. Recall the last executed expression by pressing

[2nd] [ENTRY]

The cursor is positioned at the end of the expression.

2. Use the cursor-movement keys to place the cursor over the 3 in the first line of the recalled expression and type 4 (see Fig. 3.12).

Figure 3.12 Recalling and changing that last expression.

3. Execute the command by pressing [ENTER].

The solution is displayed on the next line.

If you save $25 per month for 48 months invested at 6% annual interest, compounded monthly, you will have $1359.21 at the end of the fourth year (see Fig. 3.13).

Figure 3.13 The new solution.

What if you were to save $50 per month? The amount would double because the variable *PMT* is directly proportional to the total. To calculate how much interest you would earn under these circumstances, use the LAST ANSWER feature as follows:

1. Recall the last answer calculated from the previous expression by pressing

[2nd] [ANS]

The variable Ans appears in the display.

2. The calculate the new solution, press

[×] 2 [ENTER]

The solution is displayed on the next line.

If you save $50 per month at 6% annual interest, compounded monthly, for 4 years, at the end of the fourth year, you will have $2718.42 (see Fig. 3.14).

Figure 3.14 Using the LAST ANSWER feature.

3.2 Graphing on the TI-86

Two commands closely related to graphing are GRAPH and 2nd |SOLVER|. Each gives you access to a menu of options that enable you, among other things, to enter functions or equations for graphing, to zoom in or out on a graph, and to trace the path of a graph. Next, we summarize some of the more often used graphing options that both menus feature and follow with a more detailed discussion of them in which we use a function graphing example to illustrate.

- Edit screens
  Usually accessed by pressing

$$\text{GRAPH} \; [\text{F1:y(x)} =] \text{ or } \boxed{\text{2nd}} \; |\text{SOLVER}|$$

  They provide space in which you enter, edit, and display the functions or equations you want to graph.

  a. In Function graphing mode, you can store, graph, and analyze up to 99 functions.
  b. In Polar graphing mode, you can store, graph, and analyze up to 99 equations.
  c. In Parametric graphing mode, you can store, graph, and analyze up to 99 pairs of equations.
  d. In Differential equation graphing mode, you can store, graph, and analyze up to nine first-order differential equations.

- WIND
  Displays an edit screen on which you define the viewing window for a graph.

- ZOOM
  Displays a menu of options that enable you, among other actions, to zoom-in on a portion of the graph and to otherwise change the appearance of the viewing window.

- TRACE
  Displays the last graph generated and the **Trace cursor**, a blinking × with a blinking box in its center, that you use to trace the path of the graphed function.

- GRAPH
  Displays the graph of the currently selected functions or equations in the chosen viewing window.

3.2.1   Edit Screen: Entering a Function

In Function graphing mode, you can enter up to 99 functions for graphing. To access the $y(x) =$ edit screen, press

$$\text{GRAPH} \; [\text{F1:y(x)} =]$$

It's usually best to clear any old equations appearing on the screen before entering new equations. Clear previous equations entered on the screen as follows:

1. Position the cursor on the equation to be deleted.

2. Press

$$\boxed{\text{CLEAR}}$$

Example 2 Graphing and Solving a Function

Problem Graph and determine the solution to $y = x^3 - 2x$ and $y = 2 \cos x$.
Solution Solve this problem as follows:

1. Access the $y(x) =$ edit screen in the GRAPH feature by pressing

$$\text{GRAPH} \; [\text{F1:y(x)} =]$$

The screen displays y1 = followed by an empty field in which you enter the function. The entry cursor is positioned in the field.

2. Enter the following expressions:

a. y1 = $x^3 - 2x$; press

x-VAR (or [F1:x]) ∧ 3 − 2 x-VAR (or [F1:x]) ENTER

The function is entered in the y1 field and the cursor moves to the field next to y2. The = sign of y1 is highlighted, indicating the function has been selected for graphing.

b. *y2* = 2 cos *x*; press

2 COS x-VAR (or [F1:x]) ENTER

The function is entered in the y2 field and the cursor moves to the field next to y3. Here, too, the = sign at y2 is highlighted, indicating this function also has been selected for graphing (see Fig. 3.15).

Figure 3.15 Selecting an equation for graphing.

Do not erase these functions as they are used in later examples.

Selecting Functions for Graphing. As indicated in these steps, highlighting the = sign before the function selects that function for graphing. You may select as many of the functions you enter as you want. To select a function, do the following:

1. Position the entry cursor next to the = sign of the equation to be selected.
2. Press

[F5:SELCT]

Follow the same instructions to deselect an equation, that is, to have it not be graphed.

3.2.2 GRAPH: Displaying the Exploring the Graph

To plot and display any graph in the current viewing window, press

GRAPH [F5:GRAPH]

However, because you are already in the GRAPH feature, graph the following functions entered in Example 2 in Section 3.2.1 by pressing

2nd [M5:GRAPH]

(See Fig. 3.16. Note that you may have different viewing window. See the next section for setting a viewing window.)

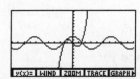

Figure 3.16 Graph of $x^3 - 2x$ and 2 cos *x*.

When the plotting is completed, you can explore the graph using the **free-moving cursor**, a plus sign (+) with a blinking center. Note that when you first graph the functions, this cursor as well as the coordinates of the cursor's position might not be visible. Press any of the cursor-movement keys and the cursor will appear near the origin of the *x*- and *y*-axes and the coordinates will appear at the bottom of the viewing screen (in Rectangular mode, these coordinates are the *x*- and *y*-coordinates and in Polar mode, they are the *r*- and *θ*-coordinates). Press any cursor-movement key and notice how the coordinates change as the cursor changes position. This cursor can be used to identify the coordinates of any location on the graph.

To view the graph without the cursor or the coordinates, press either

GRAPH or ENTER

Press a cursor-movement key to cause the cursor to reappear. It will reappear in the same position it was in when you first pressed ENTER.

This cursor moves from dot to dot on the screen, so be aware that when you move it to a dot that appears to be "on" a function, it might be near, but not on, that function. The coordinate value is accurate to within the width of the dot. To move the cursor *exactly* along a function, use the TRACE feature.

Note: Coordinate values at the bottom of the viewing screen always appear in floating decimal-point format. The numeric display settings in MODE do not affect coordinate display.

3.2.3   WINDOW: Defining the Viewing Window

The WINDOW feature enables you to choose the coordinates of the viewing window that defines the portion of the coordinate plane that appears in the display. The values of WINDOW variables determine the following:

- the size of the viewing window
- the scale units for each axis

You can view and change these values almost any time you need or want. Do this as follows for Example 2:

1. Press

GRAPH [F2:WIND]

The Window edit screen appears as shown in Fig. 3.17, which displays the default values for this feature. The entry cursor is positioned at the value of the first variable.

2. For each value you want to change,

   a. Move the cursor to the current value and
   b. type in the new value.

The new value overwrites the old.

3. After changing the values, leave the screen by pressing

2nd [QUIT]

You are returned to the Home screen.

4. To see the graph in the new window, press

GRAPH [F5:GRAPH]

The variables are defined as follows:

- *x*Min, *x*Max, *y*Min, and *y*Max
  Tell the minimum and maximum *x*- and *y*-coordinates for the desired viewing window; in Fig. 3.17, these values define the Standard window of $[-10, 10]$ by $[-10, 10]$.

- *x*Scl and *y*Scl

  Give the distance between consecutive tick marks on the coordinate axes; in Fig. 3.17, the distance is a value of 1.

- *x*Res

  Set the pixel resolution for graphs of functions. Acceptable values are 1 through 8. (See also Fig. 3.18).

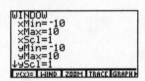

Figure 3.17 The Window edit screen.

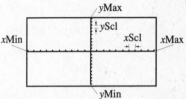

Figure 3.18 The viewing window.

3.2.4 ZOOM: Magnifying and Shrinking Parts of a Graph

The ZOOM feature enables you, among other capabilities, to adjust that portion of the viewing window that you see, for example, by magnifying a portion or retreating to give you a more global view. To access the ZOOM menu, press

GRAPH [F3:ZOOM]

(See Fig. 3.19).

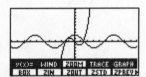

Figure 3.19 The ZOOM menu.

The Zoom-In Option. The Zoom-In ([F2:ZIN]) option allows you to zoom-in on (magnify) a portion of the graph. Using this option adjusts the viewing window in both the *x*- and *y*-directions according to the zoom factors set in the ZOOM FACTORS screen. (To default ZOOM FACTORS are 4 for *x*Fact and *y*Fact. You can access the ZOOM FACTORS screen from the ZOOM menu by pressing MORE MORE [F2:ZFACT]). To use this option on Example 2, do the following:

1. Press

GRAPH [F3:ZOOM] [F2:ZIN]

2. Place the free-moving cursor approximately in the center of the area you want to magnify. For example, move the cursor to the apparent intersection in the first quadrant as shown in Fig. 3.20.

3. Press ENTER (see Fig. 3.21).

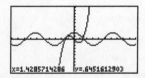

Figure 3.20 The cursor is on the apparent intersection in the first quadrant.

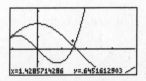

Figure 3.21 The adjusted viewing window.

The calculator adjusts the viewing window by the zoom factors and replots the selected functions with the cursor in the center of the new window.

4. To zoom in more,

   a. centered at the same point, press

   [ENTER]

   b. centered at new point,

   • move the free-moving cursor to the point you want as the center of the new viewing window, and

   • press

   [ENTER]

5. Exit the Zoom-In option by pressing

   [EXIT]

The zoomed-in graph remains on the screen and the menu lines appear at the bottom of the screen.

6. To redisplay the graph in the Standard window, press [F4:ZSTD].

The Zoom Box Option. You also can use the Zoom Box [F1:Box] option to adjust the viewing window by drawing a box anywhere on the screen display to define the size of the desired window.

To draw the box from the Graph screen, do the following:

1. Press

   [GRAPH] [F3:ZOOM] [F1:BOX]

2. Move the **Zoom-In Cursor**, a cross with a blinking center, to upper right-hand corner of the area where you want one corner of the new viewing window to be.

3. Press

   [ENTER]

*The cursor changes to the **Zoom Box cursor**, a box with a blinking center.*

4. Move the cursor to the diagonally opposite corner of the desired viewing window.

The outline of the new viewing window is drawn as you move the cursor (see Fig. 3.22).

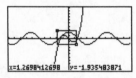

Figure 3.22 Using the Zoom Box option.

5. To accept the new cursor location, press

   [ENTER]

The graph is replotted using the box outline as the new viewing window, similar to Fig. 3.23.

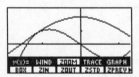

Figure 3.23 The graph replotted using the box outline.

6. To leave the graph display, press

$$\boxed{\text{EXIT}} \ \boxed{\text{EXIT}} \ \text{or} \ \boxed{\text{CLEAR}} \ \boxed{\text{CLEAR}}$$

7. To redisplay the graph, press

$$\boxed{\text{GRAPH}}$$

You can continue to draw boxes to zoom-in on even more specific portions of the graph.

3.2.5 TRACE: Moving the Cursor Along a Function's Graph

The TRACE feature enables you to trace the graph of functions. As you do this, the coordinates at the bottom of the viewing screen change to reflect the changing position of the cursor. (If the cursor moves off the top or bottom of the screen, the values continue to change.) Note that in the Rectangular coordinate system, the y-value is the calculated function value of x, that is, if $y1 = f(x)$, the value of y shown is $f(x)$.

   Trace the functions graphed in Section 5 as follows:

1. Press

$$\boxed{\text{GRAPH}} \ [\text{F4:TRACE}]$$

*The **Trace cursor**, a box with a blinking center appears on the graph of y1.*

2. a. To trace a graph, press the left or right cursor-movement keys.
   b. To move among all functions that are defined *and* selected (that is, active), press the up or down cursor-movement keys.

A number in the upper right-hand corner tells you which function is being traced.

   c. To pan in order to view graphs that disappear off the left or right of the screen, press *and hold* the left or right cursor-movement key.

3. To leave the feature and return to Home screen, press

$$\boxed{\text{EXIT}} \ \boxed{\text{EXIT}} \ \text{or} \ \boxed{\text{CLEAR}} \ \boxed{\text{CLEAR}}$$

4. To view the graph after leaving the feature, press

$$\boxed{\text{GRAPH}}$$

To view at any time the original functions entered for this graph, press

$$\boxed{\text{GRAPH}} \ [\text{F1:y(x)} =]$$

3.3 Applying Graphing and SOLVER Techniques

On the TI-86, you can explore problems in several different ways. For example, you can solve many problems either graphically or by using the SOLVER feature. To demonstrate these facilities, we use a continuing example for determining the amount of illumination. The data we need for this example follows.

   The amount of illumination on a surface is

- proportional to the intensity of the source,
- inversely proportional to the square of the distance, and
- proportional to the sine of the angle between the source and the surface.

The formula for determining the amount of illumination on a point on a surface is

$$\text{ILLUM} = \text{INTEN} \cdot \frac{\sin \theta}{\text{DIST}^2}$$

(See Fig. 3.24).

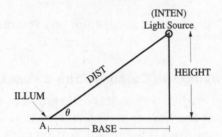

Figure 3.24 $\text{ILLUM} = \text{INTEN} \cdot \dfrac{\sin \theta}{\text{DIST}^2}$

Appropriate units for distances are as follows:

- foot-candles (ft-c) for illumination
- candlepower (CP) for intensity
- feet (ft)

From geometry,

$$\sin \theta = \frac{\text{HEIGHT}}{\text{DIST}};$$

therefore we can define illumination in terms of intensity and height as follows:

$$\text{ILLUM} = \text{INTEM} \cdot \frac{\text{HEIGHT}}{\text{DIST}^3}$$

Also from geometry, we have the following distance formula:

$$\text{DIST}^2 = \text{BASE}^2 + \text{HEIGHT}^2$$

3.3.1 Entering an Equation in the SOLVER

Using the SOLVER feature, you can solve an equation for any variable in the equation. You also can observe the effect that changing the value of one variable has on another and apply "what if" scenarios.

Recall that you can store an unevaluated expression as an equation variable. Store the distance formula, $\text{DIST}^2 = \text{BASE}^2 + \text{HEIGHT}^2$, for use in later examples as follows:

1. Return to and clear the Home screen.

2. Press

$\boxed{\text{ALPHA}}$ $\boxed{\text{ALPHA}}$ **DIST** $=$ $\boxed{\text{ALPHA}}$ $\boxed{\text{2nd}}$ $\boxed{[\sqrt{\ }]}$ $\boxed{(}$ $\boxed{\text{ALPHA}}$ $\boxed{\text{ALPHA}}$ **BASE** $\boxed{\text{ALPHA}}$ $\boxed{x^2}$

$\boxed{+}$ $\boxed{\text{ALPHA}}$ $\boxed{\text{ALPHA}}$ **HEIGHT** $\boxed{\text{ALPHA}}$ $\boxed{x^2}$ $\boxed{)}$ $\boxed{\text{ENTER}}$

(See Fig. 3.25).

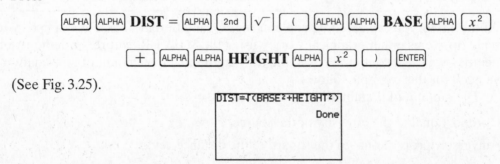

Figure 3.25 Store the distance formula, $\text{DIST}^2 = \text{BASE}^2 + \text{HEIGHT}^2$.

Example 3 Defining and Graphing a Function Using SOLVER

Problem Graph the illumination equation.

$$\text{ILLUM} = \text{INTEN} \cdot \frac{\text{HEIGHT}}{\text{DIST}^3}$$

Solution To define illumination in terms of intensity and height, we use the data given at the beginning of Section 3.3 and follow these steps:

1. Display the SOLVER edit screen by pressing

[2nd] [SOLVER] [CLEAR]

2. Enter the equation by pressing

[ALPHA] [ALPHA] **ILLUM = INTEN** [ALPHA] [×] [ALPHA] [ALPHA] **HEIGHT** [ALPHA] [÷]

(See Fig. 3.26). Notice that as you enter more than 17 characters, the equation scrolls. Ellipsis dots (...) indicate that not all of the equation is displayed on the line. To scroll the equation so you can see the rest of it, press the left and right cursor-movement keys.

Figure 3.26 Entering the equation in the SOLVER edit screen.

3. To insert the distance formula, copy the letters DIST from the menu and to the cursor location by pressing [F1:DIST].

4. Complete the equation that defines illumination in terms of intensity and height by pressing

 3

(See Fig. 3.27).

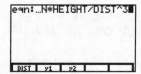

Figure 3.27 Equation defining illumination in terms of intensity and height.

5. Press [ENTER].

*The SOLVER screen appears as in Fig. 3.28. The variables are listed in the order in which they appear in the equation; for example, the variables HEIGHT and BASE, which define the equation variable DIST. The cursor is positioned after the 5 sign following the first variable. If a variable has a current value, that value is shown. **Bound** defines a limit for the value of the solution; its default values are $-1\text{E}99$ to $1\text{E}99$.*

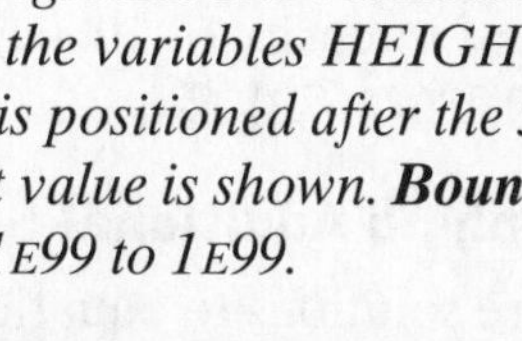

Figure 3.28 The SOLVER screen.

3.3.2 Solving for a Variable

The calculator can solve the equation for the variable on which the cursor appears. This is done using the Solve option from the SOLVE menu. Example 3 continues as an illustration.

Example 3 (continued) Determining the Illumination on a Surface

Problem Determine the illumination on a surface 25 ft from a 50-ft pole if the light intensity is 1000 CP.

Solution Solve this problem as follows:

1. Use ENTER or the cursor-movement keys to highlight the variable for which to assign a value. Entering a new value updates any that are already assigned to a variable and stored in memory. Assign the following variables:

   a. INTEN = 1000
   b. HEIGHT = 50
   c. BASE = 25

The values for each are updated on the screen and in memory (see Fig. 3.29).

Figure 3.29 Assigning values for the variables.

2. Move the cursor to the unknown variable, *ILLUM* and press

   [F5:SOLVE]

   from the SOLVE menu.

   The TI-86 will calculate the equation, display the solution (see Fig. 3.30), and update the value of the variable in memory. A square dot appears next to *ILLUM* to indicate that is the variable solved for. Notice that left–rt = 0 appears at the bottom of the screen; this shows the difference between the left-hand and right-hand sides of the equation, evaluated at the current value of the independent variable (*ILLUM*, in this case).

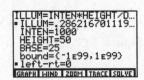

Figure 3.30 The solution .28621670111999 ft-c.

For a 50-ft pole and light intensity of 1000 CP, the illumination on the surface 25 ft from the pole is approximately 0.28621670112 ft-c.

3.3.3 Finding and Graphing Additional Solutions

You can continue to explore solutions to equations and solve for any variable within the equation using "what if" questions.

Example 3 (continued) Finding the Height at which to Place a Light

Problem If the desired illumination is exactly 0.2 ft-c and the intensity is 1000 CP, at what height on the pole should the light be placed?

Solution Solve this problem as follows:

1. Change the value of *ILLUM* to .2, as follows:

    a. Move the cursor to *ILLUM*.
    b. Press [CLEAR].
    c. Type ⎡ · ⎤ **2**.

The square dots next to ILLUM and left–rt = 0 disappear, indicating the solution is not current (see Fig. 3.31).

Figure 3.31 Square dots disappear, indicating solution is not current.

2. Move the cursor to *HEIGHT* and solve by pressing [F5:SOLVE].
    It is not necessary to clear the value of the variable for which you are solving. If it is not cleared, the value is used as the initial guess.

The equation is solved for HEIGHT and the value is displayed (see Fig. 3.32). (The solution is dependent on the initial guess and bound.)

Figure 3.32 The equation solved for *HEIGHT*.

3. Change the values of the WINDOW variables. From the SOLVER menu, do the following:

    a. Press [F2:WIND].
    b. Set the following new values for the variables:

$$x\text{Min} = 0 \qquad\qquad y\text{Min} = -1 \qquad\qquad x\text{Res} = 1$$
$$x\text{Max} = 100 \qquad\qquad y\text{Max} = 1$$
$$x\text{scl} = 10 \qquad\qquad y\text{scl} = 10$$

(see Fig. 3.33).

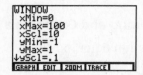

Figure 3.33 Entering the new values on the Window edit screen.

4. Graph by pressing [F1:GRAPH}

    The graph plots the selected variable as the independent variable on the *x*-axis and left–rt as the dependent variable on the *y*-axis. Solutions exist for the equation at the point on the graph where the function intersects the *x*-axis. So in this case, the calculator graphs the variable *HEIGHT* on the *x*-axis and left–rt on the *y*-axis (see Fig. 3.34). The calculation for left–rt is the following:

$$\text{left–rt} = \text{ILLUM} - \text{INTEN} \cdot \text{HEIGHT}/(\text{BASE}^2 + \text{HEIGHT}^2)^{3/2}$$

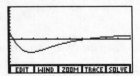

Figure 3.34 Graph of the solution.

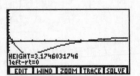

Figure 3.35 The cursor showing the value of *HEIGHT*.

Notice from the graph that this problem has at least two solutions. So far, we have found the solution for *HEIGHT* as the larger value, *x* = 63.458763246 ... (see Fig. 3.32). To solve for the other value of *HEIGHT*, we must supply a new initial guess or alter the bound. We elect to supply a new guess, as follows:

1. Move the cursor near the point at which the function crosses the *x*-axis at the smaller value. The value of *HEIGHT* identified by the cursor, as shown in Fig. 3.35, is used as the new initial guess.

2. From the SOLVER menu, press [F5:SOLVE].

The TI-86 will calculate the equation and display the new values of the variables. Note the square next to the variable HEIGHT, indicating that variable is the one solved (see Fig. 3.36).

Figure 3.36 The solution for *HEIGHT*.

When the illumination on the surface is 0.2 ft-c and the intensity is 1000 CP, the height of the light source can be approximately either 3.20222125 ft or 63.45876325 ft.

3.4 Applications in Graphing Functions

Recall that on the TI-86, functions are graphed for *x* and *y*, where *x* is the independent variable and *y* = *y*(*x*). Recall also that you can store unevaluated expressions using the [STO▶] feature. We continue Example 3 to demonstrate entering and graphing functions.

Example 3 (continued) **Defining and Graphing a Function**

Problem Graph the illumination equation

$$\text{ILLUM} = \text{INTEN} \cdot \frac{\text{HEIGHT}}{\text{DIST}^3}$$

and find the height at which the maximum illumination is achieved for a 25-ft base and an intensity of 1000 CP.

Solution To define and graph the equation, do the following:

1. Begin from the Home screen and store the unevaluated expression *x* in an equation variable *HEIGHT* by pressing

ALPHA ALPHA **HEIGHT** = ALPHA x-VAR ENTER

(See Fig. 3.37). (*INTEN* and *BASE* still contain the values 1000 and 25, respectively.)

```
DIST=√(BASE²+HEIGHT²)
                        Done
HEIGHT=x
                        Done
```

Figure 3.37 Storing the unevaluated expression *x*
in equation variable *HEIGHT*.

2. Select the $y(x)$ = edit screen from the GRAPH menu by pressing

GRAPH [F1:y(x)=]

3. Clear the expressions in the $y(x)$ = edit screen by pressing

CLEAR ENTER CLEAR

4. Recall the expression stored in an equation variable and place it at the cursor location. Do this using the RCL feature.

   a. Press

   2nd [RCL]

Rcl appears in the lower left-hand corner of the screen, followed by the cursor (see Fig. 3.38).

   b. Type the equation variable *eqn*. Press

   2nd ALPHA **E** 2nd ALPHA **Q** 2nd ALPHA **N**

   Recall that the illumination equation was stored in the equation variable *eqn*.

   c. Press

   ENTER

The equation is copied into the y1 = field. The highlighted = sign indicates the equation is selected for graphing (see Fig. 3.39).

Figure 3.38 Using the RCL feature.

Figure 3.39 Copying the illumination equation into the *y*1 = field.

5. Move the cursor to the beginning of the equation and delete ILLUM =.

6. Graph the function by pressing

2ND [M5:GRAPH]

HEIGHT is replaced by x and the current value of x is used. In Fig. 3.40, the graph of the function for $0 \leq x \leq 100$ is plotted. The graph shows there is one maximum value of ILLUM for a height between 0 and 100.

7. To display the current and *x*- and *y*-coordinates values, press the right cursor-movement key.

8. Move the cursor to the apparent maximum of the function (see Fig. 3.41).

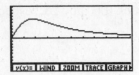

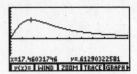

Figure 3.40 Graph of function for $0 \leq x \leq 100$.

Figure 3.41 The apparent maximum of the function.

The display shows the maximum illumination is .61290322581 CP for heights from 14.285714286 ft to 21.428271429 ft, within an accuracy of one pixel width.

In this example, accuracy$_x$ is .793650793651 and accuracy$_y$ is .032258064516, calculated as follows:

$$\text{Accuracy}_x = \frac{(x\text{Max} - x\text{Min})}{126} = .793650793651$$

$$\text{Accuracy}_y = \frac{(y\text{Max} - y\text{Min})}{62} = .032258064516$$

9. Use the TRACE feature to move along a function until you reach the largest y-value. The maximum illumination is .61577762623 CP if the height is 17.46031746 ft (see Fig. 3.42). This value of y is the function value $f(x)$ at the x-value displayed. Note that this value differs from that found with the free-moving cursor, which is based on the values of the WINDOW variables.

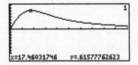

Figure 3.42 The maximum illumination of .61577762623 CP.

3.4.1 Finding a Maximum Graphically

With the operations on the GRAPH [Math] menu, you can determine the location of the minimum and maximum values, inflection points, and intercepts of a graph. For example, use the graph plotted in Section 3.4 to determine the maximum of the graph. Follow these steps:

1. Select the FMAX option by pressing

GRAPH MORE [F1:MATH] [F5:FMAX]

The Trace cursor appears on the function, with a request for a Left Bound in the flower left-hand corner.

2. Move the cursor to the left of the maximum value (see Fig. 3.43).

3. To accept the left bound press

ENTER

A prompt for a Right Bound replaces the Left Bound prompt in the lower left-hand corner.

4. Move the cursor to the right of the maximum value (see Fig. 3.44).

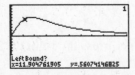

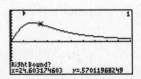

Figure 3.43 Finding the Maximum.

Figure 3.44 The Right Bound.

5. To accept the Right Bound, press

ENTER

A prompt for a Guess? for the maximum replaces the Right Bound prompt in the lower left-hand corner.

6. Move the cursor between the Left and Right Bounds where it is close to the maximum.

7. To calculate the maximum, press

ENTER

The calculator computes the maximum and displays it in the cursor coordinates at the bottom of the display, that is, .61584028714 at an x-value of 17.677668581 (see Fig. 3.45).

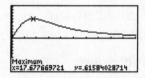

Figure 3.45 The maximum .61584028714 at an
x-value of 17.677668581.

Note that this value of *y* is larger than that found with the Trace cursor in the previous subsection. This is the most accurate of the three graphical solutions we have found.

Note: *The FMAX and FMIN calculator algorithms search between left and right bounds and use tol from the Toler edit screen to control accuracy.*

The procedures to find the minimum (MIN), inflection (INFLC), and intercepts (YICPT) are essentially the same as these.

3.4.2 Graphing the Derivative of a Function

The maxima and minima of a continuous differentiable function, if they exist, occur on the point on which the first derivative is equal to 0. On the TI-86, you can graph the exact derivative of a function. For example, using the graph found earlier in this section, follow these steps:

1. Access the $y(x)$ = edit screen by pressing GRAPH [F1:y(x) =].

2. To move to the y2 = field, press ENTER. (See Fig. 3.46.)

3. Display the CALCULUS menu by pressing 2nd |CALC|.

4. To copy the function name for the exact first derivative to the cursor location, press [F3:der1] (See Fig. 3.47).

Figure 3.46 Moving to the y2 = field.

Figure 3.47 Copying the function name
for the exact first derivative.

5. Enter the name of the first equation, y1, next to der1 as follows:

   a. Copy *y* from the first-level options to the cursor location by pressing

   2nd [M2:y]

   b. Press **1**.

   c. Press , .

You can evaluate calculus functions with respect to any variable; however, to be meaningful in graphing, the variable of differentiation or integration should be *x*.

6. Copy *x* from the first-level options and enter the equation by pressing [2nd] [M1:x] [ )] (See Fig. 3.48).

Figure 3.48 Entering more equations.

7. To evaluate both equations and obtain the derivative, press [GRAPH] [F5:GRAPH].

Because derl (y1, *x*) is the exact derivative, evaluated at the current value of *x*, then when this equation is graphed, the derivative is calculated and graphed for each value of *x*.

3.4.3 Finding a Root Graphically

The TI-86 can find the root (zero) of a graphed function and can calculate the value of the function for any value of *x*. For example, find the *x*-value where the root of the derivative function derl(y1, *x*) occurs and use it to calculate the maximum of the function. Follow these steps:

1. Access the Root option from the GRAPH [Math] menu by pressing

[MORE] [F1:MATH] [F1:ROOT]

The Trace cursor is near the middle y-value on the y1 function, with a request for a Left Bound in the lower left-hand corner.

2. Move the cursor to the derivative function y2 to a point near the root by pressing [▼], then move the cursor to the left until you get a positive *y*-value for your left bound (see Fig. 3.49).

3. To accept the left bound, press

[ENTER]

A prompt for a Right Bound replaces the Left Bound prompt in the lower left-hand corner.

4. Move the cursor to the right of the root (see Fig. 3.50).

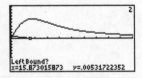

Figure 3.49 Finding the Root.

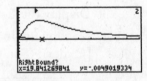

Figure 3.50 The Right Bound.

5. To accept the Right Bound press

[ENTER]

A prompt for a Guess? for the root replaces the Right Bound prompt in the lower left-hand corner.

6. Move the cursor between the Left and Right Bounds where it is close to the root.

7. To calculate the root, press

[ENTER]

The calculated root is displayed in the cursor coordinates: $y = -1.21363e - 15$ at an x-value of 17.67766953 (see Fig. 3.51).

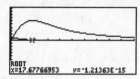

Figure 3.51 The calculated root.

8. Press

EXIT MORE [F1:EVAL].

9. Press

2nd [ANS] ENTER

to enter the solution to the root as the value for x.

In section 3.4.1, the Fmax option found a maximum of $y = .61584028714$ at $x = 17.677668581$. Corresponding to the maximum, the root found by the Root option is of the derivative at $x = 17.67766953$, which evaluated to a maximum, $y = .61584028714$.

3.5 Graphing Parametric Equations

3.5.1 Defining and Displaying a Parametric Graph

Parametric equations consist of an x-component and y-component, each expressed in terms of the same independent variable t. Up to 99 pairs of parametric equations can be defined and graphed simultaneously. You define a parametric graph in the same way as a function graph.

1. Press

2nd [MODE]

and select Parametric (Param) mode.

2. Display the E(t) = edit screen by pressing

GRAPH [F1:E(t) =]

The E(t) = edit screen displays labels for a pair of x-y parametric equations. After each label is an empty field in which you enter the function. The entry cursor is positioned in the first field (see Fig. 3.52).

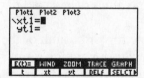

Figure 3.52 The E(t) = edit screen.

3. Enter the x- and y-components in the same manner as for functions. In this case, note the following:

 • You must define both the x- and y-components in a pair.

 • The independent variable in each component must be t.

The procedures for editing and clearing parametric equations and for exiting the screen are the same as for function graphing. Selecting equations for graphing, also, is the same as for function graphing. You can select up to 99 pairs of equations at a time and only those selected are graphed. Note that when you enter, edit, or select either component of an equation, the *pair* of equations is selected.

4. a. To display the current values of the WINDOW variables press

[2nd] [M2:WIND]

The standard values in Radian mode are shown in Table 3.1. Notice that there are three view variables: tMin, tMax, and tStep.

Table 3.1

Setting	Meaning
tMin = 0	The smallest t-value to be evaluated
tMax 5 2π	The largest t-value to be evaluated
tStep 5 $\pi/24$	The increment between t-values

Note: The display shows the numeric value of 2π (6.28318530718) for tMax and $\pi/24$ (0.130899693899) for tStep. The other Range variables have the same role as described in Section 3.2.3.

When you graph parametric equations, the calculator plots the selected parametric equations, evaluates the x- and y-components for each value of t (taken from tMin to tMax in intervals of tStep), and then plots each point defined by x and y. The values of the Range variables define the viewing window. As the graph is plotted, the calculator updates the x- and y-coordinates and the values of the parameter t.

3.5.2 Exploring a Parametric Graph

As in function graphing, you have three tools for exploring a graph:

- Using a free-moving cursor
- Tracing an equation
- Zooming

The free-moving cursor works in parametric graphing in the same manner as it does in function graphing: As the cursor moves, the displayed coordinate values of x and y in Rectangular mode—r and θ in Polar mode—are updated.

Using the TRACE feature, you can move the cursor along the graph one $t$step at a time. When you begin a trace, the cursor is on the first selected equation at the minimum t-value and the coordinate values of x, y, and t are displayed at the bottom of the screen. As you trace the graph, the displayed values of x, y, and t are updated, where the x- and y-values are calculated from t.

If the cursor moves off the top or bottom of the screen, the coordinate values continue to change and be displayed. However, panning is not possible on parametric curves. To see a section of the equations not displayed on the graph, you must change the values of the Window variables.

The ZOOM features work in parametric graphing as they do in function graphing. Only the values of the x Window variables (xMin, xMax, and xScl) and y Window variables (yMin, yMax, and yScl) are affected. The values of the t Window variables (tMin, tMax, and tStep) keep their default values. You might want to change the values of the t Window variables to ensure sufficient points are plotted.

3.5.3 Applying Parametric Graphing

Example 4 Simulating Motion

Problem Graph the position of a ball kicked from ground level at an angle of 60° with an initial velocity of 40 ft/sec. (Ignore air resistance.) What is the maximum height, and when is it reached? How far away and when does the ball strike the ground?

Solution If v_0 is the initial velocity and θ is the angle, then the horizontal component of the position of the ball as a function of time is described by

$$x(t) = tv_0 \cos \theta.$$

The vertical component of the position of the ball as a function of time is described by

$$y(t) = -16t^2 + tv_0 \sin \theta.$$

To graph the equations, do as follows:

1. Press

$$\boxed{\text{2nd}} \; \boxed{\text{MODE}}$$

and select Degree and Parametric modes.

2. Press

$\boxed{\text{GRAPH}} \boxed{\text{MORE}}$ [F3:FORMT] $\boxed{\blacktriangledown} \; \boxed{\blacktriangledown} \; \boxed{\text{ENTER}}$ to select the Draw Line option.

3. Access the $E(t) =$ edit screen in the **GRAPH** feature by pressing

$$[\text{F1:E(t) =}]$$

4. Enter the following expressions to define the parametric equation in terms of t:

   a. $xt1 = 40t \cos 60$; press

   $$\boxed{\text{CLEAR}} \; 40 \; [\text{F1:t}] \; \boxed{\text{COS}} \; 60 \; \boxed{\text{ENTER}}$$

   The function is entered in th field next to $xt1 =$ and the cursor moves to the field next to $yt1 =$.

   b. $yt1 = 40t \sin 60 - 16t^2$; press

   $$\boxed{\text{CLEAR}} \; 40 \; [\text{F1:t}] \; \boxed{\text{SIN}} \; 60 - 16 \; [\text{F1:t}] \; \boxed{x^2} \; \boxed{\text{ENTER}}$$

   The function is entered in the field next to $yt1 =$ and the cursor moves to the field next to $xt2 =$. Note that the $=$ signs of the pair of equations are highlighted, indicating they are selected for graphing.

5. Set the values of the Window variables appropriately for this problem by pressing

$$\boxed{\text{2nd}} \; [\text{M2:WIND}]$$

and entering the following values as needed:

$t\text{Min} = 0$	$x\text{Min} = -5$	$y\text{Min} = -5$
$t\text{Max} = 2.5$	$x\text{Max} = 50$	$y\text{Max} = 20$
$t\text{step} = .02$	$x\text{scl} = 5$	$y\text{scl} = 5$

6. To graph the equations, press [F5:GRAPH].

7. To explore the graph, press [F4:TRACE].

As the cursor moves along the ball's path, observe the changing x, y, and t values at the bottom of the screen. Notice you have a "stop action" picture at each 0.02 sec (see Fig. 3.53).

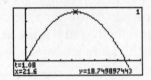

Figure 3.53 The ball's path.

3.6   Graphing Polar Equations

You can enter up to 99 equations for graphing.

Example 5 Graphing a Spiral

Problem Graph the spiral of Archimedes, that is, the curve defined by the polar equation $r = a\theta$.

Solution A polar equation $r = f(\theta)$ can be graphed using the calculator's polar graphing features. Thus the spiral of Archimedes (with $a = 0.5$) can be expressed as follows:

1. Press

[2nd] [MODE]

   a. Select Polar (Pol) mode.

   b. Choose the default settings, including Normal and Radian for the other modes.

2. Access the $r(\theta) =$ edit screen by pressing

[GRAPH] [F1:r(θ) =]

and enter the polar equation $r_1 = .5\theta$ in terms of θ by pressing

[CLEAR] [•] **5** [F1:θ]

3. To graph the equations in the Standard default viewing window, press

[2nd] [M3:ZOOM] [F4:ZSTD]

The graph shows only the first loop of the spiral because the standard default values for the Window variables define θMax as 2π (see Fig. 3.54).

4. To explore the behavior of the graph further,

   a. press

[F2:WIND]

   b. and change θMax to 25.

5. To display the new graph as shown in Fig. 3.55, press

[F5:GRAPH]

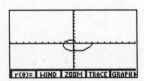

Figure 3.54 The first loop of the spiral.

Figure 3.55 The spiral of Archimedes.

6. Press

$$[F3:ZOOM] \boxed{MORE} [F2:ZSQR]$$

and notice what happens (see Fig. 3.56).

Figure 3.56 The spiral of Archimedes.

Compare Figs. 3.55 and 3.56.

Example 6 Graphing a Leafed Rose

Problem Graph a leafed rose defined by the polar equation $r = a \sin(n\theta)$.
Solution Graph a four-leafed rose with $a = 7$ and $n = 2$ as follows:

1. Press

$$\boxed{2nd} \boxed{MODE}$$

  a. Select the Polar (Pol) mode.
  b. Choose the defaults for the other modes, including Radian and Connected modes.

2. Access the $r(\theta)$ = edit screen by pressing

$$\boxed{GRAPH} [F1:r(\theta) =]$$

and clear the previous expression by pressing $\boxed{CLEAR}$.

3. Enter the expression r1 $= 7 \sin 2\theta$ by pressing:

$$7 \boxed{SIN} \boxed{(} \ 2 [F1:\theta] \boxed{)}$$

4. To graph the rose in the Standard default viewing window, press

$$\boxed{2nd} [M3:ZOOM] [F4:ZSTD]$$

(See Fig. 3.57).

5. Press

$$[F3:ZOOM] \boxed{MORE} [F2:ZSQR]$$

and observe what happens. Press $\boxed{CLEAR}$ to erase the menus.

The rose is graphed in the correct proportions. The graph should look like that in Fig. 3.57.

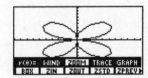

Figure 3.57 Graph of a four-leafed rose in the Standard default viewing window.

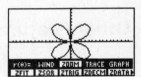

Figure 3.58 Graph of a four-leafed rose in the correct proportions.

3.7   Graphing Piecewise Functions

Piecewise functions like

$$f(x) = \begin{cases} 2x - 1 & if \ x \leq 1 \\ x^2 - 2x + 2 & if \ x > 1 \end{cases}$$

can be graphed on the TI-86 using the boolean functions in the TEST menu. To graph this function, do as follows:

1. Press 2nd |MODE| and select the Function mode.
2. Access the y(x) = edit screen by pressing GRAPH [F1:y(x) =] and enter the following expressions:

   a. $y_1 = (2x - 1)/(x \leq 1)$; press

      CLEAR (2 x-VAR — 1) ÷ (x-VAR 2nd |TEST| [F4:≤] 1) ENTER

   b. $y_2 = (x^2 - 2x + 2)/(x > 1)$; press

      CLEAR (x-VAR x^2 — 2 x-VAR + 2) ÷ (x-VAR 2nd |TEST| [F3:>] 1)

3. Change the values of the Window variables as needed to correspond to a $[-2, 2]$ by $[-2, 2]$ viewing window.
4. Graph the equations pressing

   [F5:GRAPH]

The graph should look like that in Fig. 3.59.

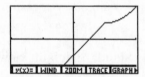

Figure 3.59 Graph of a piecewise function.

The Boolean expression $x \leq 1$ returns the value 1 when x is less than or equal to 1 and it returns the value 0 when x is greater than 1. So the function y1 is equal to $2x - 1$ when x is less than or equal to 1 and is undefined when x is greater than 1. Because the Boolean expression $x > 1$ has the value 1 when it is true and 0 when it is false, y2 is equal to $x^2 - 2x + 2$ when $x > 1$ and y2 is undefined when $x \leq 1$.

3.8   Other Features of the TI-86

References to chapters in the TI-86 User's Guide are noted in parentheses as follows: (TI-86 chapter).

1. a. In function graphing, you can store, graph, and analyze up to 99 functions (Ch. 5).

   b. In polar graphing, you can store, graph, and analyze up to 99 equations (Ch. 8).

   c. In parametric graphing, you can store, graph, and analyze up to 99 pairs of equations (Ch. 9).

   d. In differential equation graphing, you can store, graph, and analyze up to nine first-order differential equations (Ch. 10).

2. You can use drawing and shading features to add emphasis or perform additional analysis on function, polar, parametric, and differential equation graphs (Ch. 5).

3. You can solve an equation for any variable, solve a system of up to 30 simultaneous linear equations, and find the real complex roots of a polynomial equation (Ch. 15).

4. You can enter and store an unlimited number of matrices and vectors with dimensions up to 255. The TI-86 has standard matrix operations, including elementary row operations and standard vector operations (Ch. 12 and 13).

5. The TI-86 performs one-variable and two-variable statistical analysis. You can enter the store an unlimited number of data points. Seven regression models are available: linear, logarithmic, exponential, power, and second-, third-, and fourth-order polynomial. You can analyze data graphically with histograms, scatter plots, and line drawings and plot regression equation graphs (Ch. 14).

6. Programming capabilities include extensive control and I/O (input/output) instructions. You can enter and store an unlimited number of programs (Ch. 16).

7. The calculator has 32K of RAM available for storing variables, programs, pictures, and graphical databases (Ch. 17).

8. With the TI-86, you can share data and programs with another TI-86. You can print graphs and programs, enter programs, and save data on a disk through a personal computer (Ch. 18).

CHAPTER

4

Exploring Calculus with the TI-84 Plus Silver Edition

The following toolbox programs and examples are useful in exploring and visualizing concepts in calculus. In some cases, you will be given a program that must be entered in the calculator before you can explore a particular concept. In other cases, the program is a built-in part of the TI-84, so you will not have to program the calculator in order to explore the concept. In either case, the program will be described by a name in uppercase letters and you will be given the input and output parameters. If it is built in on either calculator you will be given the keys and functions necessary to execute the program.

The instructions in this chapter refer to the TI-84; but the TI-83 is compatible with most of the instructions given.

4.1   Numerical Derivative

Program 1

NDER (numerical derivative)

Input: $f(x)$, A and h (step size)

Output: (approximate) value of $f'(A)$

This is a built-in program on the TI-84. It appears as the NDeriv option in the MATH menu. To find $f'(A)$ do the following:

- Store the desired value in A.
- Press [MATH] [8:nDeriv(].
- Enter the function, followed by the independent variable, followed by A, and by the value of the step size (h).

Each parameter must be separated by commas. The last parameter (h) is optional, however; if you don't include it, the default step size is 0.001.

Example 1

If $f(x) = x - 2 \sin x, A = 0$, and $h = 0.01$, then $f'(A)$ is approximated by nDeriv ($x - 2 \sin x, x, A, 0.01$), which can be found by the key sequence shown in Table 4.1.

Table 4.1

Comments	Input (keystrokes)	Screen Display
1. Store the desired value in A.	0 [STO▶] [ALPHA] **A** [ALPHA] [:]	0→A:
2. Select the nDeriv option from the MATH menu; enter the function followed by the independent variable, then by A, and by the value of the step size (h).	[MATH] **8** [X,T,θ,n] [—] **2** [SIN] [X,T,θ,n] [ )] [,] [X,T,θ,n] [,] [ALPHA] A [,] [.] **01** [ )]	0→A:nDeriv(X − 2sin(X), X, A, .01)
	[ENTER]	−.9999666668

The step size determines the accuracy of the approximation. A step size of 0.0001 will give a closer approximation of the derivative than a step size of 0.01. The values in Table 4.2 were found by using NDER $(x − 2 \sin x, x, A, h)$ with various values of A and h. Compare the results obtained using different step sizes with the exact value (to nine decimal places) listed in the last column of Table 4.2. See if you can obtain similar results using the nDeriv option on your calculator.

Table 4.2 Numerical derivatives of $x − 2 \sin x$.

A	NDER(f) $h = 0.1$	NDER(f) $h = 0.01$	NDER(f) $h = 0.0001$	EXACT $f'(A)$
−10	2.675347551	2.678115089	2.678143055	2.678143058
−7	−.5052927574	−.5077793787	−.507804506	−.507804509
−2	1.83090721	1.832279802	1.832293672	1.832293673
0	−.9966683329	−.9999666668	−.9999999967	−1.000000000
1	−.0788045043	−.0805866018	−.08060461	−.080604612
5	.433620697	.4326850844	.43267563	.432675629
10	2.675347551	2.678115089	2.67814305	2.678143058

4.2 Graph of Numerical Derivative

Program 2

NDERGRAF (graph of numerical derivative)

Input: $f(x)$

Output: graph of $y = f'(x)$

This is a built-in function on the TI-84, so no programming is required. To overlay the graph of $f'(x)$ on the graph of $f(x)$, do the following:

- Enter the function in Y_1.

- Enter $Y_2 = \text{nDeriv}(Y_1, X, X)$.

- Select an appropriate viewing window.

- Graph.

If you don't want the graph of $f(x)$ to appear, unselect Y_1 before you press GRAPH. You can increase the accuracy of the graph by reducing the step size in nDeriv, but the graph might be drawn more slowly.

Example 2

To graph $y = x - 2 \sin x$ and its derivative, do the following:

1. Enter $Y_1 = X - 2 \sin (X)$.
2. Enter $Y_2 = \text{nDeriv}(Y_1, X, X)$.
3. Graph using a $[-10, 10]$ by $[-10, 10]$ window.

These steps produce the graph shown in Fig. 4.1.

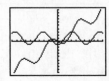

Figure 4.1 $x - 2 \sin x$ and its derivative.

Notice the roots of the derivative have the same x-coordinates as the extrema of $f(x)$. Notice also that $f(x)$ is increasing on the intervals where $f'(x)$ is positive and decreasing on the intervals where $f'(x)$ is negative. To see the second derivative, enter $Y_3 = \text{nDeriv}$ $(\text{nDeriv}(Y_1, X, X), X, X)$ or $Y_3 = \text{nDeriv}(Y_2, X, X)$ and press GRAPH.

4.3 Draw a Line Tangent to a Curve

Program 3

TANLINE (draws a line tangent to a curve)
Input: $f(x), a$
Output: overlays tangent line at $(a, f(a))$ on the graph of $y = f(x)$
A function in the DRAW menu does the job directly, either from the Home screen or from the graph interactively.

Example 3

Lines tangent to the curve $y = x - 2 \sin x$ at $x = -6, -5.24$, and -4 can be overlaid on the curve.
Directions:

1. Graph $Y_1 = X - 2 \sin X$ in the $[-10, 10]$ by $[-10, 10]$ window.
2. Press

$$\boxed{\text{2nd}} \;\; \boxed{\text{DRAW}} \;\; [5:\text{Tangent(}]$$

3. Use the cursor movement keys to move the cursor until X is approximately -6, then press ENTER. Or, instead of using the cursor keys, you can enter -6 directly using the keypad.

A tangent line is drawn at approximately $X = -6$.

4. Press

$$\boxed{\text{2nd}} \;\; \boxed{\text{QUIT}}$$

to return to the Home screen.

5. Press

$$\boxed{\text{2nd}} \;\; \boxed{\text{DRAW}} \;\; [5\text{:Tangent(]} \;\; \boxed{\text{VARS}} \;\; [\text{Y-Vars}] \;\; [1\text{:Function}] \;\; [1\text{:Y}_1]$$

$$\boxed{\text{,}} \;\; \boxed{(-)} \;\; \mathbf{5} \;\; \boxed{\text{.}} \;\; \mathbf{24} \;\; \boxed{\text{)}}$$

to enter the command Tangent $(Y_1, -5.24)$ on the Home screen.

6. Press $\boxed{\text{ENTER}}$.

You should see a tangent line drawn to the curve $X - 2 \sin (X)$ at the point where X is -5.24.

7. Press

$$\boxed{\text{2nd}} \;\; \boxed{\text{DRAW}} \;\; [5\text{:Tangent(]}$$

move the cursor until X is approximately -4, then press $\boxed{\text{ENTER}}$. Or, instead of using the cursor keys, you can enter -4 directly using the keypad.

These steps produce the graph shown in Fig. 4.2.

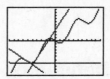

Figure 4.2 Lines tangent to $x - 2 \sin x$.

Notice in the steps for Example 3 that the x-coordinate of the point of tangency can be entered by tracing to the desired point on the graph or by entering the value directly with a command on the Home screen.

4.4   Definite Integral

Program 4

NINT (definite integral)
Input: $f(x)$, a, and b
Output: (approximate) value of $\displaystyle\int_a^b f(x)\,dx$

This is a built-in function found in the MATH menu.

Example 4A

A proper integral such as $\displaystyle\int_0^{\pi/2} \cos x \, dx$ can be evaluated. Press

$$\boxed{\text{MATH}} \;\; [9\text{:fnInt(]} \;\; \boxed{\text{COS}} \;\; \boxed{\text{X,T,}\theta\text{,}n} \;\; \boxed{\text{)}} \;\; \boxed{\text{,}} \;\; \boxed{\text{X,T,}\theta\text{,}n} \;\; \boxed{\text{,}}$$

$$\mathbf{0} \;\; \boxed{\text{,}} \;\; \boxed{\text{2nd}} \;\; \boxed{\pi} \;\; \boxed{\div} \;\; \mathbf{2} \;\; \boxed{\text{)}} \;\; \boxed{\text{ENTER}}$$

This key sequence creates the command fnInt(cos (X), X, 0, $\pi/2$) on the Home screen followed by the value of the definite integral (1). The first parameter in the fnInt command is the function to be integrated. The second parameter is the variable with respect to which the function is to be integrated. The third and fourth parameters are the lower and upper limits of integration.

Example 4B

An improper integral such as $\int_{-1}^{3} \frac{\sin x}{x}\, dx$ can be approximated if we assume $\frac{\sin x}{x} = 1$ at $x = 0$.

Press

$$\boxed{\text{MATH}}\ [9\text{:fnInt(}]\ \boxed{\text{SIN}}\ \boxed{\text{X,T,}\theta\text{,n}}\ \boxed{)}\ \boxed{\div}\ \boxed{\text{X,T,}\theta\text{,n}}\ \boxed{,}$$
$$\boxed{\text{X,T,}\theta\text{,n}}\ \boxed{,}\ \boxed{(-)}\ \mathbf{1}\ \boxed{,}\ \mathbf{3}\ \boxed{)}\ \boxed{\text{ENTER}}$$

The definite integral is approximately 2.794735598

The fnInt command is a very robust numerical algorithm with accuracy controlled by an optional fifth parameter. The default parameter is 1E-5, which guarantees accuracy to at least 1E-5 and usually much more. The fnInt command not only is designed to evaluate proper definite integrals but also can often return accurate approximations to convergent improper integrals. If you encounter an error message while attempting to evaluate one of these improper integrals, try changing either the fifth parameter of the fnInt function or the limits of integration slightly.

4.5 Graph a Function Defined by an Integral

Program 5

NINTGRAF (graph a function defined by an integral)
Input: $f(x), a$

Output: graph of $\int_{a}^{x} f(t)\, dt$

The built-in function fnInt(found in the MATH menu can be used to graph an antiderivative. No program is necessary.

Example 5A

The function $\int_{0}^{x} \frac{\sin t}{t}\, dt$ can be graphed if we assume $\frac{\sin x}{x} = 1$ at $x = 0$.

Enter $Y_1 = \text{fnInt}(\sin(X)/X, X, 0, X)$ in the $Y =$ edit screen and graph in the $[-10, 10]$ by $[-3, 3]$ window. As is, this method is somewhat slow. To speed up graphing, change *x*res in the WINDOW setting screen to higher number. For example, changing *x*res from 1 to 3 will triple the speed, but the function will be evaluated and graphed at every 3rd pixel, so increasing *x*res too much may affect the resolution of the graph.

These steps (xres = 1) produce the graph shown in Fig. 4.3.

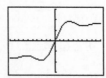

Figure 4.3 Antiderivative of (sin *x*)/*x*.

Adjusting the limits of integration slightly or changing the optional fifth parameter in the fnInt function may help to graph a convergent improper integral if an error is encountered.

Example 5B

Graph $\int_0^x (1 - 2\cos t)\, dt$ and compare with the exact antiderivative.

1. Select the Function mode.

2. Enter $Y_1 = \text{fnInt}(1 - 2\cos(X), X, 0, X)$.

3. Enter $Y_2 = X - 2\sin(X)$.

4. Press [WINDOW] and make a $[-10, 10]$ by $[-10, 10]$ viewing window. Change the $x$res to speed up the graphing if so desired.

5. Graph.

These steps produce the graph shown in Fig. 4.4.

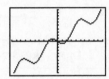

Figure 4.4 Antiderivative of $1 - 2\cos x$.

4.6 Solve an Equation

Program 6

SOLVE (find a root of an expression or a zero of a function)
Input: $f(x)$, left bound, right bound, initial approximation of a zero
Output: (approximate) zero of $f(x)$

Example 6

Solve $x = 2\sin x$ (find the zeros of $x - 2\sin x$).
Directions:

1. Select the Function mode and enter $Y_1 = X - 2\sin(X)$.

2. Graph using a $[-10, 10]$ by $[-10, 10]$ window.

3. Press [2nd] [CALC] [2:zero].

You will see a prompt for a left bound.

4. Press [◄] to move the cursor to $X = -2.12766$ and press [ENTER].

Doing this marks the left bound. You will see a prompt for a right bound.

5. Move the cursor to $X = -1.06383$ and press [ENTER].

This selects the right bound. You will see a prompt for an initial guess for the zero.

6. Move the cursor to $X = -1.914894$ and press [ENTER].

The zero is -1.895494.

7. Press [2nd] [CALC] [2:zero] again.

8. Move the cursor and press [ENTER] to mark $X = -.8510638$ for the left bound, $X = .8510686$ for the right bound, and $X = .21276$ for the initial guess.

Another zero is 0.

The TI-84 zero algorithm will find a zero close to the initial guess that is between the left and right bounds.

4.7 Rectangle Approximation Method

Program 7

RAM (rectangle approximation method)
Input: $f(x)$, a, b, and n (number of subintervals)

Output: (approximate) value of $\int_a^b f(x)\,dx$ using left, right, and midpoint rectangles

Table 4.3

Comments	Input (keystrokes)	Screen Display
1. Enter the Programming mode to create a new program.	[PRGM] [▶] [▶] [ENTER] **RAM** [ENTER]	Prgm: RAM
2. Enter A, B and N.	[PRGM] [▶] [1:Input] [ALPHA] " [ALPHA] **A** [2nd] [TEST] [1: =] [ALPHA] " [，] [ALPHA] **A** [ENTER]	:Input "A =", A
	[PRGM] [▶] [1:Input] [ALPHA] " [ALPHA] **B** [2nd] [TEST] [1: =] [ALPHA] " [，] [ALPHA] **B** [ENTER]	:Input "B =", B
	[PRGM] [▶] [1:Input] [2nd] [A-LOCK] " **NO** [ALPHA] [•] [2nd] [A-LOCK] _ **SUBINT** [2nd] [TEST] [1: =] [ALPHA] " [，] [ALPHA] **N** [ENTER]	:Input "NO. SUBINT=" , N
3. Calculate step size.	[( ] [ALPHA] **B** [—] [ALPHA] **A** [ )] [÷] [ALPHA] **N** [STO▶] [ALPHA] **H** [ENTER]	:(B−A)/N→H
4. Initialize variables.	0 [STO▶] [ALPHA] **L** [ENTER]	:0→L
	0 [STO▶] [ALPHA] **M** [ENTER]	:0→M
5. Calculate left rectangle areas.	[PRGM] [4:For(] [ALPHA] **K** [，] 1 [，] [ALPHA] **N** [，] 1 [ )] [ENTER]	:For(K, 1, N, 1)
	[VARS] [Y-VARS] [1:Function] [1:Y₁] [( ] [ALPHA] **A** [+] [( ] [ALPHA] **K** [—] 1 [ )] [ALPHA] **H** [ )] [+] [ALPHA] **L** [STO▶] [ALPHA] **L** [ENTER]	:Y_1(A + (K−1)H) +L→L

(Continued)

Comments	Input (keystrokes)	Screen Display
6. Calculate mid rectangle areas.	[VARS] [Y-VARS] [1:Function] [1:Y$_1$] ([ALPHA] **A** + ([ALPHA] **K** − . **5**) [ALPHA] **H**) + [ALPHA] **M** [STO▸] [ALPHA] **M** [ENTER] [PRGM] [7:End] [ENTER]	:Y$_1$(A + (K−.5)H) +M→M :End
7. Calculate right rectangle areas.	[ALPHA] **L** − [VARS] [Y-VARS] [1:Function] [1:Y$_1$] ([ALPHA] **A**) + [VARS] [Y-VARS] [1:Function] [1:Y$_1$] ([ALPHA] **B**) [STO▸] [ALPHA] **R** [ENTER]	:L − Y$_1$(A) + Y$_1$(B)→R
8. Output results.	[PRGM] [▸] [3:Disp] [2nd] [A-LOCK] " **LEFT** [2nd] [TEST] [1: =] [ALPHA] " [ENTER]	:Disp "LEFT ="
	[PRGM] [▸] [3:Disp] [ALPHA] **H** [ALPHA] **L** [ENTER]	:Disp HL
	[PRGM] [▸] [3:Disp] [2nd] [A-LOCK] " **MID** [2nd] [TEST] [1: =] [ALPHA] " [ENTER]	:Disp "MID ="
	[PRGM] [▸] [3:Disp] [ALPHA] **H** [ALPHA] **M** [ENTER]	:Disp HM
	[PRGM] [▸] [3:Disp] [2nd] [A-LOCK] " **RIGHT** [2nd] [TEST] [1: =] [ALPHA] " [ENTER]	:Disp "RIGHT ="
	[PRGM] [▸] [3:Disp] [ALPHA] **H** [ALPHA] **R** [ENTER] [2nd] [QUIT]	:Disp HR

Example 7A

An integral such as $\int_{-1}^{3} \dfrac{\sin x}{x}\,dx$ can be approximated if we assume $\dfrac{\sin x}{x} = 1$ at $x = 0$.

Directions:

1. Enter $Y_1 = \sin(X)/X$ and select Radian mode.
2. Execute Prgm RAM.
3. Enter $-.99999$ for A, 3 for B, and 4 for the number of subintervals.

These steps produce the three approximations to the definite integral given in the first row of Table 4.4.

Repeat the steps in Example 7A, replacing n with 10, 50, 100, and 1000, to produce the remainder of the table.

Table 4.4 Rectangular approximations to $\int_{-1}^{3} \frac{\sin x}{x}\, dx$.

N	Left	Mid	Right
4	3.137583256	2.822079015	2.343151249
10	2.944977508	2.799049551	2.627204705
50	2.826159464	2.794899691	2.762604903
100	2.810529577	2.794770307	2.778752297
1000	2.796315185	2.794727615	2.793137457

Because the integrand in Example 7A is not defined at $x = 0$, the lower limit of integration was replaced with $-.99999$. This creates a subdivision of the interval from -1 to 3 that doesn't require the program to evaluate $(\sin x)/x$ at $x = 0$. Try repeating the steps in Example 7A using -1 instead of $-.99999$. In this case, notice that the program encounters a Math error while it is running because it attempts to evaluate $(\sin x/x)/x$ at $x = 0$.

Example 7B

Compare rectangular approximations of $\int_{0}^{\pi/2} \cos x\, dx$ using 10, 100, and 1000 subdivisions with the exact solution.

Directions:

1. Enter $Y_1 = \cos(X)$.

2. Execute Prgm RAM.

3. Enter 0 for A and $\pi/2$ for B.

4. Enter 10 for the number of subintervals.

5. Repeat Prgm RAM using 100, and then 1000, for the number of subintervals.

These steps produce the results shown in Table 4.5.

Table 4.5 Rectangular approximations to $\int_{0}^{\pi/2} \cos x\, dx$.

N	Left	Mid	Right	Exact
10	1.076482803	1.001028824	.91940317	1.0
100	1.00783342	1.000010281	.9921254566	1.0
1000	1.000785193	1.000000103	.9992143962	1.0

Increasing the number of subintervals improves the accuracy of the approximation.

4.8 Trapezoidal Method

Program 8

TRAP (trapezoidal method)

Input: $f(x)$, a, b, and n (number of subintervals)

Output: trapezoidal approximation of $\int_a^b f(x)\,dx$

```
Prgm: TRAP
:Input "NO. OF SUBINT =", N
:Input "A =", A
:Input "B =", B
:(B − A)/N→D
:0→S
:For(K, 1, N − 1, 1)
:2Y₁(A + KD) + S→S
:End
:Y₁(A)→L
:Y₁(B)→R
:(D/2) (S + R + L)→S
:Disp "TRAP="
:Disp S
```

Example 8A

An integral such as $\int_{-1}^{3} \frac{\sin x}{x}\,dx$ can be approximated if we assume $\frac{\sin x}{x} = 1$ at $x = 0$.

Directions:

1. Enter $Y_1 = \sin(X)/X$.
2. Execute Prgm TRAP.
3. Enter 10 for the number of subintervals, $-.99999$ for A, and 3 for B.
4. Repeat steps 2 and 3 using 100, and then 1000, for the number of intervals.

These steps produce the results shown in Table 4.6.

Table 4.6 Trapezoidal approximations to $\int_{-1}^{3} \frac{\sin x}{x}\,dx$.

N	10	100	1000
TRAP	2.786091106	2.794640937	2.794726321

A trapezoid approximation requires a partition of the interval $[A, B]$. The function is evaluated at points in the partition. Because the integrand in Example 8A is not defined at $x = 0$, the lower limit of integration was replaced with $-.99999$. Doing this creates a subdivision of the interval from -1 to 3 that doesn't require the program to evaluate $(\sin x)/x$ at $x = 0$. Try repeating the steps in Example 8A using -1 instead of $-.99999$. In this case, notice that the program encounters a Math error while it is running because it attempts to evaluate $(\sin x)/x$ at $x = 0$. This is similar to the difficulty encountered in using Prgm RAM to evaluate the same integral.

Example 8B

Compare trapezoidal approximations of $\int_0^{\pi/2} \cos x\,dx$ using 10, 100, and 1000 subdivisions with

the exact solution.

Directions:

1. Enter $Y_1 = \cos(X)$.

2. Execute Prgm TRAP.

3. Enter 10 for the number of subintervals.

4. Enter 0 for A and $\pi/2$ for B.

5. Repeat steps 2–4 using 100, and then 1000, for the number of subintervals.

These steps produce the results shown in Table 4.7.

Table 4.7 Trapezoidal approximations to $\int_0^{\pi/2} \cos x \, dx$.

N	10	100	1000	Exact
TRAP	.9979429864	.9999794382	.9999997944	1.0

Increasing the number of subintervals improves the accuracy of approximation. The error estimate for the trapezoidal rule can be used to determine the accuracy of this program.

4.9 Simpson's Method

Program 9

SIMP (Simpson's method)

Input: $f(x)$, a, b, and n (the number of subintervals (n) must be an even number.)

Output: Simpson's approximation of $\int_a^b f(x) \, dx$

```
Prgm: SIMP
:Input "NO. OF SUBINT=", N
:Input "A=", A
:Input "B=", B
:(B − A)/N→D
:0→S
:For(K, 1, N/2, 1)
:4Y₁(A+(2K−1)D) + 2Y₁(A+2KD) + S→S
:End
:Y₁→L
:B→X
:Y₁→R
:(D/3) (S+Y₁(A)−Y₁(B))→S
:Disp "SIMP="
:Disp S
```

Example 9A

An integral such as $\int_{-1}^{3} \dfrac{\sin x}{x} \, dx$ can be approximated if we assume $\dfrac{\sin x}{x} = 1$ at $x = 0$.

Directions:

1. Enter $Y_1 = \sin(X)/X$.

2. Execute Prgm SIMP.

3. Enter 10 for the number of subintervals, $-.99999$ for A, and 3 for B.

4. Repeat steps 2 and 3 using 100, and then 1000, for the number of subintervals.

These steps produce the results shown in the second row of Table 4.8. The trapezoidal and rectangular approximations have been included in the table for comparison.

Table 4.8 Comparison of numerical solutions to $\int_{-1}^{3} \frac{\sin x}{x} dx$.

N	10	100	1000
SIMP	2.794773788	2.794727188	2.794727184
LEFT	2.944977508	2.810529577	2.796315185
MID	2.799049551	2.794770307	2.794727615
RIGHT	2.627204705	2.778752297	2.793137457
TRAP	2.786091106	2.794640937	2.794726321

Simpson's approximation requires a partition of the interval $[A, B]$. The function is evaluated at points in the partition. Because the integrand in Example 9A is not defined at $x = 0$, the lower limit of integration was replaced with $-.99999$. Doing this creates a subdivision of the interval from -1 to 3 that doesn't require the program to evaluate $(\sin x)/x$ at $x = 0$. Try repeating the steps in Example 9A using -1 instead of $-.99999$. In this case, notice that the program encounters a math error while it is running because it attempts to evaluate $(\sin x)/x$ at $x = 0$. This is similar to the difficulty encountered in using Prgms RAM and TRAP to evaluate the same integral.

Example 9B

Compare trapezoidal approximations of $\int_{0}^{\pi/2} \cos x\, dx$ using 10, 100, and 1000 subdivisions with the exact solution.

Directions:

1. Enter $Y_1 = \cos(X)$.

2. Execute Prgm SIMP.

3. Enter 10 for the number of subintervals.

4. Enter 0 for A and $\pi/2$ for B.

5. Repeat steps 2–4 using 100, and then 1000, for the number of subintervals.

These steps produce the results shown in Table 4.9. The trapezoidal and rectangular approximations have been included for comparison.

Table 4.9 Comparison of numerical solutions to $\int_{0}^{\pi/2} \cos x\, dx$

N	10	100	1000	Exact
SIMP	1.000003392	1.00000000	1.00000000	1.0
LEFT	1.076482803	1.00783342	1.000785193	1.0
MID	1.001028824	1.000010281	1.000000103	1.0
RIGHT	.91940317	.9921254566	.9992143962	1.0
TRAP	.9979429864	.9999794382	.9999997944	1.0

Increasing the number of subintervals improves the accuracy of the approximation in a dramatic way. Simpson's method gives a 10-place accuracy with just 100 subdivisions. The error estimate for Simpson's method can be used to determine the accuracy of this program.

4.10 Euler Table

Program 10

EULERT (Euler table)

Input: $f'(x, y)$; initial x, y; step size (h); number of ordered pairs in table (n)
Output: table of ordered pairs (x, y), where each pair is an element of $y = f(x)$ and $f(x)$ is a solution to the initial value problem.

```
Prgm: EULERT
:Input "INITIAL X=", X
:Input "Y (INITIAL X) =", Y
:Input "STEP SIZE=", H
:Input "NO. OF POINTS=", N
:0→J
:Lbl 1
:Disp "X="
:Disp X
:Disp "Y="
:Disp Y
:Pause
:Y + HY₁→Y
:X + H→X
:J + 1→J
:If J≤N
:Goto 1
```

Example 10

Prgm EULERT can be used to find a numerical solution to the initial value problem $\dfrac{dy}{dx} = -2xy^2$ with initial conditions $f(-2) = 0.2$

Directions:

1. Enter $Y_1 = -2XY^2$.

2. Execute Prgm EULERT.

3. Enter an initial x-value of -2.

4. Enter an initial y-value of 0.2.

5. Enter a step size of 0.1.

6. Enter 40 for the number of points.

The program will produce the ordered pairs found in Table 4.10. The x-values are in the first column and the y-values are in the third column. To see the next pair, you must press ENTER *after each ordered pair.*

The exact solution to this differential equation is $y = \dfrac{1}{1+x^2}$. The second column of

Table 4.10 contains the exact values of the solution. Compare these with the values obtained by Prgm EULERT. As x moves away from the initial value, the difference between the exact value and the EULERT solution increases.

Table 4.10 Numerical solutions to $\dfrac{dy}{dx} = -2xy^2$.

X	EXACT	EULERT $1/(1 + X^2)$	IMPEULT	RUNKUTT
−2.0	.20000000	.2000	.2000	.2000000
−1.9	.21691974	.2160	.2169	.2169197
−1.8	.23584906	.2337	.2357	.2358490
−1.7	.25706941	.2534	.2568	.2570692
−1.6	.28089888	.2752	.2805	.2808986
−1.5	.30769231	.2995	.3071	.3076918
−1.4	.33783784	.3264	.3370	.3378371
−1.3	.37174721	.3562	.3706	.3717462
−1.2	.40983607	.3892	.4083	.4098346
−1.1	.45248869	.4255	.4504	.4524866
−1.0	.50000000	.4654	.4972	.4999972
−0.9	.55248619	.5087	.5489	.5524824
−0.8	.6097561	.5553	.6051	.6097511
−0.7	.67114094	.6046	.6652	.6711346
−0.6	.73529412	.6558	.7279	.7352863
−0.5	.80000000	.7074	.7910	.7999905
−0.4	.86206897	.7574	.8514	.8620579
−0.3	.91743119	.8033	.9052	.9174188
−0.2	.96153846	.8420	.9480	.9615250
−0.1	.99009901	.8704	.9757	.9900849
0	1.0000000	.8855	.9852	.9999857
0.1	.99009901	.8855	.9755	.9900849
0.2	.96153846	.8699	.9477	.9615249
0.3	.91743119	.8396	.9048	.9174186
0.4	.86206897	.7973	.8510	.8620576
0.5	.80000000	.7464	.7905	.7999901
0.6	.73529412	.6907	.7275	.7352858
0.7	.67114094	.6335	.6649	.6711342
0.8	.6097561	.5773	.6048	.6097508
0.9	.55248619	.5240	.5487	.5524822
1.0	.50000000	.4746	.4972	.4999970
1.1	.45248869	.4295	.4504	.4524865
1.2	.40983607	.3889	.4083	.4098346
1.3	.37174721	.3526	.3707	.3717462
1.4	.33783784	.3203	.3371	.3378372
1.5	.30769231	.2916	.3072	.3076919
1.6	.28089888	.2661	.2806	.2808986
1.7	.2506941	.2434	.2569	.2570693
1.8	.23584906	.2233	.2358	.2358490
1.9	.21691974	.2053	.2170	.2169198
2.0	.20000000	.1893	.2001	.2000001

To see the approximation error for each ordered pair of output do the following.

1. Enter $Y_2 = 1/(1 + X^2)$. This is the exact solution.
2. Edit Prgm EULERT

3. After the x and y-values are displayed, and before the ":Pause" command, enter the following lines

:Disp "Y$_2$, ERROR"

:Disp Y$_2$(X)

:Disp abs(Y − Y$_2$(X))

4. Execute Prgm EULERT with parameters as stated in Example 10.

4.11 Euler Graph

Program 11

EULERG (Euler graph)

Input: $f'(x, y)$; initial x, y; step size (h);

Output: graph of solution to initial value differential equation problem using Euler's method

```
Prgm: EULERG
:0→J
:FnOff
:ClrDraw
:Input "INITIAL X=", X
:Input "Y (INITIAL X)=", Y
:Input "STEP SIZE=", H
:(Xmax−Xmin)/abs(H)→N
:Lbl 1
:Y→Z
:Pt−On (X, Y, 1)
:Z→Y
:Y + HY₁→Y
:X + H→X
:J + 1→J
:If J≤N
:Goto 1
```

Notice that the Pt−On command has three parameters; X, Y, and 1. The first two parameters are the X and Y values of the point. The third parameter specifies the mark: 1 = dot ($\cdot$), 2 = box ($\square$), and 3 = cross ($+$).

Example 11A

Use Prgm EULERG to graph the solution to the initial problem $\dfrac{dy}{dx} = -2xy^2$ with $y(-2) = 0.2$ and then compare with the exact solution.

Directions:

1. Enter Y$_1$ = $-2XY^2$.

2. Enter Y$_2$ = $1/(1 + X^2)$.

3. Enter a $[-2, 2]$ by $[-1, 1]$ window.

4. Execute Prgm EULERG.

5. Enter an initial x-value of -2.

6. Enter an initial *y*-value of 0.2.

7. Enter a step size of 0.1.

8. Press ⌊2nd⌋ |DRAW| [6:DrawF] then press |VARS| [Y-VARS] [1:Function] [2:Y$_2$] |ENTER| to draw the exact solution.

These steps produce the graph shown in Fig. 4.5.

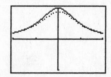

Figure 4.5 Euler's Method.

Notice the difference between the exact solution and Euler's method for *x* near zero.

Example 11B

Use Prgm EULERG to graph $\int_0^x \cos t \, dt$ and compare with the exact solution.
Directions:

1. Enter Y$_1$ = cos(*X*).

2. Enter Y$_2$ = sin(*X*).

3. Enter a $[0, 2\pi]$ by $[-2, 2]$ window.

4. Execute Prgm EULERG.

5. Enter an initial *x*-value of 0.

6. Enter an initial *y*-value of 0.

7. Enter a step size of 0.1.

8. Press ⌊2nd⌋ |DRAW| [6:DrawF] then press |VARS| [Y-VARS] [1:Function] [2:Y$_2$].

These steps produce the graph shown in Fig. 4.6.

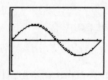

Figure 4.6 Antiderivative of cos *x*; Euler's Method.

Notice the difference between the exact solution and the Euler graph.

4.12 Improved Euler Table

Program 12

IMPEULT (improved Euler table)
Input: $f'(x, y)$; initial *x*, *y*; step size (*h*); number of ordered pairs in table (*n*)
Output: table of ordered pairs (x, y), where each pair is an element of $y = f(x)$ and $f(x)$ is a solution to the initial value problem

Prgm: IMPEULT
:0→J
:Input "INITIAL X=", X

```
:Input "Y (INITIAL X) =", Y
:Input "STEP SIZE=", H
:Input "NO. OF POINTS=", N
:Lbl 1
:Y→Z
:Disp "X="
:Disp X
:Disp "Y="
:Disp Y
:Pause
:HY₁→D
:Y + D→Y
:X + H→X
:Z + (D + HY₁)/2→Y
:1 + J→J
:If J ≤ N
:Goto 1
```

Example 12

Prgm IMPEULT can be used to find a numerical solution to the initial value problem $\frac{dy}{dx} = -2xy^2$ with initial conditions $f(-2) = 0.2$.

Directions:

1. Enter $Y_1 = -2XY^2$.

2. Execute Prgm IMPEULT.

3. Enter an initial x-value of -2.

4. Enter an initial y-value of 0.2.

5. Enter a step of 0.1.

6. Enter 40 for the number of points.

The program will produce the ordered pairs found in Table 4.10 (in Example 10).

The x-values are in the first column and the y-values are in the fourth column. You must press ENTER after each ordered pair to see the next pair. Compare the results of Prgm IMPEULT with Prgm EULERT and with the exact results.

The approximation error can also be added to IMPEULT. Follow the steps at the end of Section 4.10.

4.13 Improved Euler Graph

Program 13

IMPEULG (improved Euler graph)
Input: $f'(x, y)$; initial x, y; step size (h)
Output: graph of solution to initial value differential equation problem using the improved Euler's method

Prgm: IMPEULG
:0→J

```
:FnOff
:ClrDraw
:Input "INITIAL X=", X
:Input "Y (INITIAL X) =", Y
:Input "STEP SIZE=", H
:(Xmax − Xmin)/abs(H)→N
:Lbl 1
:Y→Z
:Pt−On (X, Y, 1)
:Z→Y
:HY₁→D
:Y + D→Y
:X + H→X
:Z + (D + HY₁)/2→Y
:1 + J→J
:If J ≤ N
:Goto 1
```

Example 13A

Use Prgm IMPEULG to graph the solution to the initial value problem $\dfrac{dy}{dx} = -2xy^2$, with $y(-2) = 0.2$, and then compare with the exact solution.

Directions:

1. Enter $Y_1 = -2XY^2$.
2. Enter $Y_2 = 1/(1 + X^2)$.
3. Enter $[-2, 2]$ by $[-1, 1]$ window.
4. Execute Prgm IMPEULG.
5. Enter an initial x-value of -2.
6. Enter an initial y-value of 0.2.
7. Enter a step size of 0.1.
8. Press [2nd] [DRAW] [6:DrawF] then press [VARS] [Y-VARS] [1:Function] [2:Y_2] [ENTER].

These steps produce the graph shown in Fig. 4.7.

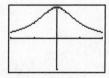

Figure 4.7 Improved Euler's method.

Compare this graph with the graph produced by Euler's method in Example 11A. Notice the improved agreement with the exact solution.

Example 13B

Use Prgm IMPEULG to graph $\displaystyle\int_0^x \cos t \, dt$ and compare with the exact solution.

Directions:

1. Enter $Y_1 = \cos(X)$.
2. Enter $Y_2 = \sin(X)$.

3. Enter a $[0, 2\pi]$ by $[-2, 2]$ window.

4. Execute Prgm IMPEULG.

5. Enter an initial *x*-value of 0.

6. Enter an initial *y*-value of 0.

7. Enter a step size of 0.1.

8. Press $\boxed{\text{2nd}}$ $\boxed{\text{DRAW}}$ [6:DrawF] then press $\boxed{\text{VARS}}$ [Y-VARS] [1:Function] [2:Y$_2$].

These steps produce the graph shown in Fig. 4.8.

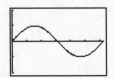

Figure 4.8 Antiderivative of cos *x*;
improved Eulers' method.

Compare this graph with that produced by Euler's method in Example 11B. Notice the improved agreement with the exact solution.

4.14 Runge-Kutta Table

Program 14

RUNKUTT (Runge-Kutta table)
Input: $f'(x, y)$; initial *x*, *y*; step size (h); number of ordered pairs in table (n)
Output: table of ordered pairs (x, y), where each pair is an element of $y = f(x)$ and $f(x)$ is a solution to the initial value problem.

```
Prgm: RUNKUTT
:0→M
:Input "INITIAL X=", X
:Input "Y (INITIAL X) =", Y
:Input "STEP SIZE=", H
:Input "NO. OF POINTS=", N
:Lbl 1
:Y→Z
:Disp "X="
:Disp X
:Disp "Y="
:Disp Y
:Pause
:HY₁→I
:X + H/2→X
:Z + I/2→Y
:HY₁→J
:Z + J/2→Y
:HY₁→K
:X + H/2→X
:Z + K→Y
:HY₁→L
```

```
:Z + (I + 2J + 2K + L)/6→Y
:M + 1→M
:If M ≤ N
:Goto 1
```

Example 14

Prgm RUNKUTT can be used to find a numerical solution to the initial value problem $\frac{dy}{dx} = -2xy^2$ with initial conditions $f(-2) = 0.2$.

Directions:

1. Enter $Y_1 = -2XY^2$.

2. Execute Prgm RUNKUTT.

3. Enter an initial x-value of -2.

4. Enter an initial y-value of 0.2.

5. Enter a step size of 0.1.

6. Enter 40 for the number of points.

The program will produce the ordered pairs found in Table 4.10 (in Example 10).

The x-values are in the first column and the y-values are in the fifth column. You must press ENTER after each ordered pair to see the next pair. Compare the results of Prgm RUNKUTT with Prgms IMPEULT, EULERT, and the exact results. The Runge-Kutta method is analogous to Simpson's method, while the improved Euler's method uses trapezoidal approximations and Euler's method uses rectangular approximations. It is not surprising that the Runge-Kutta method is the most accurate of the three numerical techniques.

The approximation error can also be added to RUNKUTT. Follow the steps at the end of Section 4.10.

4.15 Runge-Kutta Graph

Program 15

RUNKUTG (Runge-Kutta graph)

Input: $f'(x, y)$; initial x, y; step size (h)
Output: graph of solution to initial value differential equation problem using the Runge-Kutta method

```
Prgm: RUNKUTG
:ClrDrw
:FnOff
:0→M
:Input "INITIAL X=", X
:Input "Y (INITIAL X) =", Y
:Input "STEP SIZE=", H
:(Xmax−Xmin)/abs (H)→N
:Lbl 1
:Y→Z
:Pt−On (X, Y, 1)
:Z→Y
:HY₁→I
```

```
:X + H/2→X
:Z + I/2→Y
:HY₁→J
:Z + J/2→Y
:HY₁→K
:X + H/2→X
:Z + K→Y
:HY₁→L
:Z + (I + 2J + 2K + L)/6→Y
:M + 1→M
:If M ≤ N
:Goto 1
```

Example 15A

Use Prgm RUNKUTG to graph the solution to the initial value problem $\dfrac{dy}{dx} = -2xy^2$ with $y(-2) = 0.2$ and then compare with the exact solution.

Directions:

1. Enter $Y_1 = -2XY^2$.
2. Enter $Y_2 = 1/(1 + X^2)$.
3. Enter a $[-2, 2]$ by $[-1, 1]$ window.
4. Execute Prgm RUNKUTG.
5. Enter an initial x-value of -2.
6. Enter an initial y-value of 0.2.
7. Enter a step size of 0.1.
8. Press [2nd] [DRAW] [6:DrawF] then press [VARS] [Y-VARS] [1:Function] [2:Y_2] [ENTER].

These steps produce the graph shown in Fig. 4.9.

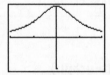

Figure 4.9 Runge-Kutta Method.

Compare this graph with the graphs produced by Euler's method in Example 11A and the improved Euler's method in Example 13A. Notice the close agreement between the Runge-Kutta graph and the exact solution.

Example 15B

Use Prgm RUNKUTG to graph $\displaystyle\int_0^x \cos t\, dt$ and compare with the exact solution.

Directions:

1. Enter $Y_1 = \cos(X)$.
2. Enter $Y_2 = \sin(X)$.
3. Enter a $[0, 2\pi]$ by $[-2, 2]$ window.
4. Execute Prgm RUNKUTG.
5. Enter an initial x-value of 0.

6. Enter an initial *y*-value of 0.

7. Enter a step size of 0.1.

8. Press [2nd] [DRAW] [6:DrawF] and then press [VARS] [Y-VARS] [1:Function] [2:Y$_2$] [ENTER].
These steps produce the graph shown in Fig. 4.10.

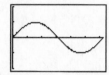

Figure 4.10 Antiderivative of cos *x*;
Runge-Kutta method.

Compare the graph with the graphs produced by Euler's method in Example 11B and the improved Euler's method in Example 13B. Notice the close agreement between the Runge-Kutta graph and the exact solution.

4.16 Make a Table of the Sequence of Partial Sums of a Series that Is Defined by an *n*th-term Formula

Program 16

PARTSUMT (partial sums of a series in tabular form)
Input: *n*th term of a series, initial value of *n*, number of terms in the sequence of partial sums
Output: sequence of partial sums
You can make the table with the sum and sequence commands.

Example 16

Make a table of the first 10 partial sums of the series

$$\sum_{n=1}^{10} 1/2^n.$$

Directions:

1. Enter $Y_1 = \text{sum}(\text{seq}(1/2{\wedge}N, N, 1, X, 1))$.

Note: The sum and seq commands are found in the LIST menu: Press

[2nd] [LIST] [Math] [5:sum] *and* [2nd] [LIST] [OPS] [5:seq].

The sum command adds up the terms in a sequence. The seq (sequence) command makes a sequence. The first parameter in the seq command is the formula for the *n*th term of a sequence. The second parameter is the index. The third and fourth parameters are the initial and final values of the index. The last parameter is the amount by which the index will change between terms in the sequence.

2. Press

[2nd] [TBLSET]

and make TblStart and ΔTbl both equal to 1. Indpnt and Depend should both be "Auto".

3. Press

$$\boxed{\text{2nd}} \; \boxed{\text{TABLE}}$$

4. Press ▼ to see more of the table.

These steps produce the following output:

N	Nth partial sum
1	.5
2	.75
3	.875
.	.
.	.
.	.
10	.99902

4.17 Graph the Sequence of Partial Sums of a Series that Is Defined by an *n*th-term Formula

Program 17

PARTSUMG (partial sums of a series in graphical form)
Input: *n*th term of a series, initial value of *n*, number of terms in the sequence of partial sums
Output: graph of the sequence of partial sums
You can draw the graph with the SUM and SEQ commands in Parametric mode, as follows:

$$X_{1T} = T$$

$$Y_{1T} = sum(seq(a_N, N, 1, T, 1))$$

Example 17

Graph the first 10 partial sums of the series $\sum_{n=1}^{10} 1/2^n$.

Directions:

1. Select the Parametric [Par] and Dot [Dot] modes.

2. Enter the following equations:

$$X_{1T} = T$$

$$Y_{1T} = sum(seq(1/2^{\wedge}N, N, 1, T, 1))$$

Example 16 describes how to enter the sum and seq commands.

3. Enter the following WINDOW values:

$t$min = 1	$x$min = 0	$y$min = 0
$t$max = 10	$x$max = 10	$y$max = 1
$t$step = 1	$x$scl = 1	$y$scl = 0

4. Graph.

These steps produce the graph shown in Fig. 4.11.

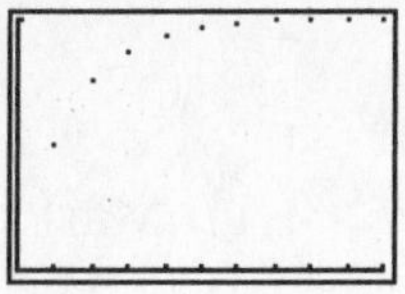

Figure 4.11 Sequence of partial sums for $\sum 1/2n$.

4.18 Make a Table of the Sequence of Partial Sums of a Series that Is Defined Recursively

Program 18

PSUMRECT (sequence of partial sums of a recursive series in tabular format)
Input: recursive definition of nth term of the series, initial n, initial term in series, number of terms in the sequence of partial sums
Output: sequence of partial sums
You can make the table by using the TABLE feature while in the sequence graphing mode. To generate a table, do the following:

- In the Mode settings window select Seq.
- In the Y = window, enter the recursive definition of the nth term for u(n), the initial term in the series for u(nMin), u + v($n - 1$) for v(n), and the first partial sum (i.e., the initial term in the series) for v(nMin).
- Generate a table using the TABLE feature.

Example 18A

Make a table of the sequence of partial sums for the series
$\frac{1}{2} + \frac{1}{4} + \frac{1}{8} + \frac{1}{16}$ ... defined recursively as $\sum a_n$ where $a_n = \left(\frac{1}{2}\right) a_{n-1}, a_1 = \left(\frac{1}{2}\right)$.

1. Press MODE and select Seq.
2. Press Y= .
3. Enter u(n) = .5u($n - 1$), u(nMin) = {.5}, v(n) = u + v($n - 1$), and v(nMin) = {.5}.
4. Press

2nd TBLSET

and make TblStart and ΔTbl both equal to 1. Indpnt and Depend should both be "Auto".
5. Press

2nd TABLE

to generate the table. The sequence of partial sums is in the third column.
6. Press ▼ to see more of the table.

These steps produce the values listed at the end of Example 16.

Example 18B

Find the sequence of partial sums for the series $1^2 + 2^2 + 3^2 + 4^2 + $ ..., which can be recursively defined as $\sum a_n$, where $a_n = a_{n-1} + 2n - 1, a_1 = 1$.

1. Press [MODE] and select Seq.
2. Press [Y=].
3. Enter u(n) = u(n − 1) + 2n − 1, u(nMin) = {1}, v(n) = u + v(n − 1), and v(nMin) = {1}.
4. Press

[2nd] [TBLSET]

   and make TblStart and ΔTbl both equal to 1. Indpnt and Depend should both be "Auto".
5. Press

[2nd] [TABLE]

   to generate the table. The sequence of partial sums is in the third column.
6. Press [▼] to see more of the table.

These steps produce the values listed below:

N	Nth partial sum
1	1
2	5
3	14
4	30
⋮	⋮
10	385

4.19 Graph the Sequence of Partial Sums of a Series that Is Defined Recursively

Program 19

PSUMRECG (graphs a sequence of partial sums of a recursive series)
Input: recursive definition of the nth term of the series, initial n, initial term in series, number of terms in the sequence of partial sums
Output: graph of the sequence of partial sums
On the TI-84 you can graph a sequence of partial sums by using the sequence graphing mode.

Example 19

Graph the sequence of partial sums for the series $\frac{1}{2} + \frac{1}{4} + \frac{1}{8} + \frac{1}{16} \ldots$

defined recursively as $\sum a_n$, where $a_n = \left(\frac{1}{2}\right)a_{n-1}$, $a_1 = \frac{1}{2}$.

1. Press [MODE] and select Seq.
2. Press [Y=].
3. Enter u(n) = .5u(n − 1), u(nMin) = {.5}, v(n) = u + v(n − 1), and v(nMin) = {.5}. Unselect u(n).

4. Press WINDOW and set nMin = 1, nMax = 10, PlotStart = 1, and PlotStep = 1. Set the viewing window to [0, 10] by [0, 1].

5. Press GRAPH.

These steps produce the same graph as Fig. 4.11.

4.20 Graph the *n*th Partial Sum of a Power Series

Program 20

GRAPHSUM (graph *n*th partial sum of a power series)
Input: nth term of series, initial n, number of terms in the series
Output: graph of the nth partial sum of the series
The graph can be drawn using the SUM and SEQ commands.

Example 20
Graph the power series for sin x, $\displaystyle\sum_{N=1}^{10} \frac{(-1)^{N+1}X^{2N-1}}{(2N-1)!}$.

Directions:

1. Enter Y_1 = sum(seq((-1)^(N + 1)X^($2N$ − 1)/($2N$ − 1)!, N, 1, 10, 1)). The sum and seq commands are found in the LIST menu: press

$\boxed{\text{2nd}}$ $\boxed{\text{LIST}}$ [Math] [5:sum] and $\boxed{\text{2nd}}$ $\boxed{\text{LIST}}$ [Ops] [5:seq].

2. You can graph Y_1 in dot mode without changing in the MODE menu. Place your cursor to the left of Y_1 by pressing ◄. Then press ENTER until the graph display icon shows the dot mode icon ($\cdot\cdot$). This will only apply to Y_1.

3. Enter $Y_2 = \sin(X)$.

4. Graph in the [−10, 10] by [−2, 2] viewing window.

These steps produce the graph shown in Fig. 4.12.

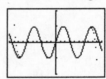

Figure 4.12 Power series for sin x.

This is the tenth partial sum of the MacLaurin series for sin x.

4.21 Graph a Slope Field for a Differential Equation

Program 21

SLOPEFLD (graph the slope field for a differential equation y′ = f(x, y))
Input: Differential equation $y' = f(x, y)$
Output: Slope field for the differential equation

Prgm SLOPEFLD
:10→L
:10→W

```
:(Ymax−Ymin)/L→V
:(Xmax−Xmin)/W→H
:ClrDraw
:FnOff
:0→R
:Ymin+V/2→Y
:Lbl 1
:R+1→R
:0→C
:Xmin+H/2→X
:Lbl 2
:C+1→C
:Y₁→M
:−M∗H/4}+Y→S
:M∗H/4+Y→T
:X−H/4→P
:X+H/4→Q
:If abs (T−S)>.7V
:Goto 3
:Lbl 4
:Y→Z
:Line (P, S, Q, T)
:Z→Y
:X+H→X
:If C<W
:Goto 2
:Y+V→Y
:If R<L
:Goto 1
:Stop
:Lbl 3
:Y+.35V→T
:Y−.35V→S
:(T−Y)/M+X→Q
:(S−Y)/M+X→P
:Goto 4
```

Program by: Mark Howell, Gonzaga School, Washington, D.C.

The variables L and W are both initialized to 10 in the first two lines of the program. These initial values can be adjusted to change the number of rows and columns in the output of the Slopefld program.

Example 21A

Use Prgm SLOPEFLD to illustrate the family of solutions to the differential equation $y' = \sin x/x$.

Directions:

1. Enter $Y_1 = \sin(X)/X$

2. Enter a $[-7, 7]$ by $[-2, 2]$ viewing window.

3. Execute Prgm SLOPEFLD.

These steps produce the slope field shown (see Fig. 4.13).

Figure 4.13 Slope field for $y' = \sin x/x$.

Example 21B

Graph the slope field for the differential equation $y'=x+y$.

Directions:

1. Enter $Y_1 = X + Y$.
2. Enter a $[-2, 2]$ by $[-1, 1]$ viewing window.
3. Execute Prgm SLOPEFLD.

You should see the following slope field (see Fig. 4.14).

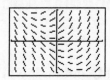

Figure 4.14 Slope field for $y' = x + y$.

Example 21C

Graph the slope field for $y' = -2xy^2$.

1. Enter $Y_1 = -2XY^2$.
2. Enter a $[-2, 2]$ by $[-1, 1]$ viewing window and execute Prgm SLOPEFLD.

Compare this slope field (Fig. 4.15) with the results of Prgms EULERG, IMPEULG, and RUNGKUTG in Examples 11A, 13A, and 15A.

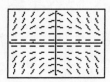

Figure 4.15 Family of solutions to $y = -2xy^2$.

Example 21D

Graph the slope field for $y' = -2xy^2$, then use Prgm EULERG to superimpose the solution to the initial value problem $\dfrac{dy}{dx} = -2xy^2$ with $y(-2) = 0.2$.

1. Enter $Y_1 = -2XY^2$.
2. Enter $Y_2 = 1/(1 + X^2)$.
3. Enter a $[-2, 2]$ by $[-1, 1]$ viewing window and execute Prgm SLOPEFLD.
4. Edit Prgm EULERG.
5. Delete line 3 (:ClrDraw).
6. Go to line 13 (:Pt$-$On $(X, Y, 1)$) and change the third parameter from 1 to 3 (:Pt$-$On $(X, Y, 3)$).
7. Execute Prgm EULERG.

8. Enter an initial *x*-value of -2.

9. Enter an initial *y*-value of .2.

10. Enter a step size of 0.1.

These steps produce the graph shown in Figure 4.16.

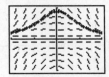

Figure 4.16 Slope field for $y' = -2xy^2$ and Euler's method.

Note: This example will also work with Prgm IMPEULG and Prgm RUNKUTG.

4.22 Visualizing Rectangular Approximation Methods for Areas

Program 22

AREA (graph left, right, and midpoint rectangles used for area approximation)
Input: $f(x), a, b, n$ (number of rectangles)
Output: numeric results and graphs of rectangles used to approximate areas bounded by $f(x), a, b$, and the *x*-axis

```
Prgm: AREA
:Input "A=", A
:Input "B=", B
:Input "NO. OF SUBINT=", N
:(B − A)/N→H
:H/2→D
:0→L
:0→M
:0→R
:ClrDraw
:DispGraph
:0→J
:A→X
:Lbl 1
:Y₁ + L→L
:Line (X, 0, X, Y₁)
:Line (X, Y₁, X + H, Y₁)
:Line (X + H, 0, X + H, Y₁)
:X + H→X
:J + 1→J
:If J < N
:Goto 1
:Pause
:HL→L
:ClrHome
:Disp "LEFT="
:Disp L
:Pause
```

```
:ClrDraw
:DispGraph
:0→J
:A + H→X
:Lbl 2
:Y₁ + R→R
:Line (X − H, 0, X − H, Y₁)
:Line (X − H, Y₁, X, Y₁)
:Line (X, 0, X, Y₁)
:X + H→X
:J + 1→J
:If J < N
:Goto 2
:Pause
:HR→R
:ClrHome
:Disp "LEFT="
:Disp L
:Disp "RIGHT="
:Disp R
:Pause
:ClrDraw
:DispGraph
:0→J
:A + D→X
:Lbl 3
:Y₁ + M→M
:Line (X − D, 0, X − D, Y₁)
:Line (X − D, Y₁, X + D, Y₁)
:Line (X + D, Y₁, X + D, 0)
:X + H→X
:1 + J→J
:If J < N
:Goto 3
:Pause
:HM→M
:ClrHome
:Disp "LEFT="
:Disp L
:Disp "RIGHT="
:Disp R
:Disp "MIDPOINT="
:Disp M
```

Example 22

Graph the left, right and midpoint rectangles that approximate the area bounded by the function $y = 4x − x^2$.

Directions:

1. Enter $Y_1 = 4X − X^2$
2. Enter a $[−1, 5]$ by $[−1, 4]$ viewing window.
3. Execute Prgm AREA.

4. Enter 0 for A.

5. Enter 4 for B.

6. Enter 4 for the number of subintervals.

You should see a graph like Fig. 4.17 that illustrates the left-hand rectangles.

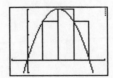

Figure 4.17 Left-rectangles.

7. Press ENTER to see the sum of the areas of the left-hand rectangles (10) and then press ENTER again to continue.

Now you should see the right-hand rectangles (see Fig. 4.18).

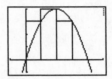

Figure 4.18 Right-rectangles.

8. Press ENTER to see the sums of the left-hand and right-hand rectangles (10 again) and then press ENTER to continue.

You should see midpoint rectangles like those in Fig. 4.19.

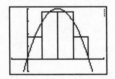

Figure 4.19 Midpoint rectangles.

9. Press ENTER once more to see the numerical results of the summations.

4.23 Investigating Limits

Example 23A

Graphically investigate $\lim\limits_{x \to -\infty} \tan^{-1} x$, $\lim\limits_{x \to \infty} \tan^{-1} x$.

   Directions:

1. Enter $Y_1 = \tan^{-1}(x)$.

2. Enter $Y_2 = -\pi/2$.

3. Enter $Y_3 = \pi/2$.

4. Graph in a $[-100, 100]$ by $[-3, 3]$ viewing window.

These steps produce the graph shown in Fig. 4.20.

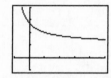

Figure 4.20 End behavior of arctan *x*.

This graph provides evidence that $\lim\limits_{x \to -\infty} tan^{-1}x = -\dfrac{\pi}{2}$ and $\lim\limits_{x \to \infty} tan^{-1}x = \dfrac{\pi}{2}$.

Example 23B

Graphically investigate $\lim\limits_{x \to 0+} (1+x)^{1/x}$.

Directions:

1. Enter $Y_1 = (1 + X)\verb|^|(1/X)$.
2. Graph in a $[-1, 5]$ by $[-1, 4]$ viewing window.

These steps produce the graph shown in Fig. 4.21.

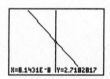

Figure 4.21 $y = (1 + x)\verb|^|(1/x)$.

Zoom in several times on the *y*-intercept of the graph and then trace towards the *y*-intercept from the positive side. Zoom-in produces something similar to the graph shown in Fig. 4.22.

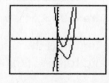

Figure 4.22 Zoom in on $y = (1 + x)\verb|^|(1/x)$.

This graph provides evidence that $\lim\limits_{x \to 0+}(1+x)^{1/x} = e$. This limit is the *y*-coordinate of a removable discontinuity in the graph.

Example 23C

Find a local minimum value of $f(x) = x^3 - 4x^2 + 3x - 4$.

Directions:

1. Enter $Y_1 = X\verb|^|3 - 4X^2 + 3X - 4$.
2. Enter $Y_2 = \text{nDeriv}(Y_1, X, X)$.
3. Graph in a $[-10, 10]$ by $[-10, 10]$ viewing window.

These steps should produce the graph shown in Fig. 4.23. Notice that the zeros of the derivative correspond to the x-coordinates of the extrema of f(x).

Figure 4.23 $y = x^3 - 4x^2 + 3x - 4$ and its derivative.

4. Press

$$\boxed{\text{2nd}} \; \boxed{\text{CALC}} \; [2\text{:zero}]$$

to find the zero of Y_2 near $X = 2.2$.

(Remember to use the up cursor-movement key to move the cursor to Y_2 before you enter the left and right bounds and the initial guess.)

The value of the zero should be 2.2152502.

5. You can evaluate $f(2.2152502)$ by using the CALCULATE [1:value] feature.

Press

$$\boxed{\text{2nd}} \; \boxed{\text{CALC}} \; [1\text{:value}] \; \mathbf{2} \; \boxed{\cdot} \; \mathbf{2152502} \; \boxed{\text{ENTER}}$$

The value of Y_1 should be -6.112612.

The exact local minimum is $f\left(\dfrac{8 + \sqrt{28}}{6}\right) = -6.112611791$ (to nine decimal places).

4.24 Find Local Extrema

Program 23

MAXFIND, MINFIND (find local extrema)
Input: $f(x)$, initial approximation of extreme point
Output: (approximate) coordinates of local extreme point

Example 26

Find local minimum and maximum values of $f(x) = x^3 - 4x^2 + 3x - 4$.
  Directions:

1. Enter $Y_1 = X^3 - 4X^2 + 3X - 4$.

2. Graph in a $[-10, 10]$ by $[-10, 10]$ viewing window.

3. Press $\boxed{\text{2nd}} \; \boxed{\text{CALC}}$ [3:minimum].

4. Move the cursor until it is slightly left of the minimum and press $\boxed{\text{ENTER}}$.

This marks the left bound.

5. Move the cursor until it is slightly right of the minimum and press $\boxed{\text{ENTER}}$.

This marks the right bound.

6. Move the cursor as close as possible to the local minimum and press $\boxed{\text{ENTER}}$.

This marks your guess.
The local minimum is at $x \approx 2.22$ (see Figure 4.24).

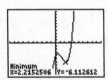

Figure 4.24 Local Minimum

The procedure to find a local maximum is the same as the procedure to find a local minimum. Press $\boxed{\text{2nd}} \; \boxed{\text{CALC}}$ [4:maximum and follow steps 4, 5, and 6 above.

C H A P T E R
5

Exploring Calculus
with the TI-86

The following toolbox programs and examples are useful in exploring and visualizing
concepts in calculus. In some cases, you will be given a program that must be entered in
the calculator before you can explore a particular concept. In other cases, the program is a
built-in part of the TI-86, so you will not have to program the calculator in order to explore
the concept. In either case, the program will be described by a name in uppercase letters and
you will be given the input and output parameters. If it is built in, you will be given the keys
and functions necessary to execute the program.

5.1 Numerical Derivative

Program 1

NDER (numerical derivative)
Input: $f(x)$, A and h (step size)
Output: (approximate) value of $f'(A)$
This is a built-in program on the TI-86. It appears as the nDer option in the CALC menu,
or you can always find it in the CATALOG menu. To find the derivative of $f(x)$ with respect
to x, evaluated at $x = a$, enter nDer $(f(x), x, a)$. The step size (h) is determined by the δ variable in the Tolerance screen.

Example 1

If $f(x) = x - 2 \sin x$, then $f'(0)$ is approximated by the following key sequence:

Table 5.1

Comments	Input (keystrokes)	Screen Display
1. Access the Tolerance screen and enter the step size.	[2nd] [MEM] [F4:TOL] [·] 01 [ENTER] [·] 01	TOLERANCE tol = .01 δ = .01
2. Exit the Tolerance screen.	[EXIT]	
3. Select the nDer option from the CALC menu and input the derivative of $f(x)$ with respect to x, evaluated at $x = a$.	[2nd] [CALC] [F2:nDER] [x-VAR] [—] 2 [SIN] [x-VAR] [,] [x-VAR] [,] 0 [ )] [ENTER]	nDER $(x - 2 \sin x, x, 0)$ $-.999966666833$

Table 5.2 Numerical derivatives of $x - 2 \sin x$.

A	NDER(f) $h = 0.1$	NDER(f) $h = 0.01$	NDER(f) $h = 0.0001$	EXACT $f'(A)$
−10	2.675347551	2.678115089	2.67814305	2.678143058
−7	−.5052927574	−.5077793787	−.50780451	−.507804509
−2	1.83090721	1.832279802	1.832293672	1.832293673
0	−.9966683329	−.9999666668	−.9999999967	−1.000000000
1	−.0788045043	−.0805866018	−.08060461	−.080604612
5	.433620697	.4326850844	.43267563	.432675629
10	2.675347551	2.678115089	2.67814305	2.678143058

5.2 Graph of Numerical Derivative

Program 2

NDERGRAF (graph of numerical derivative)
Input: $f(x)$
Output: graph of $y = f'(x)$
This is a built-in function on the TI-86, so no programming is required. To overlay the graph of $f'(x)$ on the graph of $y = f(x)$, do the following:

- Enter the function y in y_1.
- Enter $y_2 = \text{nDer}(y_1, x, x)$
- Select an appropriate viewing window.
- Graph.

If you don't want the graph of $f(x)$ to appear, unselect y_1 before you press [GRAPH]. You can increase the accuracy of the graph by reducing the step size, (d), but the graph might be drawn more slowly. Generally d = .001 will give accurate results.

Example 2

To graph $y = x - 2 \sin x$ and its derivative, do the following:

1. Select Radian mode, and then enter $y_1 = x - 2 \sin x$.
2. Enter $y_2 = \text{nDer}(y_1, x, x)$.
3. Graph using a $[-10, 10]$ by $[-10, 10]$ window.

These steps produce the graph shown in Fig. 5.1.

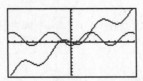

Figure 5.1 $x - 2 \sin x$ and its derivative.

Notice the roots of the derivative have the same x-coordinates as the extrema of $f(x)$. Notice also that $f(x)$ is increasing on the intervals where $f'(x)$ is positive and decreasing on the intervals where $f'(x)$ is negative. To see the second derivative, enter $y_3 = \text{nDer}(\text{nDer}(y_1, x, x), x, x)$ and press [GRAPH].

5.3 Draw a Line Tangent to a Curve

Program 3

TANLINE (draws a line tangent to a curve)

Input: $f(x), a$

Output: overlays tangent line at $(a, f(a))$ on the graph of $y = f(x)$

A function in the DRAW menu does the job directly, either from the Home screen or from the graph interactively.

Example 3

Lines tangent to the curve $y = x - 2 \sin x$ at $x = -6, -5.24$, and -4 can be overlaid on the curve. Directions:

1. Graph $y_1 = x - 2 \sin x$ in the $[-10, 10]$ by $[-10, 10]$ window.

2. From the GRAPH [Math] menu select [F1:TANLN].

3. Use the cursor movement keys to move the cursor until x is approximately -6, then press ENTER. Or, instead of using the cursor keys, you can enter -6 directly using the keypad.

A tangent line is drawn at approximately $x = -6$.

4. Press EXIT to return to the GRAPH menu at the bottom of the screen.

5. Select [F2:Draw] and [F2:TANLN] and provide the parameters y_1 and -5.24. The command on the Home Screen should read "TanLn $(y_1, -5.24)$". Press ENTER

A tangent line is drawn at $x = -5.24$.

6. Return to the GRAPH [Math] menu and select [F1:TANLN].

7. Use the cursor movement keys to move the cursor until x is approximately -4, then press ENTER. Or, instead of using the cursor keys, you can enter -4 directly using the keypad.

These steps produce the graph shown in Fig. 5.2.

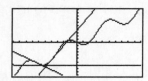

Figure 5.2 Lines tangent to $x - 2 \sin x$.

Notice in the steps for Example 3 that the x-coordinate of the point of tangency can be entered by tracing to the desired point on the graph or by entering the value directly with a command on the Home screen.

5.4   Definite Integral

Program 4

NINT (definite integral)

Input: $f(x)$, a, and b

Output: (approximate) value of $\displaystyle\int_a^b f(x)\,dx$

This is a built-in program. It appears as the fnInt option in the CALC menu. The expression fnInt $(f(x), x, a, b)$ will return the approximate value of $\displaystyle\int_a^b f(x)\,dx$. The accuracy of the numerical approximation is determined by the tol variable in the Tolerance screen.

Example 4A

A proper integral such as $\displaystyle\int_0^{\pi/2} \cos x\,dx$ can be evaluated by the following key sequence.

Table 5.3

Input (keystrokes)	Screen Display
[2nd] [MEM] [F4:TOL] [•] **01**	TOLERANCE tol = .01
[EXIT]	
[2nd] [CALC] [F5:fnInt]	fnInt (
[COS] [x-VAR] [,] [x-VAR] [,] **0**	fnInt (cos $x, x, 0, \pi/2$)
[,] [2nd] [π] [÷] **2** [ )] [ENTER]	1

This key sequence creates the command fnInt(cos $x, x, 0, \pi/2$) on the Home screen followed by the value of the definite integral (1). The first parameter in the fnInt command is the function to be integrated. The second parameter is the variable with respect to which the function is to be integrated. The third and fourth parameters are the lower and upper limits of integration.

Example 4B

An improper integral such as $\displaystyle\int_{-1}^{3} \frac{\sin x}{x}\,dx$ can be approximated if we assume $\dfrac{\sin x}{x} = 1$ at $x = 0$.

Directions:

1. Press

$$[2nd]\ [MEM]\ [F4:TOL]$$

and set the tol variable to .01.

2. In the Home screen enter fnInt $((\sin x)/x, x, -1, 3)$.

The definite integral is approximately 2.79473559858.

Although Prgm NINT is designed to evaluate proper definite integrals, it can sometimes approximate improper integrals by the proper selection of the tol variable or by making adjustments in the limits of integration. Try repeating the steps in Example 4B using a tolerance of .0001 instead of .01. The program encounters a 'DIV BY ZERO' error while it is running because it attempts to evaluate $(\sin x)/x$ at $x = 0$.

If a tolerance cannot be found that will allow the calculator to evaluate the improper integral, the limits of integration may be adjusted to approximate the solution. Repeat the steps in Example 4B using a tolerance of .0001 but replace the lower limit of integration of -1 with $-.99999$. This creates a partition of the interval of integration that will not cause division by zero. The new approximation to the integral is 2.79472718364.

5.5 Graph a Function Defined by an Integral

Program 5

NINTGRAF (graph a function defined by an integral)
Input: $f(x), a$
Output: graph of $\int_a^x f(t)\,dt$

The built-in program appearing as the fnInt option in the CALC menu can be used to graph a function defined by an integral. To visualize $\int_a^x f(t)\,dt$, enter y1 = fnInt $(f(t), t, a, x)$ and graph.

Example 5A

The function $\int_0^x \dfrac{\sin t}{t}\,dt$ can be graphed if we assume $\dfrac{\sin x}{x} = 1$ at $x = 0$.
Directions:

1. Press $\boxed{\text{2nd}}$ $\boxed{\text{MEM}}$ [F4:TOL] and set the tolerance to .01.

2. Enter y1 = fnInt$((\sin t)/t, t, 0, x)$.

3. Select [F2:WIND] in the GRAPH menu and create a $[-10, 10]$ by $[-3, 3]$ viewing window.

4. Graph. To speed up graphing, change xres in the WINDOW setting screen to higher number. For example, changing xres from 1 to 3 will triple the speed, but the function will be evaluated and graphed at every 3rd pixel, so increasing xres too much may affect the resolution of the graph.

These steps produce the graph shown in Fig. 5.3.

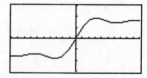

Figure 5.3 Antiderivative of $(\sin x)/x$.

This program is designed to graph functions defined by proper integrals; however, it can sometimes graph functions defined by improper integrals. You might need to make adjustments in the tolerance or in the limits of integration. If you encounter an error while attempting to graph the antiderivative, try using a different value for the tol variable in the Tolerance screen or changing the lower limit of integration by a very small amount, such as .00001. These adjustments might allow the program to avoid the cause of the discontinuity in the function that is being integrated. This is similar to the problem encountered while using fnInt in Example 4B.

Example 5B

Graph $\int_0^x (1-2\cos t)\, dt$ and compare with the exact antiderivative.

Directions:

1. Set the tolerance to .01 and select the Radian mode.

2. Enter $y1 = \text{fnInt}(1-2\cos t, t, 0, x)$.

3. Enter $y2 = x - 2\sin x$.

4. Select [F3:ZOOM] in the GRAPH menu then [F4:ZSTD] in the ZOOM menu to create a standard $[-10, 10]$ by $[-10, 10]$ viewing window.

These steps produce the graph shown in Fig. 5.4.

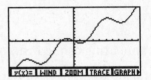

Figure 5.4 Antiderivative of $1-2\cos x$.

The accuracy of the graph might be improved by decreasing the tolerance. This change might improve accuracy at the expense of speed.

5.6 Solve an Equation

Program 6

SOLVE (solve an equation)

Input: $f(x)$ initial approximation of root

Output: (approximate) root of $f(x)$

This built-in feature is the Root option in the GRAPH [Math] menu. To approximate the root of a function, do the following:

• Graph the function.

• Select [F1:ROOT] in the GRAPH [Math] menu.

• Use the cursor-movement keys to select a left bound, a right bound, and a guess for the root.

Example 6

Solve $x = 2\sin x$ (find the roots of $x - 2\sin x$).

Directions:

1. Enter $y1 = x - 2\sin x$.

2. Graph using a $[-10, 10]$ by $[-10, 10]$ window.

3. Select [F1:ROOT] in the GRAPH [Math] menu.

You will see a prompt for a left bound.

4. Use the cursor movement keys to move the cursor to $x = -2.2222$ and press $\boxed{\text{ENTER}}$.

Doing this marks the left bound. You will see a prompt for a right bound.

5. Move the cursor to $x = -1.1111$ and press $\boxed{\text{ENTER}}$.

This selects the right bound. You will see a prompt for an initial guess for the root.

6. Move the cursor to $x = -1.90476$ and press ⎡ENTER⎤.

The root is -1.895494267.

7. Select [F1:ROOT] from the GRAPH [Math] menu again.

8. Select $x = -.47619$ for the left bound, $x = .47619$ for the right bound, and $x = 0$ for the initial guess. Note that you can directly enter the values for the bounds and initial guess using the keypad.

Another root is 0.

The root algorithm finds a root close to the initial guess that is between the left and right bounds.

5.7 Rectangle Approximation Method

Program 7

RAM (rectangle approximation method)
Input: $f(x)$, a, b, and n (number of subintervals)

Output: (approximate) value of $\displaystyle\int_a^b f(x)\, dx$ using left, right, and midpoint rectangles

Table 5.4

Comments	Input (keystrokes)	Screen Display
1. Enter Prgm RAM.	⎡PRGM⎤ [F2:EDIT] **RAM** ⎡ENTER⎤	PROGRAM RAM
2. Initialize sums.	**0** ⎡STO▶⎤ **S** ⎡2nd⎤ ⎡:⎤ ⎡ALPHA⎤ **0** ⎡STO▶⎤ **SM** ⎡2nd⎤ ⎡:⎤ ⎡ALPHA⎤ **0** ⎡STO▶⎤ **SR** ⎡ENTER⎤	:0→S: 0→SM: 0→SR
3. Enter A, B, N.	[F3:I/O] [F1:Input] ⎡MORE⎤ ⎡MORE⎤ [F1:"] ⎡ALPHA⎤ **A** ⎡ALPHA⎤ = [F1:"] ⎡,⎤ ⎡ALPHA⎤ **A** ⎡ENTER⎤	:Input "A =", A
	⎡MORE⎤ [F1:Input] ⎡MORE⎤ ⎡MORE⎤ [F1:"] ⎡ALPHA⎤ **B** ⎡ALPHA⎤ = [F1:"] ⎡,⎤ ⎡ALPHA⎤ **B** ⎡ENTER⎤	:Input "B =", B
	⎡MORE⎤ [F1:Input] ⎡MORE⎤ ⎡MORE⎤ [F1:"] ⎡ALPHA⎤ ⎡ALPHA⎤ **NO** ⎡ALPHA⎤ ⎡•⎤ ⎡ALPHA⎤ ⎡ALPHA⎤ **SUBINT** = [F1:"] ⎡ALPHA⎤ ⎡,⎤ ⎡ALPHA⎤ **N** ⎡ENTER⎤	:Input "NO. SUBINT =", N
4. Calculate step size.	⎡(⎤ ⎡ALPHA⎤ **B** ⎡−⎤ ⎡ALPHA⎤ **A** ⎡)⎤ ⎡÷⎤ ⎡ALPHA⎤ **N** ⎡STO▶⎤ **D** ⎡ENTER⎤	:(B−A)/N→D
5. Initialize x-coordinates of rectangles.	⎡ALPHA⎤ **A** ⎡STO▶⎤ **RA** ⎡2nd⎤ ⎡:⎤ ⎡ALPHA⎤ ⎡(⎤ 2 ⎡ALPHA⎤ **A** ⎡+⎤ ⎡ALPHA⎤ **D** ⎡)⎤ ⎡÷⎤ 2 ⎡STO▶⎤ **AM** ⎡ENTER⎤	:A→RA: (2A+D)/2→AM
	⎡ALPHA⎤ **A** ⎡+⎤ ⎡ALPHA⎤ **D** ⎡STO▶⎤ **RR** ⎡ENTER⎤	:A+D→RR

Continued on next page

(Continued)

Comments	Input (keystrokes)	Screen Display
6. Sum areas.	[EXIT] [F4:CTL] [MORE] [F4:Lbl] [ALPHA] **T1**	:Lbl T1:RA→x:y1+S→S
	[2nd] [:] [ALPHA] **R**	
	[ALPHA] **A** [STO▸] [ALPHA]	
	[x-VAR] [2nd] [:] [2nd]	
	[ALPHA] **y1** [+]	
	[ALPHA] **S** [STO▸] **S** [ENTER]	
	[ALPHA] **R** [ALPHA] **R** [STO▸]	:RR→x:y1+SR→SR
	[ALPHA] [x-VAR] [2nd] [:] [2nd]	
	[ALPHA] **y1** [+] [ALPHA] **S**	
	[ALPHA] **R** [STO▸] **SR** [ENTER]	
	[ALPHA] **R** [ALPHA] **R** [+]	:RR+D→RR
	[ALPHA] **D** [STO▸] **RR** [ENTER]	
	[ALPHA] **R** [ALPHA] **A** [+]	:RA+D→RA
	[ALPHA] **D** [STO▸] **RA** [ENTER]	
	[ALPHA] **A** [ALPHA] **M** [STO▸]	:AM→x:y1+SM→SM
	[ALPHA] [x-VAR] [2nd] [:]	
	[2nd] [ALPHA] **y1** [+]	
	[ALPHA] **S** [ALPHA] **M** [STO▸]	
	SM [ENTER]	
	[ALPHA] **A** [ALPHA] **M** [+]	:AM+D→AM
	[ALPHA] **D** [STO▸] **AM** [ENTER]	
	[MORE] [MORE] [MORE] [F1:If]	:If B−RA>.001
	[ALPHA] **B** [−] [ALPHA] **R**	
	[ALPHA] **A** [2nd] [TEST] [F3: >]	
	[·] **001** [ENTER]	
	[EXIT] [MORE] [F5:Goto] [ALPHA]	:Goto T1
	T1 [ENTER]	
7. Print results.	[EXIT] [F3:I/O] [F3:Disp]	:Disp "LEFT =", D∗S
	[MORE] [MORE] [F1:"] [ALPHA]	
	[ALPHA] **LEFT**= [ALPHA]	
	[F1:"] [,] [ALPHA] **D** [×]	
	[ALPHA] **S** [ENTER]	
	[MORE] [F3:Disp] [MORE] [MORE]	:Disp "MID =", D∗SM
	[F1:"] [ALPHA] [ALPHA] **MID**= [ALPHA]	
	[F1:"] [,] [ALPHA] **D** [×] [ALPHA] **S**	
	[ALPHA] **M** [ENTER]	
	[MORE] [F3:Disp] [MORE] [MORE]	:Disp "Right =", D∗SR
	[F1:"] [ALPHA] [ALPHA] **RIGHT**=	
	[ALPHA] [F1:"] [,] [ALPHA] **D** [×]	
	[ALPHA] **S** [ALPHA] **R** [2nd] [QUIT]	

Example 7A

An integral such as $\int_{-1}^{3} \frac{\sin x}{x} \, dx$ can be approximated if we assume $\frac{\sin x}{x} = 1$ at $x = 0$.
Directions:

1. Enter $y_1 = \sin (x)/x$ and select Radian mode.

2. Execute Prgm RAM.

3. Enter $-.99999$ for A, 3 for B, and 4 for the number of subintervals.

These steps produce the three approximations to the definite integral given in the first row of Table 5.5.

Repeat steps 2 and 3 in Example 7A, replacing n with 10, 50, 100, and 1000, to produce the remainder of the table.

Table 5.5 Rectangular approximations to $\int_{-1}^{3} \frac{\sin x}{x} \, dx$.

N	Left	Mid	Right
4	3.13758325638	2.82207901499	2.34315124866
10	2.94497750764	2.79904955137	2.62720470456
50	2.82615946391	2.79489969057	2.76260490329
100	2.81052957724	2.79477030735	2.77875229693
1000	2.7963151852	2.79472761487	2.79313745717

Because the integrand in Example 7A is not defined at $x = 0$, the lower limit of integration was replaced with $-.99999$. This creates a subdivision of the interval from -1 to 3 that doesn't require the program to evaluate $(\sin x)/x$ at $x = 0$. Try repeating steps 2 and 3 in Example 7A using -1 instead of $-.99999$. In this case, notice that the program encounters a Math error while it is running because it attempts to evaluate $(\sin x)/x$ at $x = 0$.

Example 7B

Compare rectangular approximations of $\int_{0}^{\pi/2} \cos x \, dx$ using 10, 100, and 1000 subdivisions with the exact solution.

Directions:

1. Enter $y_1 = \cos x$.

2. Execute Prgm RAM.

3. Enter 0 for A and $\pi/2$ for B.

4. Enter 10 for the number of subintervals.

5. Repeat Prgm RAM using 100, and then 1000, for the number of subintervals.

These steps produce the results shown in Table 5.6.

Table 5.6 Rectangular approximations to $\int_{0}^{\pi/2} \cos x \, dx$.

N	Left	Mid	Right	Exact
10	1.07648280269	1.00102882414	.919403170015	1.0
100	1.00783341987	1.00001028091	.992125456606	1.0
1000	1.00078519255	1.00000010281	.999214396221	1.0

Increasing the number of subintervals improves the accuracy of the approximation.

5.8 Trapezoidal Method

Program 8

TRAP (trapezoidal method)
Input: $f(x)$, a, b, and n (number of subintervals)

Output: trapezoidal approximation of $\int_a^b f(x)\,dx$

```
Prgm: TRAP
:Input "NO. OF SUBINT =", N
:Input "A =", A
:Input "B =", B
:(B−A)/N→D
:A+D→A: A→TA
:0→S
:Lbl T1: TA→x:2*y1+S→S
:TA+D→TA
:If B−TA > .001
:Goto T1
:A−D→x: y1→L: B→x: y1→R
:(D/2) (S+R+L)→T
:Disp "TRAP=", T
```

Example 8A

An integral such as $\int_{-1}^{3} \dfrac{\sin x}{x}\,dx$ can be approximated if we assume $\dfrac{\sin x}{x} = 1$ at $x = 0$.

Directions:

1. Enter $y_1 = (\sin x)/x$

2. Execute Prgm TRAP.

3. Enter 10 for the number of subintervals, $-.99999$ for A, and 3 for B.

4. Repeat steps 2 and 3 using 100, and then 1000, for the number of subintervals.

These steps produce the results shown in Table 5.7.

Table 5.7 Trapezoidal approximations to $\int_{-1}^{3} \dfrac{\sin x}{x}\,dx$.

N	10	100	1000
TRAP	2.7860911061	2.79464093708	2.79472632119

A trapezoid approximation requires a partition of the interval $[A, B]$. The function is evaluated at points in the partition. Because the integrand in Example 8A is not defined at $x = 0$, the lower limit of integration was replaced with $-.99999$. Doing this creates a subdivision of the interval from -1 to 3 that doesn't require the program to evaluate $(\sin x)/x$ at $x = 0$. Try repeating the steps in Example 8A using -1 instead of $-.99999$. In this case, notice that the program encounters a Math error while it is running because it attempts to evaluate $(\sin x)/x$ at $x = 0$. This is similar to the difficulty encountered in using Prgm RAM to evaluate the same integral.

Example 8B

Compare trapezoidal approximations of $\int_0^{\pi/2} \cos x \, dx$ using 10, 100, and 1000 subdivisions with the exact solution.

Directions:

1. Enter $y_1 = \cos x$.

2. Execute Prgm TRAP.

3. Enter 10 for the number of subintervals.

4. Enter 0 for A and $\pi/2$ for B.

5. Repeat steps 2–4 using 100, and then 1000, for the number of subintervals.

These steps produce the results shown in Table 5.8.

Table 5.8 Trapezoidal approximations to $\int_0^{\pi/2} \cos x \, dx$.

N	10	100	1000	Exact
TRAP	.997942986354	.99997943824	.999999794385	1.0

Increasing the number of subintervals improves the accuracy of approximation. The error estimate for the trapezoidal rule can be used to determine the accuracy of this program.

5.9 Simpson's Method

Program 9

SIMP (Simpson's method)

Input: $f(x)$, a, b, and n (the number of subintervals (n) must be an even number.)

Output: Simpson's approximation of $\int_a^b f(x) \, dx$

```
Prgm: SIMP
:Input "NO. OF SUBINT=", N
:Input "A=", A
:Input "B=", B
:(B−A)/N→D
:A+D→A: A→TA
:0→S
:Lbl T1: TA→x: y1→Y1
:TA+D→x: 4*Y1+2*y1+S→S
:TA+2D→TA
:If B−TA > .001
:Goto T1
:A−D→x: y1→L: B→x: y1→R
:(D/3) (S+L−R)→SIM
:Disp "SIMP=", SIM
```

The uppercase (Y1) and lowercase (y1) entries are not the same variable.

Example 9A

An integral such as $\int_{-1}^{3} \frac{\sin x}{x} dx$ can be approximated if we assume $\frac{\sin x}{x} = 1$ at $x = 0$.

Directions:

1. Enter $y_1 = (\sin x)/x$.

2. Execute Prgm SIMP.

3. Enter 10 for the number of subintervals, $-.99999$ for A, and 3 for B.

4. Repeat steps 2 and 3 using 100, and then 1000, for the number of subintervals.

These steps produce the results shown in the second row of Table 5.9. The trapezoidal and rectangular approximations have been included in the table for comparison.

Table 5.9 Comparison of numerical solutions to $\int_{-1}^{3} \frac{\sin x}{x} dx$.

N	10	100	1000
SIMP	2.79477378779	2.79472718825	2.79472718364
LEFT	2.94497750764	2.81052957724	2.7963151852
MID	2.79904955137	2.79477030735	2.79472761487
RIGHT	2.62720470456	2.77875229693	2.79313745717
TRAP	2.7860911061	2.79464093708	2.79472632119

Simpson's approximation requires a partition of the interval $[A, B]$. The function is evaluated at points in the partition. Because the integrand in Example 9A is not defined at $x = 0$, the lower limit of integration was replaced with $-.99999$. Doing this creates a subdivision of the interval from -1 to 3 that doesn't require the program to evaluate $(\sin x)/x$ at $x = 0$. Try repeating the steps in Example 9A using -1 instead of $-.99999$. In this case, notice that the program encounters a math error while it is running because it attempts to evaluate $(\sin x)/x$ at $x = 0$. This is similar to the difficulty encountered in using Prgms RAM and TRAP to evaluate the same integral.

Example 9B

Compare Simpson's method approximations of $\int_{0}^{\pi/2} \cos x \, dx$ using 10, 100, and 1000 subdivisions with the exact solution.

Directions:

1. Enter $y_1 = \cos x$.

2. Execute Prgm SIMP.

3. Enter 10 for the number of subintervals.

4. Enter 0 for A and $\pi/2$ for B.

5. Repeat steps 2–4 using 100, and then 1000, for the number of subintervals.

These steps produce the results shown in Table 5.10. The trapezoidal and rectangular approximations have been included for comparison.

Table 5.10 Comparison of numerical solutions to $\int_{0}^{\pi/2} \cos x \, dx$.

N	10	100	1000	Exact
SIMP	1.00000339222	1.00000000034	.999999999999	1.0
LEFT	1.07648280269	1.00783341987	1.00078519255	1.0
MID	1.00102882414	1.00001028091	1.00000010281	1.0
RIGHT	.919403170015	.992125456606	.999214396221	1.0
TRAP	.997942986354	.99997943824	.999999794385	1.0

Increasing the number of subintervals improves the accuracy of the approximation in a dramatic way. Simpson's method gives 10-place accuracy with just 100 subdivisions. The error estimate for Simpson's method can be used to determine the accuracy of this program.

5.10 Euler Table

Program 10

EULERT (Euler table)

Input: $f'(x, y)$; initial x, y; step size (h); number of ordered pairs in table (n)
Output: table of ordered pairs (x, y), where each pair is an element of $y = f(x)$ and $f(x)$ is a solution to the initial value problem.

```
Prgm: EULERT
:Input "INITIAL X =", x
:Input "Y (INITIAL x) =", Y
:Input "STEP SIZE =", H
:Input "NO. OF POINTS =", N
:0→J
:Lbl A
:Disp "X =", x
:Disp "Y =", Y
:Pause
:Y + H*y1→Y
:x + H→x
:J + 1→J
:If J≤N
:Goto A
```

Example 10

Prgm EULERT can be used to find a numerical solution to the initial value problem $\frac{dy}{dx} = -2xy^2$ with initial conditions $f(-2) = 0.2$

Directions:

1. Enter $y_1 = -2x * Y^2$.

2. Execute Prgm EULERT.

3. Enter an initial x-value of -2.

4. Enter an initial y-value of 0.2.

5. Enter a step size of 0.1.

6. Enter 40 for the number of points.

The program will produce the ordered pairs found in Table 5.10. The x-values are in the first column and the y-values are in the third column. To see the next pair, you must press ENTER *after each ordered pair.*

The exact solution to this differential equation is $y = \dfrac{1}{1 + x^2}$. The second column of Table 5.10 contains the exact values of the solution. Compare these with the values obtained by Prgm EULERT. As x moves away from the initial value, the difference between the exact value and the EULERT solution increases.

Table 5.10 Numerical solutions to $\frac{dy}{dx} = -2xy^2$.

x	EXACT $1/(1 + x^2)$	EULERT	IMPEULT	RUNKUTT
−2.0	.20000000	.2000	.2000	.2000000
−1.9	.21691974	.2160	.2169	.2169197
−1.8	.23584906	.2337	.2357	.2358490
−1.7	.25706941	.2534	.2568	.2570692
−1.6	.28089888	.2752	.2805	.2808986
−1.5	.30769231	.2995	.3071	.3076918
−1.4	.33783784	.3264	.3370	.3378371
−1.3	.37174721	.3562	.3706	.3717462
−1.2	.40983607	.3892	.4083	.4098346
−1.1	.45248869	.4255	.4504	.4524866
−1.0	.50000000	.4654	.4972	.4999972
−0.9	.55248619	.5087	.5489	.5524824
−0.8	.6097561	.5553	.6051	.6097511
−0.7	.67114094	.6046	.6652	.6711346
−0.6	.73529412	.6558	.7279	.7352863
−0.5	.80000000	.7074	.7910	.7999905
−0.4	.86206897	.7574	.8514	.8620579
−0.3	.91743119	.8033	.9052	.9174188
−0.2	.96153846	.8420	.9480	.9615250
−0.1	.99009901	.8704	.9757	.9900849
0	1.0000000	.8855	.9852	.9999857
0.1	.99009901	.8855	.9755	.9900849
0.2	.96153846	.8699	.9477	.9615249
0.3	.91743119	.8396	.9048	.9174186
0.4	.86206897	.7973	.8510	.8620576
0.5	.80000000	.7464	.7905	.7999901
0.6	.73529412	.6907	.7275	.7352858
0.7	.67114094	.6335	.6649	.6711342
0.8	.6097561	.5773	.6048	.6097508
0.9	.55248619	.5240	.5487	.5524822
1.0	.50000000	.4746	.4972	.4999970
1.1	.45248869	.4295	.4504	.4524865
1.2	.40983607	.3889	.4083	.4098346
1.3	.37174721	.3526	.3707	.3717462
1.4	.33783784	.3203	.3371	.3378372
1.5	.30769231	.2916	.3072	.3076919
1.6	.28089888	.2661	.2806	.2808986
1.7	.2506941	.2434	.2569	.2570693
1.8	.23584906	.2233	.2358	.2358490
1.9	.21691974	.2053	.2170	.2169198
2.0	.20000000	.1893	.2001	.2000001

To see the approximation error for each ordered pair of output do the following.

1. Enter $y_2 = 1/(1 + x^2)$. This is the exact solution.

2. Edit Prgm EULERT

3. After the *x*- and *y*-values are displayed, and before the ":Pause" command, enter the following lines

   :Disp "y2, ERROR"
   :Disp y2
   :Disp abs(Y − y2)

4. Execute Prgm EULERT with parameters as stated in Example 10.

5.11 Euler Graph

Program 11

EULERG (Euler graph)
Input: $f'(x, y)$; initial x, y; step size (h);
Output: graph of solution to initial value differential equation problem using Euler's method
This is a built-in program on the TI-86 that is accessed in DifEq mode.

Example 11A
Use Prgm EULERG to graph the solution to the initial problem $\dfrac{dy}{dx} = -2xy^2$ with $y(-2) = 0.2$ and then compare with the exact solution.

1. In the Function (Func) mode, enter $y1 = 1/(1 + x^2)$.

2. In the MODE screen, select Differential Equation (DifEq) mode.

3. In the GRAPH [Format] menu (press [GRAPH] [MORE] [F1:FORMT]), select Euler and FldOff.

4. Enter $Q'1 = -2t * Q1^2$ in the $Q'(t)=$ menu.

5. Enter the following Window values:

*t*Min = −2	*x*Min = −2	*y*Min = −1	EStep =1
*t*Max = 2	*x*Max = 2	*y*Max = 1	
*t*Step = .1	*x*Scl = 1	*y*Scl = 1	
*t*Plot = 0			

6. In the Initial Conditions (INITC) menu enter QI1 = .2.

7. In the AXES menu set $x = t$ and $y = $ Q1, then graph the solution to the differential equation by pressing [F5:GRAPH].

8. Select DrawF from the GRAPH [Draw] menu, and enter DrawF y1, then press ENTER.

These steps produce the graph shown in Fig. 5.5.

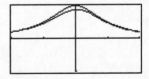

Figure 5.5 Euler's Method.

Notice the difference between the exact solution and Euler's method for *x* near zero.

Example 11B

Use Prgm EULERG to graph $\int_0^x \cos t \, dt$ and compare with the exact solution.

1. Enter $y_1 = \sin x$.
2. Select Differential Equation (DifEq) mode.
3. In the GRAPH [Format] menu, select Euler and FldOff.
4. Enter $Q'1 = \cos t$.
5. Enter the following Window values:

$t\text{Min} = 0$	$x\text{Min} = 0$	$y\text{Min} = -2$	EStep $=1$
$t\text{Max} = 2\pi$	$x\text{Max} = 2\pi$	$y\text{Max} = 2$	
$t\text{Step} = .1$	$x\text{Scl} = \pi/2$	$y\text{Scl} = 1$	
$t\text{Plot} = 0$			

6. In the Initial Conditions [INITC] menu enter QI1 = 0.
7. In the AXES menu set $x = t$ and $y = Q1$, then graph the solution to the differential equation.
8. Select DrawF from the GRAPH [Draw] menu, and enter DrawF y1, then press ENTER.

These steps produce the graph shown in Fig. 5.6.

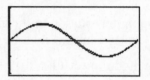

Figure 5.6 Antiderivative of cos x; Euler's Method.

Notice the difference between the exact solution and the Euler graph.

5.12 Improved Euler Table

Program 12

IMPEULT (improved Euler table)

Input: $f'(x, y)$; initial x, y; step size (h); number of ordered pairs in table (n)
Output: table of ordered pairs (x, y), where each pair is an element of $y = f(x)$ and $f(x)$ is a solution to the initial value problem

```
Prgm: IMPEULT
:0→J
:Input "INITIAL x=", x
:Input "Y (INITIAL x) =", Y
:Input "STEP SIZE=", H
:Input "NO. OF POINTS=", N
:Y→Z
:U=y1
:V=evalF(y1, Y, Z)     {The evalF option can be accessed by pressing [2nd] [CALC] F1:evalF].}
:Lbl A
:Disp "X=", x
:Disp "Y=", Y
:Pause
:H∗U→D
:Y+D→Z
:x+H→x
```

```
:Y+(D+H*V)/2→Y
:J+1→J
:If J≤N
:Goto A
```

Example 12

Prgm IMPEULT can be used to find a numerical solution to the initial value problem $\frac{dy}{dx} = -2xy^2$ with initial conditions $f(-2) = 0.2$.

Directions:

1. Enter $y1 = -2x*Y^2$.
2. Execute Prgm IMPEULT.
3. Enter an initial x-value of -2.
4. Enter an initial y-value of 0.2.
5. Enter a step of 0.1.
6. Enter 40 for the number of points.

The program will produce the ordered pairs found in Table 5.10 (in Example 10).

The x-values are in the first column and the y-values are in the fourth column. You must press ENTER after each ordered pair to see the next pair. Compare the results of Prgm IMPEULT with Prgm EULERT and with the exact results.

The approximation error can also be added to IMPEULT. Follow the steps at the end of Section 5.10.

5.13 Improved Euler Graph

Program 13

IMPEULG (improved Euler graph)

Input: $f'(x, y)$; initial x, y; step size (h)
Output: graph of solution to initial value differential equation problem using the improved Euler's method

```
Prgm: IMPEULG
:0→J: FnOff: ClrDrw
:Input "INITIAL x=", x
:Input "Y (INITIAL x)=", Y
:Input "STEP SIZE=", H
:(xMax−xMin)/abs H→N
:Y→Z
:U=y1
:V=evalF (y1, Y, Z)
:Lbl A
:PtOn (x, Y)
:H*U→D
:Y+D→Z
:x+H→x
:Y+(D+H*V)/2→Y
:J+1→J
:If J≤N
:Goto A
```

Example 13A

Use Prgm IMPEULG to graph the solution to the initial value problem $\frac{dy}{dx} = -2xy^2$, with $y(-2) = 0.2$, and then compare with the exact solution.

Directions:

1. Enter $y_1 = -2x*Y^2$.

2. Enter $y_2 = 1/(1+x^2)$.

3. Enter $[-2, 2]$ by $[-1, 1]$ window.

4. Execute Prgm IMPEULG.

5. Enter an initial x-value of -2.

6. Enter an initial y-value of 0.2.

7. Enter a step size of 0.1.

8. Select DrawF from the GRAPH [Draw] menu and enter DrawF y2.

These steps produce the graph shown in Fig. 5.7.

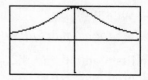

Figure 5.7 Improved Euler's method.

Compare this graph with the graph produced by Euler's method in Example 11A. Notice the improved agreement with the exact solution.

Example 13B

Use Prgm IMPEULG to graph $\int_0^x \cos t \, dt$ and compare with the exact solution.
Directions:

1. Enter $y_1 = \cos x$.

2. Enter $y_2 = \sin x$.

3. Enter a $[0, 2\pi]$ by $[-2, 2]$ window.

4. Execute Prgm IMPEULG.

5. Enter an initial x-value of 0.

6. Enter an initial y-value of 0.

7. Enter a step size of 0.1.

8. Select DrawF from the GRAPH [Draw] menu and enter DrawF y2.

These steps produce the graph shown in Fig. 5.8.

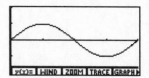

Figure 5.8 Antiderivative of cos x; improved Euler's method.

Compare this graph with that produced by Euler's method in Example 11B. Notice the improved agreement with the exact solution.

5.14 Runge-Kutta Table

Program 14

RUNKUTT (Runge-Kutta table)
Input: $f'(x, y)$; initial x, y; step size (h); number of ordered pairs in table (n)
Output: table of ordered pairs (x, y), where each pair is an element of $y = f(x)$ and $f(x)$ is a solution to the initial value problem.

```
Prgm: RUNKUTT
:0→M
:FX=evalF (y1, Y, Y)
:Input "INITIAL x=", x
:Input "Y (INITIAL x)=", Y
:Input "STEP SIZE=", H
:Input "NO. OF POINTS=", N
:Lbl A
:Y→Z
:Disp "x=", x
:Disp "Y=" Y
:Pause
:H∗FX→I
:x+H/2→x
:Z+I/2→Y
:H∗FX→J
:Z+J/2→Y
:H∗FX→K
:x+H/2→x
:Z+K→Y
:H∗FX→L
:Z+(I+2∗J+2∗K+L)/6→Y
:M+1→M
:If M≤N
:Goto A
```

Example 14

Prgm RUNKUTT can be used to find a numerical solution to the initial value problem $\dfrac{dy}{dx} = -2xy^2$ with initial conditions $f(-2) = 0.2$.

Directions:

1. Enter $y_1 = -2x * Y^2$.

2. Execute Prgm RUNKUTT.

3. Enter an initial x-value of -2.

4. Enter an initial y-value of 0.2.

5. Enter a step size of 0.1.

6. Enter 40 for the number of points.

The program will produce the ordered pairs found in Table 5.10 (in Example 10).

The x-values are in the first column and the y-values are in the fifth column. You must press [ENTER] after each ordered pair to see the next pair. Compare the results of Prgm

RUNKUTT with Prgms IMPEULT, EULERT, and the exact results. The Runge-Kutta method is analogous to Simpson's method, while the improved Euler's method uses trapezoidal approximations and Euler's method uses rectangular approximations. It is not surprising that the Runge-Kutta method is the most accurate of the three numerical techniques.

The approximation error can also be added to RUNKUTT. Follow the steps at the end of Section 5.10.

5.15 Runge-Kutta Graph

Program 15

RUNKUTG (Runge-Kutta graph)
Input: $f'(x, y)$; initial x, y; step size (h)
Output: graph of solution to initial value differential equation problem using the Runge-Kutta method
This is a built-in program on the TI-86 that is accessed in DifEq mode.

Example 15A

Use Prgm RUNKUTG to graph the solution to the initial value problem $\dfrac{dy}{dx} = -2xy^2$ with $y(-2) = 0.2$ and then compare with the exact solution.

1. In the Function (Func) mode, enter $y_1 = 1/(1 + x^2)$.

2. Select Differential Equation (DifEq) mode.

3. In the GRAPH [Format] menu select RK and FldOff.

4. Enter $Q'1 = -2t*Q1^2$.

5. Set the following variables in the Window menu:

tMin $= -2$	xMin $= -2$	yMin $= -1$	dif Tol $= .01$
tMax $= 2$	xMax $= 2$	yMax $= 1$	
tStep $= .1$	xScl $= 1$	yScl $= 1$	
tPlot $= 0$			

6. In the Initial Conditions (INITC) menu enter QI1 $= .2$.

7. In the AXES menu, set $x = t$ and $y = Q1$, then graph the solution to the differential equation.

8. Select DrawF from the GRAPH [Draw] menu, and enter DrawF y1, then press ENTER.

These steps produce the graph shown in Fig. 5.9.

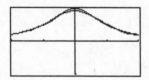

Figure 5.9 Runge-Kutta Method.

Compare this graph with the graphs produced by Euler's method in Example 11A and the improved Euler's method in Example 13A. Notice the close agreement between the Runge-Kutta graph and the exact solution.

Example 15B

Use Prgm RUNKUTG to graph $\int_0^x \cos t \, dt$ and compare with the exact solution.

1. Enter $y_1 = \sin x$.
2. Select Differential Equation (DifEq) mode.
3. In the GRAPH [Format] menu select RK and FldOff.
4. Enter $Q'1 = \cos t$.
5. Set the following variables in the Window menu:

$$
\begin{array}{llll}
t\text{Min} = 0 & x\text{Min} = 0 & y\text{Min} = -2 & \text{dif Tol} = .01 \\
t\text{Max} = 2\pi & x\text{Max} = 2\pi & y\text{Max} = 2 & \\
t\text{Step} = .1 & x\text{Scl} = \pi/2 & y\text{Scl} = 1 & \\
t\text{Plot} = 0 & & &
\end{array}
$$

6. In the Initial Conditions (INITC) menu enter $QI1 = 0$.
7. In the AXES menu, set $x = t$ and $y = Q1$, then graph the solution to the differential equation.
8. Select DrawF from the GRAPH [Draw] menu, and enter DrawF y1, then press ENTER.

These steps produce the graph shown in Fig. 5.10.

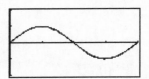

Figure 5.10 Antiderivative of cos x; Runge-Kutta method.

Compare the graph with the graphs produced by Euler's method in Example 11B and the improved Euler's method in Example 13B. Notice the close agreement between the Runge-Kutta graph and the exact solution.

5.16 Make a Table of the Sequence of Partial Sums of a Series that Is Defined by an *n*th-term Formula

Program 16

PARTSUMT (partial sums of a series in tabular form)

Input: nth term of a series, initial value of n, number of terms in the sequence of partial sums

Output: sequence of partial sums

You can make the table on the TI-86 with the sum and sequence commands.

Example 16

Make a table of the first 10 partial sums of the series $\sum_{n=1}^{10} 1/2^n$.

1. Enter $Y_1 = $ sum(seq(1/2^N, N, 1, x, 1)).

Note: The sum and seq commands are found in the LIST menu: Press

$\boxed{\text{2nd}}$ $\boxed{\text{LIST}}$ [F5:OPS] $\boxed{\text{MORE}}$ [F1:sum] *and* $\boxed{\text{2nd}}$ $\boxed{\text{LIST}}$ [F5:OPS] $\boxed{\text{MORE}}$ [F3:seq]

The sum command adds up the terms in a sequence. The seq (sequence) command makes a sequence. The first parameter in the seq command is the formula for the *n*th term of a sequence. The second parameter is the index. The third and fourth parameters are the initial and final values of the index. The last parameter is the amount by which the index will change between terms in the sequence.

2. Press

$\boxed{\text{TABLE}}$ [F2:TBLST]

and make TblStart and ΔTbl both equal to 1. Indpnt and Depend should both be "Auto".

3. Press

[F1:TABLE]

4. Press $\boxed{\blacktriangledown}$ to see more of the table.

These steps produce the following output:

N	Nth partial sum
1	.5
2	.75
3	.875
.	.
.	.
.	.
10	.99902

5.17 Graph the Sequence of Partial Sums of a Series that Is Defined by an *n*th-term Formula

Program 17

PARTSUMG (partial sums of a series in graphical form)
Input: *n*th term of a series, initial value of *n*, number of terms in the sequence of partial sums
Output: graph of the sequence of partial sums

You can draw the graph without a program with the sum and seq commands in Parametric mode, as follows:

$$x_{t1} = t$$
$$y_{t1} = \text{sum}(\text{seq}(a_n, n, 1, t, 1))$$

and using a *t*step of 1.

Example 17

Graph the first 10 partial sums of the series $\sum_{n=1}^{10} 1/2^n$.
Directions:

1. Press 2nd MODE and select the Parametric (Param) mode, then select DrawDot from the GRAPH [Formt] menu.

2. Enter the following equations in the E(t) = edit screen.

$$x_{t1} = t$$
$$y_{t1} = \text{sum seq}(1/2^\wedge\ N, N, 1, t, 1)$$

Example 16 describes how to enter the sum and seq commands.

3. Enter the following WINDOW values:

tMin = 1	xMin = 0	yMin = 0
tMax = 10	xMax = 10	yMax = 1
$t$step = 1	$x$scl = 1	$y$scl = 0

4. Graph.

These steps produce the graph shown in Fig. 5.11.

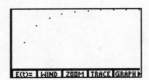

Figure 5.11 Sequence of partial sums for $\sum 1/2n$.

5.18 Make a Table of the Sequence of Partial Sums of a Series that Is Defined Recursively

Program 18

PSUMRECT (sequence of partial sums of a recursive series in tabular format)
Input: recursive definition of nth term of the series, initial n, initial term in series, number of terms in the sequence of partial sums
Output: sequence of partial sums

```
Prgm: PSUMRECT
:Input "INITIAL N =", I
:Input "INITIAL TERM =", A
:Input "NO. OF TERMS =", M
:I→N
:A→S
:Lbl A
:Disp "N =", N
:Disp "PARTIAL SUM =", S
:Pause
:1 + N→N
:y1 + S→S
:y1→A
:If (N − I) < M
:Goto A
```

Example 18A

Use Prgm PSUMRECT to make a table of the sequence of partial sums for the series $\frac{1}{2} + \frac{1}{4} + \frac{1}{8} + \frac{1}{16}$ ... defined recursively as $\sum a_n$ where $a_n = \left(\frac{1}{2}\right)a_{n-1}, a_1 = \left(\frac{1}{2}\right)$.

1. Enter $y_1 = (1/2)A$ in the Y = edit screen (You must be in Func (Function) Mode).
2. Execute Prgm PSUMRECT.
3. Enter 1 for the initial n-value.
4. Enter 1/2 for the initial term.
5. Enter 10 for the number of terms.
6. Press

$\boxed{\text{ENTER}}$

to see each element in the sequence of partial sums.

These steps produce the values listed at the end of Example 16.

Example 18B

Find the sequence of partial sums for the series $1^2 + 2^2 + 3^2 + 4^2 + ...$, which can be recursively defined as $\sum a_n$, where $a_n = a_{n-1} + 2n - 1, a_1 = 1$.

Directions:

1. Enter $y_1 = A + 2N - 1$ in the Y = edit screen.
2. Execute Prgm PSUMRECT.
3. Enter 1 for the initial n-value.
4. Enter 1 for the initial term.
5. Enter 10 for the number of terms.
6. Press

$\boxed{\text{ENTER}}$

to see each element in the sequence of partial sums.

These steps produce the values listed below:

N	Nth partial sum
1	1
2	5
3	14
4	30
.	.
.	.
.	.
10	385

5.19 Graph the Sequence of Partial Sums of a Series that Is Defined Recursively

Program 19

PSUMRECG (graphs a sequence of partial sums of a recursive series)
Input: recursive definition of the nth term of the series, initial n, initial term in series, number of terms in the sequence of partial sums
Output: graph of the sequence of partial sums

```
Prgm: PSUMRECG
:FnOff: ClDrw
:Input "INITIAL N =", I
:Input "INITIAL TERM", A
:Input "NO. OF TERMS =", M
:I→N
:A→S
:Lbl A
:PtOn(N, S)
:1+N→N
:y₁+S→S
:y₁→A
:If (N−I)<M
:Goto A
```

Example 19

Use Prgm PSUMRECG to graph the sequence of partial sums for the series $\frac{1}{2}+\frac{1}{4}+\frac{1}{8}+\frac{1}{16}...$ defined recursively as $\sum a_n$, where $a_n = \left(\frac{1}{2}\right)a_{n-1}, a_1 = \frac{1}{2}$.
Directions:

1. Enter $y_1 = (1/2)A$ in the y = edit screen.

2. Set the viewing window to $[0, 10]$ by $[0, 1]$.

3. Execute Prgm PSUMRECG.

4. Enter 1 for the initial n-value.

5. Enter 1/2 for the initial term.

6. Enter 10 for the number of terms.

These steps produce the same graph as Fig. 5.11.

5.20 Graph the *n*th Partial Sum of a Power Series

Program 20

GRAPHSUM (graph *n*th partial sum of a power series)
Input: *n*th term of series, initial *n*, number of terms in the series
Output: graph of the *n*th partial sum of the series
The graph can be drawn using the sum and seq commands in the List [Ops] menu.

Example 20

Graph the power series for sin x, $\sum_{N=1}^{10} \frac{(-1)^{N+1} X^{2N-1}}{(2N-1)!}$ and overlay with sin x.
Directions:

1. Enter $y_1 = $ sum seq$((-1)^\wedge(N + 1)x^\wedge(2N - 1)/(2N - 1)!, N, 1, 10, 1)$.

2. Enter $y_2 = \sin x$.

3. Graph in the $[-10, 10]$ by $[-2, 2]$ viewing window.

These steps produce the graph shown in Fig. 5.12.

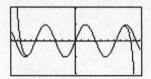

Figure 5.12 Power series for sin *x*.

This is the tenth partial sum of the MacLaurin series for sin *x* overlaid on the graph of sin *x*.

The first parameter in the seq function in Step 1 is the *n*th term of the series. The second parameter is the index for the series. The third parameter is the beginning value of the index and the fourth is the end value for the index. The last parameter is the increment for the index.

5.21 Graph a Slope Field for a Differential Equation

Program 21

SLOPEFLD (graph the slope field for a differential equation $y' = f(x, y)$)
Input: Differential equation $y' = f(x,y)$
Output: Slope field for the differential equation
This is a built-in program that is accessed in DifEq mode.

Example 21A

Use Prgm SLOPEFLD to illustrate the family of solutions to the differential equation $y' = \sin x/x$.

1. Select Differential Equation (DifEq) mode.

2. In the GRAPH [Format] menu, select SlopeField [SlpFld].

3. Enter $Q'1 = \sin t/t$.

4. Enter the following Window values:

$t\text{Min} = -7$	$x\text{Min} = -7$	$y\text{Min} = -2$
$t\text{Max} = 7$	$x\text{Max} = 7$	$y\text{Max} = 2$
$t\text{Step} = .1$	$x\text{Scl} = 1$	$y\text{Scl} = 1$
$t\text{Plot} = 0$		

5. In the Initial Conditions (INITC) menu, delete the value for QI1.

6. In the AXES menu, set $y = Q1$ and fldRes = 10, then GRAPH the slope field.

These steps produce the slope field shown (see Fig. 5.13).

Example 21B

Graph the slope field for the differential equation $y' = x + y$.

1. Select Differential Equation (DifEq) mode.

2. In the GRAPH [Format] menu select SlopeField [SlpFld].

3. Enter $Q'1 = t + Q1$

4. Enter the following window variables:

$t\text{Min} = -2$	$x\text{Min} = -2$	$y\text{Min} = -1$
$t\text{Max} = 2$	$x\text{Max} = 2$	$y\text{Max} = 1$
$t\text{Step} = .1$	$x\text{Scl} = 1$	$y\text{Scl} = 1$
$t\text{Plot} = 0$		

5. In the Initial Conditions (INITC) menu, delete the value for QI1.

6. In the AXES menu get y = Q1 and fldRes = 10, then GRAPH the slope field.

You should see the following slope field (see Fig. 5.14).

Figure 5.13 Slope field for $y' = \sin x/x$.

Figure 5.14 Slope field for $y' = x + y$.

Example 21C

Graph the slope field for $y' = -2xy^2$.

1. In DifEq and SlpFld modes, enter $Q'1 = -2t\,Q1^2$.

2. Enter a $[-2, 2]$ by $[-1, 1]$ viewing window, delete any Initial Condition for QI1, and set FldRes = 10. Then GRAPH the slope field.

Compare this slope field (Fig. 5.15) with the results of Prgms EULERG, IMPEULG, and RUNGKUTG in Examples 11A, 13A, and 15A.

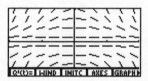

Figure 5.15 Family of solutions to $y = -2xy^2$.

Example 21D

Graph the slope field for $y' = -2xy^2$, then use Prgm EULERG to superimpose the solution to the initial value problem $\dfrac{dy}{dx} = -2xy^2$ with $y(-2) = 0.2$.

The TI-86 will overlay the Euler graph onto a slope field automatically if you assign the initial conditions.

1. In DifEq, Euler, and SlpFld modes, enter $Q'1 = -2t\,Q1^2$.

Note: This will also work in RK mode.

2. Enter a $[-2, 2]$ by $[-1, 1]$ viewing window.

3. In the INITC menu set QI1 = .2, then press [F5:GRAPH].

Note: This example will also work with Prgm IMPEULG and Prgm RUNKUTG.

These steps produce the graph shown in Figure 5.16.

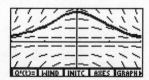

Figure 5.16 Slope field for $y' = -2xy^2$ and Euler's method.

5.22 Visualizing Rectangular Approximation Methods for Areas

Program 22

AREA (graph left, right, and midpoint rectangles used for area approximation)
Input: $f(x), a, b, n$ (number of rectangles)
Output: numeric results and graphs of rectangles used to approximate areas bounded by $f(x), a, b$, and the x-axis

```
Prgm: AREA
:Prompt A
:Prompt B
:Input "NO. OF SUBINT =", N
:(B−A)/N→H
:H/2→D
:0→L
:0→M
:0→R
:ClDrw
:DispG
:0→J
:A→x
:While J < N
:y₁+L→L
:Line (x, 0, x, y₁)
:Line (x, y₁, x+H, y₁)
:Line (x + H, 0, x+H, y₁)
:x+H→x
:J+1→J
:END
:Pause
:H∗L→L
:CILCD
:Input "LEFT =", L
:Pause
:ClDrw
:DispG
:0→J
:A+H→x
:While J < N
:y₁ + R→R
:Line (x−H, 0, x−H, y₁)
:Line (x−H, y₁, x, y₁)
:Line (x, 0, x, y₁)
:x+H→x
:J+1→J
:END
:Pause
:H∗R→R
:Disp "RIGHT =", R
:Pause
:ClDrw
```

```
:DispG
:0→J
:A+D→x
:While J < N
:y₁+M→M
:Line (x−D, 0, x−D, y1)
:Line (x−D, y1, x+D, y1)
:Line(x+D, y1, x+D, 0)
:x+H→x
:1+J→J
:End
:Pause
:H∗M→M
:Disp "MIDPOINT =", M
```

Example 22

Graph the left, right and midpoint rectangles that approximate the area bounded by the function $y = 4x - x^2$.

Directions:

1. Enter $y_1 = 4x - x^2$

2. Enter a $[-1, 5]$ by $[-1, 4]$ viewing window.

3. Execute Prgm AREA.

4. Enter 0 for A.

5. Enter 4 for B.

6. Enter 4 for the number of subintervals.

You should see a graph like Fig. 5.17 that illustrates the left-hand rectangles.

7. Press [ENTER] to see the sum of the areas of the left-hand rectangles (10) and then press [ENTER] again to continue.

Now you should see the right-hand rectangles (see Fig. 5.18).

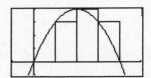

Figure 5.17 Left-rectangles.

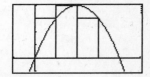

Figure 5.18 Right-rectangles.

8. Press [ENTER] to see the sums of the left-hand and right-hand rectangles (10 again) and then press [ENTER] to continue.

You should see midpoint rectangles like those in Fig. 5.19.

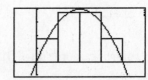

Figure 5.19 Midpoint rectangles.

9. Press [ENTER] once more to see the numerical results of the three summations.

5.23 Investigating Limits

Example 23A

Graphically investigate $\lim\limits_{x\to-\infty} \tan^{-1}x$ and $\lim\limits_{x\to\infty} \tan^{-1}x$.

Directions:

1. Enter $y_1 = \tan^{-1}x$.
2. Enter $y_2 = -\pi/2$.
3. Enter $y_3 = \pi/2$.
4. Graph in a $[-100, 100]$ by $[-3, 3]$ viewing window.

These steps produce the graph shown in Fig. 5.20.

This graph supports the fact that $\lim\limits_{x\to-\infty} \tan^{-1}x = -\dfrac{\pi}{2}$ and $\lim\limits_{x\to\infty}\tan^{-1}x = \dfrac{\pi}{2}$.

Example 23B

Graphically investigate $\lim\limits_{x\to 0+}(1+x)^{1/x}$.
Directions:

1. Enter $y_1 = (1 + x)^\wedge(1/x)$.
2. Graph in a $[-1, 5]$ by $[-1, 4]$ viewing window.

These steps produce the graph shown in Fig. 5.21.

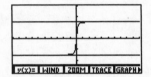
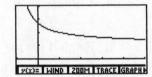

Figure 5.20 End behavior of arctan x.   **Figure 5.21** $y = (1 + x)^\wedge(1/x)$.

Zoom in several times on the y-intercept of the graph and then trace towards the y-intercept from the positive side. Zoom-in produces something similar to the graph shown in Fig. 5.22.

Figure 5.22 Zoom in on $y = (1 + x)^\wedge(1/x)$.

This graph provides evidence that $\lim\limits_{x\to 0+}(1+x)^{1/x} = e$. This limit is the y-coordinate of a removable discontinuity in the graph.

Example 23C

Find a local minimum value of $f(x) = x^3 - 4x^2 + 3x - 4$.
Directions:

1. Set the δ variable in the Tolerance screen to .01.
2. Enter $y_1 = x^\wedge 3 - 4x^2 + 3x - 4$.
3. Enter $y_2 = \text{nDer}(y_1, x, x)$.
4. Graph in a $[-10, 10]$ by $[-10, 10]$ viewing window.

These steps should produce the graph shown in Fig. 5.23. Notice that the zeros of the derivative correspond to the x-coordinates of the extrema of f(x).

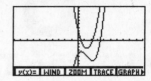

Figure 5.23 $y = x^3 - 4x^2 + 3x - 4$ and its derivative.

5. Select [F1:Root] from the GRAPH [Math] menu to find the zero of y_2 near $x = 2.2$.

(Remember to use the up cursor-movement key to move the cursor to y_2 before you enter the left and right bounds and the initial guess.)

The value of the zero should be 2.2152315386.

6. You can evaluate $f(2.2152315386)$ by printing the current value of y_1 on the Home screen. (Type y1 and press ENTER.)

The value of y_1 should be -6.11261178998.

The exact local minimum is $f\left(\dfrac{8 + \sqrt{28}}{6}\right) = -6.112611791$ (to nine decimal places). Note the high degree of accuracy of the local minimum value (even with d = 0.01)! Changing d to 0.0001 in the nDer method used in y2 will improve accuracy even more.

5.24 Find Local Extrema

Local extrema can be found using the Fmin and Fmax options from the Graph [Math] menu. The Fmin option returns the minimum value of $f(x)$, and the Fmax option returns the maximum value of $f(x)$.

The tol variable in the Tolerance screen determines the accuracy of Fmin and Fmax.

Example 24

Find local minimum and maximum values of $f(x) = x^3 - 4x^2 + 3x - 4$.
Directions:

1. Set the tol variable in the Tolerance screen to .00001.
2. Enter $Y_1 = X{\wedge}3 - 4x^2 + 3x - 4$.
3. Graph in a $[-10, 10]$ by $[-10, 10]$ viewing window.
4. Select [F4:FMIN] in the GRAPH [Math] menu.
5. Use the cursor movement keys to set the left bound at $x = 1.42857$, the right bound at $x = 3.01587$, and a guess of $x = 2.22222$, then press ENTER. Note that the bounds and guess can be entered directly from the keypad.

The output on the screen should be $x = 2.2152513371$, $y = -6.112611791$. These are the coordinates of the local minimum. Compare these results with those of Example 25.

6. Select [F5:FMAX] from the GRAPH [Math] menu.
7. Use the cursor movement keys to set the left bound at $x = 0$, the right bound at $x = 1.1111$, and a guess of $x = .47619$, then press ENTER.

The output should be $x = .45141636815$, $y = -3.368869691$. These are the coordinates of the local maximum.

C H A P T E R

6

Graphing with the TI-89 Titanium

The TI-89 Titanium is the most powerful of all of the Texas Instruments calculators. It comes with more features and preloaded applications than any previous TI calculator, yet is user-friendly. The following aspects of working with the TI-89 are covered:

- Section 1—the keypad and major features and functions
- Section 2—graphing techniques
- Section 3—parametric graphing
- Section 4—polar graphing
- Section 5—sequence graphing
- Section 6—tables to represent functions
- Section 7—finding accurate approximations to solutions
- Section 8—piecewise functions
- Section 9—graphical databases
- Section 10—drawing pictures

6.1　Getting Started on the TI-89 Titanium

The keypad of the TI-89 is divided into several sections of related keys. Note that there are often several sets of keystrokes that will provide the same result. Generally, only one method will be presented here.

6.1.1　Turning the TI-89 On and Off

To turn on the calculator, press

$$\boxed{\text{ON}}$$

which is located in the far lower left-hand corner of the TI-89.
To turn off the TI-89, press

$$\boxed{\text{2nd}}\ \boxed{\text{ON}}$$

The $\boxed{\text{2nd}}$ key is the light blue key located in the upper left-hand corner of the keypad. In this manual we will give keystrokes by their function, not by the key. For example, we write the keystrokes for turning off the TI-89 as $\boxed{\text{2nd}}\ \boxed{\text{OFF}}$, not $\boxed{\text{2nd}}\ \boxed{\text{ON}}$.

When you first turn on the TI-89, you see the **menu screen**. From here you can access many of the TI-89's functions such as the **home screen**, the **numeric solver**, or the **graphing** screen. Scroll until you find the **Home** icon and press Enter or simply press the $\boxed{\text{HOME}}$ button. The **entry line** is at the bottom of the Home screen and contains the entry cursor. The entry cursor is either a blinking rectangle (▮) or a blinking vertical line (|). In the **history area** of the Home screen you see the results of the data and instructions you entered in the entry line. When you turn off the TI-89, all data shown on the home screen are retained in memory and reappear when you again turn on the calculator. If you are in any other screen or in a menu, turning off the TI-89 by using ⌊2nd⌋ ⌊OFF⌋ removes you from both and when you turn it on again, you will see the Home screen. If you use ⌊◆⌋ ⌊OFF⌋ to turn off the TI-89, the display will be exactly as you left it. *Note: The TI-89 includes a power-saver feature that results in the calculator turning itself off after approximately three to four minutes of nonuse. To reactivate the calculator when it has powered-off on its own, press*

⌊2nd⌋

When the TI-89 turns itself off under the power-saver feature, any data on the screen at the time of power-off reappears just as it was before the calculator shut down. If you were in another screen or in a menu, you are returned to your original location.

Since the Home screen is the most used application, all instructions here will be presented with the starting point being assumed to be the Home screen, unless otherwise specified.

6.1.2 Exploring the TI-89 Titanium

The TI-89 is divided into parts according to the position and color of the keys.

The keys are grouped according to position as follows:

- Row 1 - The **Menu Keys**. Used to access the calculator's interactive graphing features.

- Rows 2 and 3 (the first three keys of each row) - The **Editing Keys**. Used to edit expressions and values.

- Row 4 - The **Advanced Function Keys** (left 3 keys). Used to access advanced functions through various full-screen menus.

- Row 5 - The **Scientific Calculator Keys**. Used to access the capabilities of a standard scientific calculator. The keys are grouped according to color as follows:

    - Cursor-Movement Keys (black)
      Notice the triangle of these four keys. Eac triangle points in the direction the cursor moves when the key is pressed.

    - Number Pad (black)
      The numbers 0-9 are set out in black, as is the negative sign (-) and the decimal point (·) .

    - Enter
      Causes the calculator to calculate the function you have entered. It is also used to accept certain variable information and perform other duties.

    - All other keys (except the ⌊2nd⌋ (blue), and ⌊ALPHA⌋ (grey) and ⌊◆⌋ (green), which we discuss in the next subsections represent the various features and functions avaaialbale on the TI-89 Titanium.

Erasing Data from the Screen and Leaving a Screen or Menu. Pressing ⌊CLEAR⌋ enables you to clear the entry line of data or expressions or to delete a particular entry/answer pair in the history area. ⌊CLEAR⌋ also serves other purposes, described as needed in these instructions. To clear the Home screen of the results of evaluating expressions, press ⌊F1⌋, and select [8:Clear Home] or enter **ClrHome** on the entry line. To close a menu and return to the previous screen, press the ⌊ESC⌋ key. To return to the Home screen from any other application press ⌊APPS⌋ and select ⌊HOME⌋, or press ⌊HOME⌋. What the ⌊ESC⌋ key does depends on the application.

Deleting and Inserting Data. The mode of the entry cursor determines the method for deleting and inserting data. You can toggle between insert and overtype mode by pressing $\boxed{\text{2nd}}$ $\boxed{\text{INS}}$.

If you have the entry cursor in overtype mode, the entry cursor will be a blinking rectangle. In this mode, you can "delete" data by entering new data over it. The new entry replaces the old, character for character. For example, to delete the number 123233 and replace it with 243556, position the entry cursor over the left-most character of 123233 and key in the new value, 243556. However, for those occasions when you need to delete data entirely, this method won't work. For example, if you want to delete the number 123233 entirely, keying in another value over it won't produce the desired result. In this case, you can use $\boxed{\leftarrow}$ or $\boxed{\text{CLEAR}}$ instead.

$\boxed{\leftarrow}$ deletes the character to the left of the entry cursor, while $\boxed{\text{CLEAR}}$ deletes all characters to the right of the entry cursor, or all characters on the entry line if there are no characters to the right of the entry cursor. To use $\boxed{\leftarrow}$, do the following:

1. a. To delete one character, position the entry cursor to the right of the character you want to delete.
   b. Press

$$\boxed{\leftarrow}$$

The character is erased.

2. a. To delete more than one *consecutive* character, position the entry cursor to the right of the left-most one.
   b. Press and hold

$$\boxed{\leftarrow}$$

until all characters you want deleted are erased.

Having the entry cursor in insert mode enables you to insert additional data between characters already on the entry line.

Suppose you have entered the following on the entry line of the Home screen:

$$5 \times 36$$

You realize it should read 5 * 316. To insert a 1 between the 3 and 6, do the following:

1. Position the entry cursor between the 3 and the 6, if the entry cursor is in insert mode, or on the 6, if the entry cursor is in overtype mode.

2. Press

$$\boxed{\text{2nd}}\ \boxed{\text{INS}}$$

until the entry cursor is in insert mode.

3. Type a **1**.

*The number 1 is inserted **to the left** of the 6.*

Unless otherwise stated, these instructions will assume that the TI-89 entry cursor is in insert mode.

6.1.3   Accessing the TI-89 Titanium's Features and Functions

The TI-89 offers numerous features and functions, so many that if each were assigned a separate key, the size of the keypad would more than double. Therefore to keep the size of a keypad manageable, most of the keys perform double or triple duty. This capability resembles that of a typewriter or computer keyboard on which each key can be used to access more than one character, number, or function.

On the TI-89, the first level of features or functions is represented by the names or symbols printed on the keys. As on a typewriter, to access one of these, simply press the key. For example, to enter the number 5, press **5**. Or to calculate the square of 5, press

$$5 \ \boxed{\wedge} \ 2 \ \boxed{\text{ENTER}}$$

For example, suppose you want to find the square root of 5. To access the square root function, press [2nd] [√]. To complete the calculation of the square root of 5, press

5. [ )] [ENTER]

Note that the TI-89 will automatically add an open parenthesis, (, to many functions. It is necessary to press [ )]. Note that the decimal point is added after the 5 so that we get a numerical approximation of the square root of 5. Depending on what mode you are in (see p. 145 about Exact/Approx modes), you may not get an approximation if you do not include the decimal point.

6.1.4   Resetting the TI-89 Titanium

Resetting the TI-89 erases all previously entered data and programs. Before beginning the sample problems in these instructions, reset the TI-89.

To reset the TI-89, do the following:

1. Turn the TI-89 on by pressing

[ON]

2. Press [2nd] [MEM] to display the MEM (memory) menu.

3. Press

[F1]

The RESET menu appears.

4. Select

[3:All Memory]

The TI-89 asks for confirmation.

5. Press

[ENTER]

Notice that the screen turns dark after resetting the memory. The next section, 6.1.5, tells you how to adjust the display contrast.

6.1.5   Setting the Contrast of the Screen's Display

The brightness and contrast of the display depend on room lighting, battery freshness, viewing angle, and adjustment of the display contrast. You can adjust the display contrast at any time to suit your viewing angle and lighting conditions. The contrast setting is retained in memory when the TI-89 is turned off. To adjust the contrast, do the following:

1. To increase the contrast,

   *   press [◆] and then
   *   press *and hold* [+].

2. To decrease the contrast,

   *   press [◆] and then
   *   press *and hold* [−].

Observe that if you decrease the contrast very far, the display might appear to go completely blank. To correct this, simply press [◆] and then press and hold [+] until the display appears.

Note: *When the batteries are low, the display begins to dim, especially during calculations. You will need to adjust the contrast to a higher setting to compensate for this. However, if you need to adjust it as frequently, you may need to replace the batteries soon.*

6.1.6 Displaying Data on the Viewing Screen

The TI-89 displays both text and graphics. For text, the history area can show up to five entry/answer pairs. When the history area is filled, the text scrolls off the top of the screen.

For simple functions, the TI-89 shows the results immediately. However, when the TI-89 is involved in a relatively lengthy calculation or graphing function, the word busy appears in the right-hand corner of the status line to signal that the calculator is busy.

Display Cursors. The TI-89 has several types of cursors, as shown in Table 6.1. In most cases, the appearance of the cursor indicates what will happen when you press the next key.

Table 6.1

Cursor	Appearance	Meaning
Entry cursor	Solid blinking rectangle	The next keystroke is entered at the cursor, overwriting any character already at that position.
Insert cursor	Blinking line cursor	The next keystroke is inserted at the cursor.
Free-moving cursor	+ sign within a circle	Moving the cursor updates the x- and y- coordinate values.
Trace cursor	Blinking + sign within a circle	Move among all functions that are defined or selected.
Zoom Box cursor	Blinking + sign within a circle	Move and enter points for a box outlining the viewing window.

Displaying Calculations. One advantage of the TI-89, in contrast to a typical scientific calculator, is that you can see the complete expression *and* its solution simultaneously on the screen. For example, enter $100(1.06)^{10}$ by pressing

100 ☐×☐ **1** ☐•☐ **06** ☐∧☐ **10**

(See Fig. 6.1.) Notice that the entire expression is shown on the entry line beginning at the left margin. Press ENTER to have the TI-89 evaluate the expression. After the evaluation, the expression is shown in the history area as the left-hand member of an entry/answer pair and the result is shown as the right-hand member, while the expression is highlighted on the entry line. Note that if an expression requires more than one line, an arrow will indicate that the expression exceeds the history area or entry line and that the entry and answer will be on separate lines in the history area.

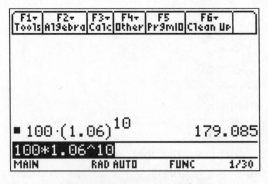

Figure 6.1 $100(1.06)^{10}$.

Using Concatenation. The TI-89 supports the combining of two or more commands. This is done using [:] to separate commands. For example, to store the number 20 in *n* and then evaluate 1000×1.06^n, press

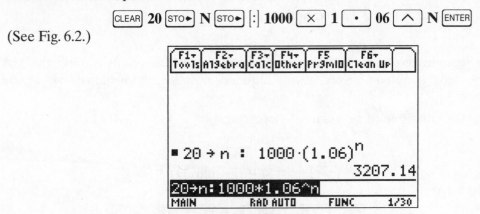

(See Fig. 6.2.)

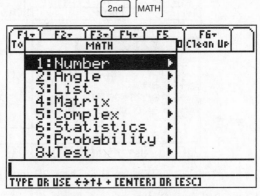

Figure 6.2 Using concatenation.

6.1.7 Accessing Advanced Functions via Menus

Through menus you can access functions and operations that you cannot access directly from the keyboard. There are several types of menus on the TI-89. When you press a menu key, the menu displaying the selections available for that menu item appears. After you select an item from a menu, the screen on which you were working is redisplayed, unless you were using the applications menu to change windows. The menus that have specific keys are the **toolbar menus** (accessed via the function keys) and the **applications menu**.

For example, the MATH menu, which is typical of all the numbered menus, is shown in Fig. 6.3. To display it, press

2nd [MATH]

Figure 6.3 The MATH menu.

Options in menus are numbered in the left-hand column, with each number (or letter) followed by a colon. For example, the MATH menu contains 14 submenus from which to choose. You can use the cursor pad to move down the list of submenus. Notice that as the cursor moves down the list of submenus, the selected submenu is highlighted. To see the options available for each submenu, press the number or letter that appears to the left of the submenu name, or use the ▶ direction on the cursor pad once the submenu is highlighted.

Sometimes more options are available that can be viewed simultaneously on the screen. For example, press 2nd [MATH] and then select [3:List]. This menu has 15 options from which to choose. Notice, however, that only 8 are displayed. To learn whether a menu has additional options, notice option 8, whose number is followed by an arrow instead of a colon. The arrow indicates there are more options. To see them, do the following:

1. Press ▼ to reach the bottom of the menu.

2. Then continue to press that key to cause the menu to scroll upward and reveal additional options.

In this case, scrolling enables you to see the last two options of the LIST [MATH] submenu.

You can select the option you want in one of two ways:

1. Press the number or letter that corresponds to the desired option. This is the easiest way.

2. Move the cursor to the desired option and press

ENTER

Keying Sequence Notation for Numbered Menus. For numbered menus like the MATH menu, we have adopted a special keying sequence notation. For instance, to compute 7!, do the following:

1. Clear the entry line (if necessary) by pressing

CLEAR

2. Press

7 [2nd] [MATH] [7:Probability] [1:!] [ENTER]

(See Fig. 6.4.)

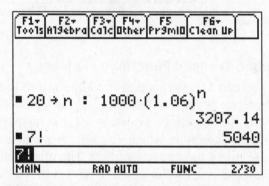

Figure 6.4 Keying sequence notation for numbered menus.

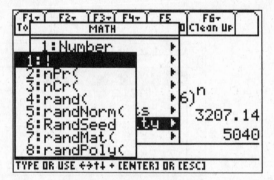

Figure 6.5 The PRB menu.

The results are shown in Fig. 6.4. You can see from the MATH and [Probability] menus, shown in Fig. 6.5, that option 1 is the factorial function (!). To indicate that you should have selected the seventh option of the MATH menu and the first option of the [Probability] submenu, we denoted the keystrokes by [7:Probability] and [1:!].

6.1.8 Changing Modes

A **mode** is one of a number of optional systems of operation. For example, you can choose to operate in Exact, Approximate, or Automatic mode with regard to how numeric results are displayed on the screen. To view the Mode screen, press

MODE

The default options on the TI-89 are: Function, main, Float 6, Radian, Normal, Real, Rectangular, On (Pretty Print), Full, Home, Auto, Dec (Decimal), SI, English and On (Apps Desktop). Note that some of the options on the second screen of modes are not legible under the default mode options of the TI-89. The following are descriptions of all of the modes (see Fig. 6.6 and 6.7):

- Graph: Function, Parametric, Polar, Sequence, 3D Diff Equations.
  These are the Function, Parametric, Polar, Sequential, 3D and Differential Equations graphing modes. **Function graphing** plots a function where y is expressed in terms of x. See Section 6.2 for more information about graphing functions. **Parametric graphing** plots a relation in which x and y are each expressed in terms of a third variable, t. See Section 6.3 for more information about graphing parametric equations. Section 6.4 contains more information about polar equations, while Section 6.5 gives more information about sequences where the nth term is defined explicitly in terms of n or where the nth term is defined recursively. **3D** and Differential Equations graphing will not be discussed here.

- Current Folder: main
  If more than one folder has been set up, this indicates which folder the TI-89 will use for data and computation.

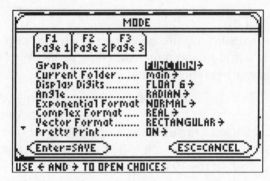

Figure 6.6 The MODE menu (page 1).

- Display Digits: Fix 0 through 12, Float 0 through 12
  Represent the Floating (Float) or Fixed (Fix) Decimal Point modes with the number indicating the number of digits shown to the right of the decimal point. Note that option [E:Float] yields a display in which the number of digits varies depending on the result being displayed.

- Angle: Radian, Degree
  Represent the Radian and Degree angle modes. **Radian mode** means that angle arguments in trigonometric functions or polar-rectangular conversions are interpreted as radians and results are displayed in radians. **Degree mode** means that angle arguments in these functions or conversions are interpreted as degrees and results are displayed in degrees.

- Exponential Format: Normal, Scientific, Engineering
  Determines how a numeric result will be formatted. You can enter a number in any format. **Normal notation** is how we usually express numbers, with digits to the left and right of the decimal point, as in 12345.67. **Scientific notation** expresses numbers in two parts. The significant digits are displayed with one digit to the left of the decimal point. The appropriate power of 10 is displayed to the right of E, as in 1.234567E4. **Engineering notation** is similar to scientific notation, except that one, two, or three digits before the decimal point may be displayed and the power-of-10 exponent is a multiple of three, as in 13.34567E3.

- Complex Format: Real, Rectangular, Polar
  Determines whether a complex result is displayed. In the **Real** mode, a complex result is not displayed unlesss complex numbers are entered as input. In the **Rectangular** mode, complex numbers are displayed in the form a + bi, where a is the real part and b is the imaginary part of the number. In the **Polar** mode, complex numbers are displayed in the form re^θi, where r is the argument and θ is the angle of the complex number.

- Vector Format: Rectangular, Cylindrical, Spherical
  Determines how 2-element and 3-element vectors are displayed. (Vectors can be entered in any of the coordinate systems.) In the **Rectangular** mode, coordinates are in terms of x, y, and z. The TI-89 also had two other modes for 3-element vectors, the **Cylindrical** mode and the **Spherical** mode.

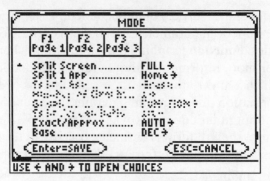

Figure 6.7 The MODE menu (page 2).

- Pretty Print: On, Off
  Determines how results are displayed on the Home screen. With Pretty Print **Off**, results are displayed in a linear, one-dimensional form. With Pretty Print **On**, results are displayed in conventional mathematical format.
- Split Screen: Full (Full Screen), Top-Bottom, Left-Right
  Stand for a Full Screen, or a screen split into two windows, either vertically or horizontally. In the **Full Screen** mode, the entire screen consists of one application. In the **Top-Bottom** mode, the upper half of the screen shows one application while the lower half shows another application. In the **Left-Right** mode, the left side of the screen shows one application while the right side shows another application (see Figs. 6.8, 6.9, and 6.10).

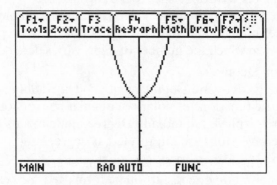

Figure 6.8 A Full Screen display.

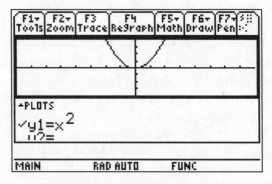

Figure 6.9 A Top-Bottom display.

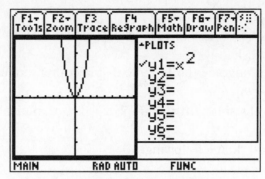

Figure 6.10 A Left-Right display.

- Split 1 App: Home, Y = Editor, Window Editor, Graph, Table, Data/Matrix Editor, Program Editor, Text Editor, Numeric Solver
  In full screen mode, this determines which of the TI-89 applications will be shown on the screen. With the screen split into two parts, this determines which application will be shown in the top or left part of the screen.

- Split 2 App: Home, Y = Editor, Window Editor, Graph, Table, Data/Matrix Editor, Program Editor, Text Editor, Numeric Solver
  Note that this option is not active in full screen mode. With the screen split into two parts, this determines which application will be shown in the bottom or right part of the screen.

- Number of Graphs: 1, 2
  Note that this option is not active in full screen mode. With the screen split into two parts, this determines whether one or both parts of the screen can display graphs at the same time. **1** allows only one part of the screen to show a graph, while **2** allows the two parts of the screen to show independent graphs simultaneously.

- Graph 2: Function, Parametric, Polar, Sequence, 3D, Differential Equations
  Note that this option is not active unless the screen is split into two parts and two graphs can be displayed. With the screen split into two parts, this determines the graphing mode for the second graph. See above for a description of the graphing modes.

- Split Screen Ratio: 1:1, 1:2, 2:1
  Note that this option is not active in full screen mode. With the screen split into two parts, this determines the proportional sizes of the two parts of the screen. **1:1** divides the screen equally, either top-bottom or left-right. **1:2** sets the bottom or right part of the screen as approximately twice the size of the top or left part of the screen. **2:1** sets the top or left part of the screen as approximately twice the size of the bottom or right part of the screen.

- Exact/Approx: Auto, Exact, Approximate
  Specifies how fractional and symbolic expressions are calculated and displayed. When rational and symbolic forms are used, precision is increased by eliminating most numeric rounding errors. **Auto** uses Exact settings in most cases. However, if an entry contains a decimal point, Auto will use Approximate settings. **Exact** displays non-whole-number results in their rational or symbolic form. **Approximate** displays numeric results in floating-point form. For example, pressing $\boxed{\text{2nd}}$ $\boxed{\pi}$ $\boxed{\text{ENTER}}$ from the Home screen in Auto or Exact modes results in an entry/answer pair which both show π, while the same keystrokes in Approximate mode results in an entry/answer pair which shows π and 3.14159, respectively.

- Base: Dec, Hex Bin
  Allows for output to be displayed in the Decimal, Hexadecimal, or Binary Unit System: Unit System: SI, ENG/US, Custom Specifies the units that expressions will be displayed in. Note that to receive an answer with units; the input must also have units.

- Custom Units
  Note that this option is only active when the Unit System is set to custom.
- Language: English
  It is possible to upgrade the TI-89 to display other languages.
- Apps Desktop: Off, On
  With the Apps Desktop off, the grapher will automatically be at the Home Screen when turned on.

To change a mode, do the following:

1. Press

$$\boxed{\text{MODE}}$$

2. Move the cursor down to the mode you want to change.
3. Press

$$\boxed{\blacktriangleright} \text{ and } \boxed{\blacktriangledown}$$

until the mode that you want is highlighted.

4. Press

$$\boxed{\text{ENTER}}$$

5. Follow the same sequence if you want to change other modes.
6. Press

$$\boxed{\text{ENTER}}$$

to accept the new modes.

For example, to change the Auto to the Exact mode, do the following:

1. Press

$$\boxed{\text{MODE}}$$

2. Use the cursor pad to move the cursor to Exact.
3. Press

$$\boxed{\text{ENTER}}$$

twice to change the mode and accept the new mode.

New selections are saved in the TI-89's memory, even when it is turned off, until you change them again.

6.1.9 Recalling a Previous Entry

After an expression has been evaluated, TI-89 stores it in a special storage area called Last Entry. It will still be displayed on the Entry Line and be highlighted until you begin entering another expression. However, even after you have begun entering another expression, you can recall the last expression by pressing

$$\boxed{\text{2nd}} \; \boxed{\text{ENTRY}}$$

The recalled expression replaces the newer one on the Entry Line.

Perform the following steps:

1. Press

$$7 \boxed{\times} 5 \boxed{\text{ENTER}}$$

The expression is calculated and the screen shows the result: 35.

2. Press

$$2 \boxed{\times} 5$$

Do **not** press $\boxed{\text{ENTER}}$.

3. Press

2nd [ENTRY]

The expression 2 × 5 is replaced by the first one—7 × 5—which was saved in Last Entry (see Fig. 6.11).

In Example 1, we show you how you can use Last Entry.

The TI-89 stores as many of the most recent entries in memory as can be stored in the history area (up to a total of 99 entries), even when it is turned off. To further see how this feature works, do the following:

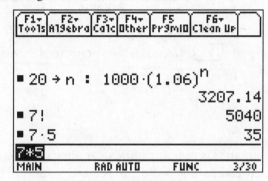

Figure 6.11 The Last Entry Storage area.

1. Calculate the Last Entry expression by pressing

ENTER

2. Press

2nd [ENTRY] 2nd [ENTRY] 2nd [ENTRY] 2nd [ENTRY]

Notice that after each time you press 2nd [ENTRY], a preceding calculation appears on the screen. Before continuing to Example 1, press F1 [8:Clear Home] to clear the Home screen.

Example 1 Last Entry

Problem Determine when an investment earning interest at 8.5% compounded monthly will double in value. The applicable compound interest equation is

$$2 = (1 + .085/12)^N.$$

Solution We want to solve this equation for N. We start by estimating N = 100. Press

(1 + · 085 ÷ 12) ^ 100 ENTER

The result is shown in Fig. 6.12. From this result, we see that our estimate of 100 was too high, so we try again with another, smaller estimate, say N = 99. This time, we use the LAST ENTRY feature, as follows:

1. Press

2nd [ENTRY]

The original equation remains on the Entry Line. Notice that the entire equation is highlighted.

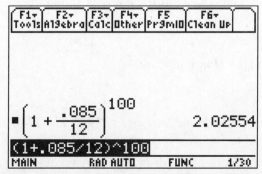

Figure 6.12 The compound interest equation entered.

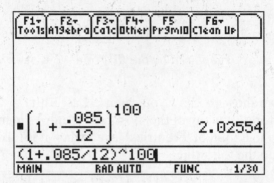

Figure 6.13 Using the LAST ENTRY feature.

2. Use the cursor pad (▶) to move the cursor to the end of the expression. (See Fig. 6.13)

3. Use the ⬅ key to erase the 100.

4. Type **99**.

5. Press

ENTER

Continue estimating in this manner until your answer is as accurate as you want; for example, make your next estimate $N = 98$ and see the result in Fig. 6.14.

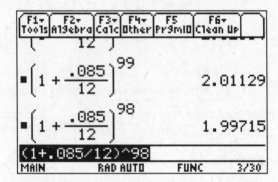

Figure 6.14 Solution for N of $2 = (1 + .085/12)^N$.

6.1.10   Recalling the Last Answer

You also can recall answers obtained from previous calculations. Each previous answer is stored in memory as a variable (Ans(#)), where # refers to the number of the entry/answer pair to which the answer belongs. These previous answers can be used in computations. To recall the previous answer, press

2nd |ANS|

The following example shows how to use this feature:

1. Press

7 × 5 ENTER

   The expression is calculated and the screen shows the result: 35.

2. Press

4 +

   4 + appears on the Home screen.

3. Press

2nd |ANS|

   Ans(1) appears to the immediate right of 4+. The TI-89 then waits for you to either accept or reject insertion of the last answer.

4. a. To accept the stored answer (variable Ans), press

ENTER

The last saved answer—35—is retrieved from memory and added to 4. 4 + 35 appears as the left-hand entry in the history area and the result of adding 4 to the saved answer of 35, that is, 39, appears as the right-hand entry.

b. To reject the stored answer,

1. Press

4 ☐+☐ ☐2nd☐ ⌊ANS⌋

2. Use the ⌊←⌋ key to erase ans(1) from the entry line.

Ans(1) is erased, but 4 + remains on the screen.

c. To reject the stored answer and erase the current expression on the Entry Line, press

⌊CLEAR⌋

6.2   Graphing on the TI-89 Titanium

6.2.1   Basic Graphing Functions

The main graphing functions are listed in green above the F1, F2, and F3 keys and are accessed by using the ⌊◆⌋ key. We summarize each of these next and follow with a more-detailed discussion of these functions and others that are available from toolbar menus on graphing screens:

- ⌊◆⌋ ⌊Y=⌋
  Displays an edit screen on which you enter, edit, and display the functions you want to graph.
- ⌊◆⌋ ⌊WINDOW⌋
  Displays an edit screen on which you define the viewing window for a graph.
- ⌊◆⌋ ⌊GRAPH⌋
  Displays the graph of the currently selected functions in the chosen viewing window.

6.2.2   ⌊◆⌋ Y =: Entering a Function

Entering functions involves the following steps. It's usually best to clear any old equations appearing on the screen before entering new equations. Clear previous equations entered on the Y = edit screen as follows:

1. Position the cursor on the equation to be deleted.

2. Press

⌊CLEAR⌋

To illustrate, we use an example with two functions (see Fig. 6.15).

1. Ensure the TI-89 is in Function mode by pressing

⌊MODE⌋

to display the MODE menu and select

[Function]

as the Graph option.

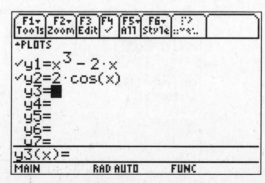

Figure 6.15 Entering functions.

2. Accept the Function mode and return to the previous application by pressing ENTER

3. If the TI-89 is not showing the Y = edit screen press
◆ [Y=]

The screen displays labels for up to 8 functions, Y_1 through Y_8, with more functions available. After each label is an empty field. The entry cursor is on the first field.

4. Enter the function $f(x) = x^3 - 2x$ by pressing
X [∧] 3 [−] 2 X ENTER

Note: *The function is entered in the Y_1 field and the cursor moves to the field next to Y_2. A check-mark appears to the left of Y_1, indicating the function has been selected for graphing.*

5. Enter the function $g(x) = 2 \cos x$ by pressing
2 [2nd] [COS] X [ )] ENTER

The function is entered in the Y_2 field and the cursor moves to the field next to Y_3. A check-mark appears to the left of Y_2, indicating this function also has been selected for graphing.

Note: *These functions are used in demonstrating principles in later sections.*

Selecting functions for graphing. As indicated in these steps, the check-mark left of the function indicates that the function is selected for graphing. You may select as many of the functions entered as you want. To deselect a function, that is, to have it not graphed, do the following:

1. Position the cursor on the applicable function.

2. Press
F4

The check-mark disappears and the function is no longer selected for graphing.

6.2.3   WINDOW: Defining the Viewing Window

The WINDOW screen enables you to choose the coordinates of the viewing window that define the portion of the coordinate plane that appears in the display.

Using the Window edit screen. The values of the Window edit screen variables determine the following:

• The size of the viewing window

• The scale units for each axis

    You can view and change these values easily. Do this as follows:

1. Press ◆ [WINDOW].

The Window edit screen appears as shown in Fig. 6.16, which displays the default values for this feature. The entry cursor is positioned at the value of the first variable.

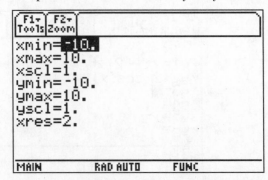

Figure 6.16 The default values for the Window edit screen.

2. For each value you want to change,

    a. move the cursor to the current value,

    b. clear the current value by pressing

$$\boxed{\text{CLEAR}}$$

    c. type in the new value.

3. After changing the values, leave the screen and return to the Home screen by pressing

$$\boxed{\text{HOME}}$$

The variables are defined as follows:

- $x$min, $x$max, $y$min, and $y$max
  Tell the minimum and maximum x- and y-coordinates for the desired viewing window.

In Fig. 6.16, these values define the Standard window of $[-10, 10]$ by $[-10, 10]$.

- $x$scl and $y$scl
  Give the distance between consecutive tick marks on the coordinate axes; in Fig. 6.16, the distance is a value of 1.

Expressions, such as $\pi/2$, $-1 + \sqrt{3}$, and $x{\wedge}2$, can be entered directly as values for Window variables.

6.2.4   GRAPH: Formats for the Graph

Using the FORMAT menu, you can determine how information on the screen is presented, for example, whether the coordinates at the bottom of the screen are displayed in Rectangular or Polar mode.

Using the FORMAT menu. The FORMAT menu offers six options from which you can choose to affect the way data are displayed in the window. To access this menu, do the following:

1. From the Y = or Window screen, press

$$\boxed{\text{F1}} \; [9{:}\text{Format}]$$

or

 F

The six options of the FORMAT menu are displayed.

3. Move the cursor to highlight the option you want to select.

4. Select an option by pressing

$$\boxed{\text{ENTER}}$$

The options in the FORMAT menu are defined as follows:

- Coordinates: Rect (Rectangular), Polar, Off
  Determine whether the free-moving or Trace cursors display Rectangular coordinates, Polar coordinates, or no coordinates at the bottom of the screen.
- Graph Order: Seq (Sequential), Simul (Simultaneous)
  When more than one function is selected, this determines whether the functions are plotted Sequentially (one function is plotted completely before the next function is evaluated) or Simultaneously (all functions evaluated and plotted at a single point before the functions are evaluated for the next point).
- Grid: Off, On
  Activate and deactivate the grid of points that appear on a graph. The grid points correspond to the axis tick marks.

- Axes: On, Off
  Determine whether the *x*- and *y*-axes will appear on the graph.
- Leading Cursor: Off, On
  Determine whether a reference cursor will track the functions as they are graphed.
- Labels: Off, On
  Tell whether the *x*- and *y*-axes will be labeled.

6.2.5 GRAPH: Displaying and Exploring the Graph

To plot and display a graph in the current viewing window with default values, press

$$\boxed{\blacklozenge} \; \lfloor \text{GRAPH} \rfloor$$

This will graph the functions entered in Section 6.2.2 (Fig. 6.17). When the plotting is completed, you can explore the graph using the **free-moving cursor**, a blinking plus sign (+) inside a circle. Note that when you first press $\boxed{\blacklozenge}$ ⌊GRAPH⌋, this cursor isn't visible. To see it, press any direction on the Cursor pad and the cursor will appear near the origin of the *x*- and *y*-axes. Along the bottom of the viewing screen are displayed the coordinates of the cursor's current position.

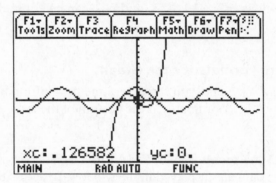

Figure 6.17 Graphing functions.

If the coordinates are not displayed, you can turn them on as follows. Press a direction on the Cursor pad.

a. If the Coordinate option in the FORMAT menu is Rect (Rectangular) or Polar, pressing a direction on the Cursor pad causes the coordinates to reappear on the screen. Note that the direction that you press determines which coordinate values are shown. To erase the coordinate display from the screen, press

$$\boxed{\text{ESC}}$$

b. If the Coordinate option in the FORMAT menu is Off, pressing a direction on the Cursor pad will not cause the coordinates to reappear on the screen. To see the coordinates, the Coordinate option must be Rect or Polar. See Section 6.2.4 for instructions on working with Coordinate options.

If the Coordinate option of the FORMAT menu is Rectangular (Rect), the *x*- and *y*-coordinates are displayed; if the option is Polar, the *R*- and θ-coordinates are displayed. Press any direction on the Cursor pad and notice how the coordinates change as the cursor changes position. The free-moving cursor can be used to identify the coordinates of any location on the graph and operates in both FullScreen, Top-Bottom, and Left-Right modes (see Figs. 6.18, 6.19 and 6.20, respectively).

This cursor moves from dot to dot on the screen, so be aware that when you move it to a dot that appears to be "on" a function, it might be near, but not on, that function. The coordinate value is accurate to within the width of the dot. To move the cursor *exactly* along a function, use the TRACE feature.

Note: *Coordinate values at the bottom of the viewing screen always appear in floating decimal-point format. The numeric display settings in MODE do not affect coordinate display.*

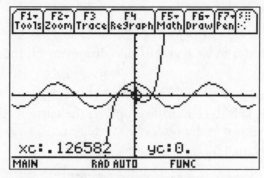

Figure 6.18 The free-moving cursor in the Full Screen mode.

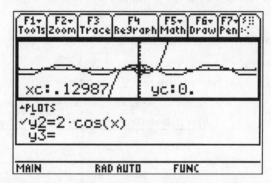

Figure 6.19 The free-moving cursor in the Top-Bottom Screen mode.

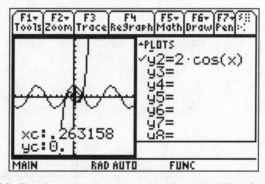

Figure 6.20 The free-moving cursor in the Left-Right Screen mode.

6.2.6 TRACE: Moving the Cursor along a Function's Graph

The TRACE feature enables you to trace the graph of a function. As you do this, the coordinates at the bottom of the viewing screen change to reflect the changing position of the cursor. (If the cursor moves off the top or bottom of the screen, the values continue to change.) Note that in the Rectangular coordinate system, the *y*-value is the calculated function value $f(x)$.

Trace the functions graphed in Section 6.2.4 as follows:

1. Press

$\boxed{\text{F3}}$

The Trace cursor appears near the origin of the axes.

2. a. To trace a graph, press

$\boxed{\blacktriangleright}$ or $\boxed{\blacktriangleleft}$

on the Cursor pad.

b. To move among all functions that are defined *and* selected (that is, active), press

$$\boxed{\blacktriangle} \text{ or } \boxed{\blacktriangledown}$$

on the Cursor pad.

A number in the upper right-hand corner tells you which function is being traced.

c. To pan in order to view graphs that disappear off the left or right of the screen, press and hold

$$\boxed{\blacktriangleright} \text{ or } \boxed{\blacktriangleleft}$$

on the Cursor pad. To center the graph on the current cursor location at any time, press $\boxed{\text{ENTER}}$. This is known as the *QuickCenter* feature.

3. To leave the feature, press

$$\boxed{\text{HOME}}$$

4. To view the graph after quitting the feature, press

$$\boxed{\blacklozenge} \; [\text{GRAPH}]$$

To view at any time the original functions entered for this graph, press

$$\boxed{\blacklozenge} \; [\text{Y=}]$$

Figures 6.21 and 6.22 show tracing the Y_1 and Y_2 graphs, respectively.

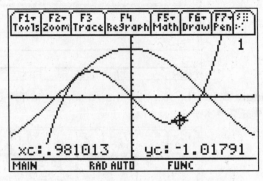

Figure 6.21 Using the TRACE feature.

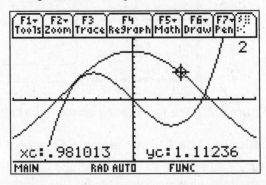

Figure 6.22 Tracing along a function's graph.

Note: The TI-89 stores in memory the set of functions and the graph involved with this problem, provided you have not entered a new set of variables, even after you turn off the calculator. Entering new data replaces the old data that is stored in memory.

6.2.7 ZOOM: Magnifying and Shrinking Parts of a Graph

The ZOOM feature enables you, among other capabilities, to adjust that portion of the viewing window that you see, for example, by magnifying a portion (zoom in) or retreating (zoom out) to give you a more global view. To access the feature, press

$$\boxed{\text{F2}}$$

Figure 6.23 shows the ZOOM menu. Several of the options shown on this menu are discussed in the next several subsections.

When the TI-89 executes a Zoom option, it updates the values of the Window variables to reflect the new viewing window. The modified values depend on the exact cursor position when you executed the option. To see these new values, press

◆ [WINDOW]

To return to the graph without having to replot it, press

◆ [GRAPH]

To practice the following features, use the functions graphed in Section 6.2.5.

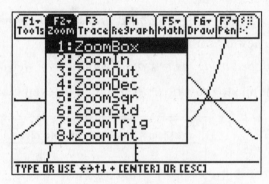

Figure 6.23 The ZOOM menu.

The Zoom Box Option. This option lets you adjust the viewing window by drawing a box anywhere on the screen display to define the size of the desired window. To draw the box, do the following:

1. Press

F2 [1:ZoomBox]

You are returned to the graph. The cursor is in the middle of the screen at the origin of the axes.

2. Move the cursor to the place where you want one corner of the new viewing window to be (see Fig. 6.24).

3. Press ENTER

*The cursor changes to the **Zoom Box cursor**, a blinking square.*

4. Move the cursor to the diagonally opposite corner of the desired viewing window (see Fig. 6.25). Note that you can use the Cursor pad to move diagonally.

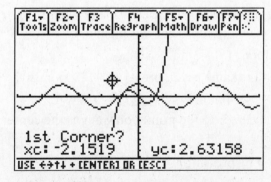

Figure 6.24 Using the Zoom Box option.

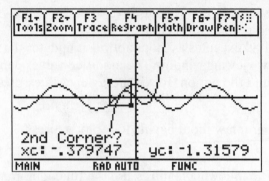

Figure 6.25 Drawing a box to define the new viewing window.

The outline of the new viewing window is drawn as you move the cursor.

5. To accept the new cursor location, press ENTER.

The graph is replotted using the box outline as the new viewing window (see Fig. 6.26).

You can continue to draw boxes to zoom in on even more specific portions of the graph.

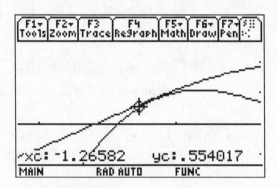

Figure 6.26 A new viewing window.

The Zoom-In Option. This option allows you to zoom in on (magnify) a portion of the graph. Using this option adjusts the viewing window in both the *x*- and *y*-directions according to the zoom factors set in the SET FACTORS menu (see later in this section for details on setting zoom factors). To use this option, do the following:

1. Press

F2 [2:ZoomIn]

You are returned to the graph. The cursor is in the middle of the screen.

2. Place the cursor approximately in the center of the area you want to magnify.

3. Press ENTER.

The TI-89 adjusts the viewing window by the zoom factors, replots the selected functions with the cursor in the center of the new window, and updates the values of the Window variables.

4. To zoom in more,

    a. centered at the same point, press F2 [2:ZoomIn] ENTER.

    b. centered at new point, press F2 [2:ZoomIn]

        • move the cursor to the point you want as the center of the new viewing window, and

        • press ENTER.

5. Exit the screen by pressing HOME.

You also can select another application by pressing the appropriate keys.

For example, Figs. 6.27 and 6.28 show the before and after of using the Zoom-In feature. In Fig. 6.27, the cursor is placed at an intersection of the two graphs; in Fig. 6.28, that intersection with the cursor on it has become the center of a new viewing window.

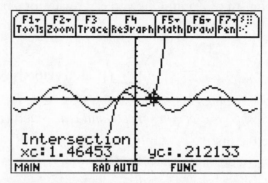

Figure 6.27 Before using the Zoom-In feature.

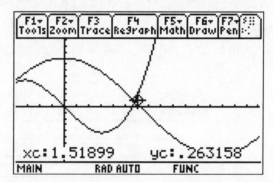

Figure 6.28 After using the ZOOM-IN feature.

The Zoom-Out Option. Zoom-out displays a greater portion of the graph to present a more global view of the graph. Using this option adjusts the viewing window in both the *x*- and *y*-directions according to the zoom factors set in the SET FACTORS menu (see the next subsection for details on setting zoom factors). To use this option, do the following:

1. Press

[F2] [3:ZoomOut]

You are returned to the graph. The cursor is in the middle of the screen at the origin of the graphs.

2. Place the cursor at the point you want as the center of the new viewing window.

3. Press

[ENTER]

The TI-89 adjusts the viewing window by the zoom factors, replots the selected functions with the cursor in the center of the new window, and updates the values of the Window variables.

4. To zoom-out more,
    a. centered at the same point, press [F2] [3:ZoomOut] [ENTER]
    b. centered at new point, press [F2] [3:ZoomOut] move the cursor to the point you want as the center of the new viewing window, and
        • press [ENTER]

5. Exit the screen by pressing

[HOME]

You also can select another application by pressing the appropriate keys.

The Set Factors Option. Zoom factors determine the scale of the magnification for the Zoom-In and Zoom-Out options. These factors are numbers (not necessarily integers) greater than or equal to one.

Before using Zoom-In or Zoom-Out, you can review or change the current values. To use this feature, do the following:

1. Press

$$\boxed{\text{F2}}\ \text{[C:SetFactors]}$$

The Zoom Factors box appears, as shown in Fig. 6.29. In that figure, the default factors of 4 in the x-direction (xFact), y-direction (yFact), and z-direction (zFact) are shown.

2. To change the factors.
   a. enter a new value in the *x*Fact field,

   or

   b. use $\boxed{\blacktriangledown}$ to reach *y*Fact or *z*Fact and enter a new value.

The new value overwrites the old.

3. Accept the new values and exit the feature by pressing

$$\boxed{\text{ENTER}}$$

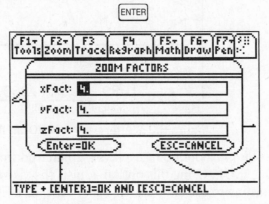

Figure 6.29 The Zoom Factors box.

Other ZOOM Features. Several of the ZOOM features either reset the values of the Window variables to predefined values or use factors to adjust those values. Two of the MEMORY features save and recall Window variables.

- ZoomDec
  Adjusts the values of the Window variables to the following values and replots the functions; for example:

  $$x\text{min} = -7.9 \qquad y\text{min} = -3.9$$
  $$x\text{max} = 7.9 \qquad y\text{max} = 3.9$$
  $$x\text{scl} = 1 \qquad y\text{scl} = 1$$

  In the window with these coordinates, the *x*-coordinate changes in units of 0.1 when you use either the Trace or free-moving cursor. The *y*-coordinate also changes in units of 0.1 as the free-moving cursor moves but not when you trace. This latter situation is because the *y*-coordinate is determined by the function being traced.

- ZoomSqr
  Replots the selected functions as soon as the option is selected. It redefines the viewing window using values that are based on the current values of the Window variables but adjusted to equalize the width of the dots on the *x*- and *y*-axes. The center of the current graph becomes the center of the new graph. This feature makes the graph of a circle look like a circle (see Example 2).

- ZStandard

  Updates the values of the Window variables to the standard default values and then replots the graph. The standard default values of the Window variables are as follows:

$$xmin = -10 \qquad ymin = -10$$
$$xmax = 10 \qquad ymax = 10$$
$$xscl = 1 \qquad yscl = 1$$

- ZoomTrig

  Updates the values of the Window variables using present values appropriate for trigonometric functions and then replots the graph. The values of the trig Window variables in Radian mode are as follows:

$$xmin = -10.3410758181... \qquad ymin = -4$$
$$xmax = 10.3410758181... \qquad ymax = 4$$
$$xscl = 1.5707963267949 \qquad yscl = 0.5$$

Note: The display shows the numeric value of $\pi/2$, (1.5707963267949).

- ZoomInt

  Enables you to move the cursor to the point you want as the center of the new viewing window. Press [ENTER] to have the functions replotted, with the new viewing window redefined so that the midpoint of each dot on the x- and y-axes is an integer. $xscl$ and $yscl$ are equal to 10.

- ZoomData

  Updates the values of the Window variables in order to display all statistical data points.

- ZoomFit

  Replots the selected functions as soon as the option is selected. The Ymin and Ymax variables are updated to include the minimum and maximum y-values of the selected functions between the current Xmin and Xmax values. The Xmin and Xmax values are not changed.

The following are the Memory features available by pressing [F2] [B:Memory]:

- ZoomPrev

  Toggles you back and forth between the graph currently on the screen and the previous graph that was on the screen.

- ZoomSto

  Saves the values of the current window variables for later recall by the ZoomRcl option. After the values are saved, you are returned automatically to the Graph screen.

- ZoomRcl

  Recalls the values of the Window variables that were saved with the ZoomSto option and then draws the current functions in the new window.

Example 2 Graphing a Circle

Problem Graph a circle of radius 10, centered around the origin $x^2 + y^2 = 10$.

Solution To graph a circle, you must enter separate formulas for the upper and lower portions of the circle. Do as follows:

1. Press [♦] [Y=] and use [CLEAR] to erase any existing functions, then enter the expressions to define two functions.

   a. The top half of the circle is defined by $Y_1 = \sqrt{100 - X^2}$, so press

   [2nd] [√] **100** [−] **X** [^] **2** [ )] [ENTER]

b. The bottom half of the circle is defined by $Y_2 = -Y_1$, so press

[(−)] **Y1** [( ] **X** [ )] [ENTER]

2. Press

[F2] [6:ZoomStd]

This is a quick way to reset the values of the Window variables to the standard default values. As this option also graphs the functions, you don't need to press [◆] [GRAPH]. Notice that the graph appears to be an ellipse (see Fig. 6.30).

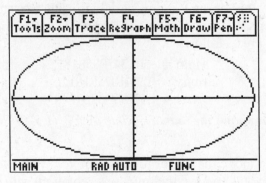

Figure 6.30 Graph of $x^2 + y^2 = 10$.

3. To adjust the display so that each "dot" has an equal width and height, press

[F2] [5:ZoomSqr]

The functions are replotted and now appear as a circle on the display (see Fig. 6.31).

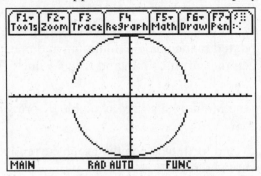

Figure 6.31 Graph of a circle.

4. To see the effect of the ZSquare option on the values of the Window variables, press

[◆] [WINDOW]

and notice how the *x*min, *x*max, *y*min, and *y*max values change.

6.3 Graphing Parametric Equations

6.3.1 Defining and Displaying a Parametric Graph

Parametric equations consist of an *x*-component and a *y*-component, each expressed in terms of the same independent variable, *t*. You can define and graph up to 99 *pairs* of parametric equations simultaneously. The steps for defining a parametric graph are similar to those for defining a function graph. To define a parametric graph, do the following:

1. Press

[MODE]

and from the Graph option select [2:PARAMETRIC].

2. To accept the new mode press

Note: *You must set the TI-89 in Parametric mode before you enter the values of the Window variables or enter the components of parametric equations.*

3. Press

The Y = edit screen displays labels for up to 99 pairs of x-y parametric equations. After each label is an empty field in which you enter the function. The entry cursor is positioned at the first field.

4. Enter the two equations in the same manner as for functions, as follows (see Fig. 6.32):

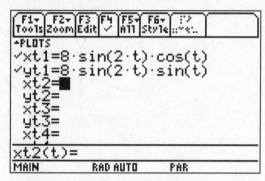

Figure 6.32 Enter parametric equations.

a. $8 \sin 2T \cos T$; press

8 [SIN] 2 T [ )] [COS] T [ )] [ENTER]

b. $8 \sin 2T \sin T$; press

8 [SIN] 2 T [ )] [SIN] T [ )] [ENTER]

In this case, note the following:

-   You must define both the *x*- and *y*-components in a pair.
-   The independent variable in each component must be *t*.

The procedures for editing and clearing parametric equations and for exiting the screen are the same as for function graphing. Selecting equations for graphing, also, is the same as for function graphing. Only the selected equations are graphed.

5. To display the current values of the Window variables, press

[♦] [WINDOW]

The standard values in Radian mode are shown in Table 6.2.

6. As needed, change the values on your screen to match those in Table 6.2.

Table 6.2

Setting	Meaning
WINDOW	
$t$min = 0	The smallest *t*-value to be evaluated
$t$max = 2π	The largest *t*-value to be evaluated
$t$step = $\pi/24$	The increment between *t*-values
$x$min = -10	The smallest *x*-value to be displayed
$x$max = 10	The largest *x*-value to be displayed
$x$scl = 1	The spacing between *x* tick marks
$y$min = -10	The smallest *y*-value to be displayed
$y$max = 10	The largest *y*-value to be displayed
$y$scl = 1	The spacing between *y* tick marks

Note: The display shows the numeric value of 2π, 6.28318530718, for tMAX and π/24, .13089969389958, for tstep.

Notice the three new variables: tmin, tmax, and tstep.

7. To graph the equations, press

◆ [GRAPH]

(See Fig. 6.33.)

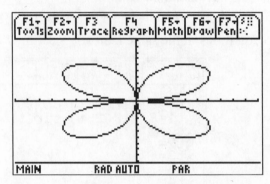

Figure 6.33 Graphing parametric equations.

Pressing ◆ [GRAPH] causes the TI-89 to plot the selected parametric equations. It evaluates both the *x*- and *y*-components for each value of *t* (taken from *t*min to *t*max in intervals of *t*step) and then plots each point defined by *x* and *y*. The values of the Window variables define the viewing window. As the graph is plotted, the TI-89 updates the *x*- and *y*-coordinates and the values of the parameter *t*.

6.3.2 Exploring a Parametric Graph

As in function graphing, you have three tools for exploring a graph:

- Using the free-moving cursor
- Tracing an equation
- Zooming

The free-moving cursor works in parametric graphing in the same manner as it does in function graphing: As the cursor moves, the displayed coordinate values of *x* and *y* in Rectangular (Rect) mode—R and θ in Polar (Polar) mode—are updated.

Using the TRACE feature, you can move the cursor along the graph one *t*step at a time. When you begin a trace, the cursor is on the first selected equation at the initial *t*-value and the coordinate values of *x, y*, and *t* are displayed at the bottom of the screen. As you trace the graph, the displayed values of *x, y*, and *t* are updated, where the *x*- and *y*-values are calculated from *t*.

If the cursor moves off the top or bottom of the screen, the coordinate values continue to change and be displayed. Panning is not possible on parametric curves. However, you can use the QuickCenter feature to see sections. You can also change the values of the Window variables.

The ZOOM features work in parametric graphing as they do in function graphing. Only the values of the *x* Window variables (*x*min, *x*max, and *x*scl) and *y* Window variables (*y*min, *y*max, and *y*scl) are affected. The values of the *t* Window variables (*t*min, *t*max, and *t*step) are affected only when you select [ZoomStd], in which case, they become *t*min = 0, *t*max = 2π, and *t*step = π/24. You might want to change the values of the *t* Window variables to ensure sufficient points are plotted.

6.3.3 Applying Parametric Graphing

Example 3 Simulating Motion

Problem Graph the position of a ball kicked from ground level at an angle of 60° with an initial velocity of 40 ft/sec. (Ignore air resistance.) What is the maximum height, and when is it reached? How far away and when does the ball strike the ground?

Solution If v_0 is the initial velocity and θ is the angle, then the horizontal component of the position of the ball as a function of time is described by

$$X(T) = Tv_0 \cos \theta.$$

The vertical component of the position of the ball as a function of time is described by

$$Y(T) = -16T^2 + Tv_0 \sin \theta.$$

To graph the equations, do as follows:

1. Press $\boxed{\text{MODE}}$ and select Parametric and Degree modes.

2. Press $\boxed{\blacklozenge}$ $\boxed{\text{Y=}}$, use $\boxed{\text{CLEAR}}$ to erase any previous functions, then enter the following expressions to define the parametric equation in terms of t:

   a. $X_{1T} = 40T \cos 60$; press

   $$\textbf{40 T} \boxed{\times} \boxed{\text{2nd}} \boxed{[\text{COS}]} \textbf{60} \boxed{)} \boxed{\text{ENTER}}$$

   b. $Y_{1T} = 40T \sin 60 - 16T^2$; press

   $$\textbf{40 T} \boxed{\times} \boxed{\text{2nd}} \boxed{[\text{SIN}]} \textbf{60} \boxed{)} \boxed{-} \textbf{16 T} \boxed{\wedge} \textbf{2} \boxed{\text{ENTER}}$$

Note: You must press $\boxed{\times}$ *between T and* [COS] *or* [SIN] *or the TI-89 will interpret what you have entered as containing new functions called tcos and tsin.*

3. Set the values of the Window variables appropriately for this problem by pressing $\boxed{\blacklozenge}$ $\boxed{\text{WINDOW}}$ and entering the following values as needed:

$t\text{min} = 0$	$x\text{min} = -5$	$y\text{min} = -5$
$t\text{max} = 2.5$	$x\text{max} = 50$	$y\text{max} = 20$
$t\text{step} = .02$	$x\text{scl} = 5$	$y\text{scl} = 5$

4. To graph the equations, press $\boxed{\blacklozenge}$ $\boxed{\text{GRAPH}}$.

5. To explore the graph, press $\boxed{\text{F3}}$.

As the cursor moves along the ball's path, observe the changing x-, y-, and t-values at the bottom of the screen. Notice you have a "stop action" picture at each 0.02 sec. See Fig. 6.34.

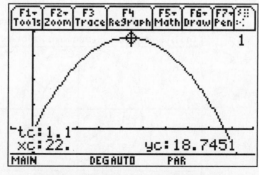

Figure 6.34 Simulating motion.

6.4 Graphing Polar Equations

You can enter up to 99 equations for graphing.

Example 4 Graphing a Spiral

Problem Graph the spiral of Archimedes, that is, the curve defined by the polar equation $r = a\theta$.

Solution A polar equation $r = f(\theta)$ can be graphed using the TI-89's polar graphing features. Thus the spiral of Archimedes (with $a = 0.5$) can be expressed as follows:

1. Press MODE
   a. Select Polar mode.
   b. Choose the default settings, including Radian and Normal, for the other modes.

2. Press ◆ [Y=], clear any existing functions, then enter the polar equation in terms of θ:

$$r_1 = .5\theta$$

   by pressing

   · 5 ◆ [Θ] ENTER

3. To graph the equations in the Standard default viewing window, press

   F2 [6:ZoomStd]

The graph shows only the first loop of the spiral because the standard default values for the Window variables define θmax as 2π.

4. To explore the behavior of the graph further, press ◆ [WINDOW] and change θ max to 25.

5. To display the new graph as shown in Fig. 6.35, press

   ◆ [GRAPH]

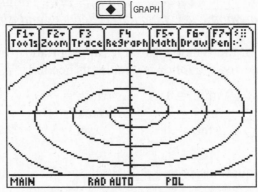

Figure 6.35 Graphing a spiral.

6. Press

   F2 [5:ZoomSqr]

   and notice what happens (see Fig. 6.36).
   Compare Figs. 6.35 and 6.36.

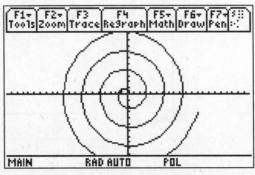

Figure 6.36 The spiral of Archimedes.

Example 5 Graphing a Leafed Rose

Problem Graph a leafed rose defined by the polar equation $r = a \sin(n\theta)$.
Solution Graph a four-leafed rose with $a = 7$ and $n = 2$ as follows:

1. Press

$$\boxed{\text{MODE}}$$

    a. Select Polar mode.
    b. Choose the defaults for the other modes.

2. Press $\boxed{\blacklozenge}$ $\boxed{\text{Y=}}$, clear any existing functions, then enter the expression

$$r_1 = 7 \sin(2\theta)$$

by pressing

$$\boxed{\text{CLEAR}} \; \mathbf{7} \; \boxed{\text{2nd}} \; \boxed{\text{SIN}} \; \mathbf{2} \; \boxed{\blacklozenge} \; \boxed{\theta} \; \boxed{\;)\;} \; \boxed{\text{ENTER}}$$

3. To graph the rose in the Standard default viewing window, press

$$\boxed{\text{F2}} \; [\text{6:ZoomStd}]$$

4. Press

$$\boxed{\text{F2}} \; [\text{5:ZoomSqr}]$$

and observe what happens.

The graph should look that in Fig. 6.37.

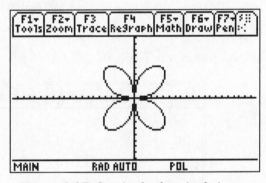

Figure 6.37 Graph of a four-leafed rose.

6.5 Graphing a Sequence

The TI-89 can graph sequences defined recursively or with an nth-term formula. For example, the sequence $\{1/2, 1/4, 1/8, 1/16 \ldots\}$ can be defined by the nth-term formula $a_n = 1/2^n$ or by the recursive formula $a_n = (1/2)a_{n-1}, a_1 = 1/2$.

Example 6 Graphing an *n*th-term Formula Sequence

Problem Graph a sequence defined by $a_n = 1/2^n$.
Solution To graph this sequence, do the following steps

1. Press $\boxed{\text{MODE}}$ and select the Sequential [4:Sequence] mode.

2. Press $\boxed{\blacklozenge}$ [Y=], clear any existing functions, then enter the expression

$$a_n = 1/2^n$$

by pressing

$$1 \boxed{\div} 2 \boxed{\wedge} \boxed{\text{ALPHA}} \boxed{\blacklozenge} \boxed{\text{ENTER}}$$

(See Fig. 6.38.)

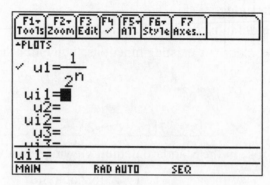

Figure 6.38 Entering the nth-term formula.

3. Press $\boxed{\blacklozenge}$ [WINDOW]
and enter the following values for the Window variables:

$n\text{min} = 1$	plotstrt = 1	$x\text{min} = 0$	$y\text{min} = 0$
$n\text{max} = 10$	plotstep = 1	$x\text{max} = 10$	$y\text{max} = 1$
		$x\text{scl} = 1$	$y\text{scl} = 1$

4. Press $\boxed{\blacklozenge}$ [GRAPH].

Your graph should look like that in Fig. 6.39.

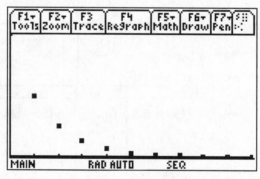

Figure 6.39 Graph of a sequence Defined by $a_n = 1/2^n$.

Example 7 Graphing a Recursive Sequence

Problem Graph the recursive sequence defined by $a_n = (1/2)a_{n-1}; a_1 = 1/2$.
Solution To graph this sequence, do the following:

1. Press $\boxed{\text{MODE}}$ and select the Sequential [4:Sequence] mode.

2. Press $\boxed{\blacklozenge}$ [Y=], clear any existing functions, then enter the expression

$$a_n = (1/2)a_{n-1}$$

by pressing

$$\boxed{(} 1 \boxed{\div} 2 \boxed{)} \boxed{\text{ALPHA}} [\text{u}] 1 \boxed{(} \boxed{\text{ALPHA}} [\text{N}] \boxed{-} 1 \boxed{)} \boxed{\text{ENTER}}$$

3. Enter the value of

$$a_1 = 1/2$$

by entering 1/2 for ui 1 on the second line of the Y = screen.

3. Enter the following values for the WINDOW variables:

$n$min = 1	plotstrt = 1	$x$min = 0	$y$min = 0
$n$max = 10	plotstep = 1	$x$max = 10	$y$max = 1
		$x$scl = 1	$y$scl = 1

4. Press [◆] |GRAPH|.

Your graph should look like that in Fig. 6.40.

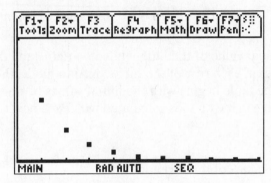

Figure 6.40 Graph of the recursive sequence defined by $a_n = 1/2a_{n-1}$; $a_1 = 1/2$.

6.6 Representing Functions Numerically Using Tables

The TI-89 can represent functions numerically by making a table of selected values for the independent and dependent variables. To create such a table, you enter the function in Y_1 and then designate the initial value and the increment for the independent variable.

Example 8 Describing a Function in a Table; Building the Table Automatically

Problem Describe the function $f(x) = 1/2^x$ in a table and use the automatic feature to build the table.

Solution To solve this problem, do the following:

1. Press |MODE| and select Function mode.

2. Press |Y=|, clear any existing functions, then enter the function

$$Y_1 = 1/2^x$$

by pressing

1 [÷] **2** [∧] **X** |ENTER|

3. Access the TABLE SETUP menu by pressing

[◆] |TBLSET|

4. To make the independent variable (X) begin at 0 and increase by 1, press

0 [▼] **1** |ENTER|

Note: [Independent] *shows* AUTO, *indicating the table will be generated automatically. See Fig. 6.41.*

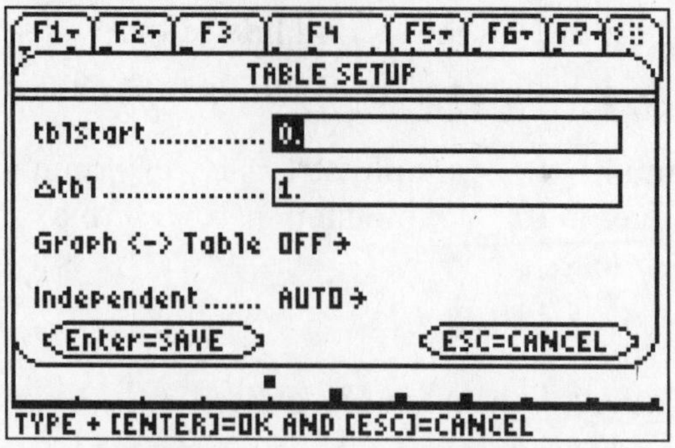

Figure 6.41 The TABLE SETUP menu.

tblStart is the initial value of the independent variable and Δtbl is the amount by which that variable increases in each row of the table. In Auto mode, the rows of the table are filled in automatically. The table begins with the initial values of x and Y_1 and increments x by Δtbl. The corresponding value of Y_1 is calculated with each new row.

5. Press

ENTER

to accept the values of tblStart and Δtbl.

6. To build the table, press

◆ [TABLE]

The result should be the table shown in Fig. 6.42.

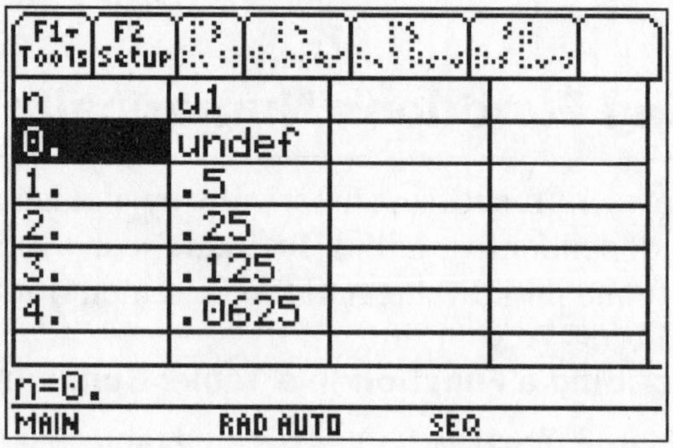

Figure 6.42 Describing a function in a table.

You can use the cursor pad to scroll through more of the table that lies beyond the bottom and top of the screen.

7. To leave the table, press

HOME

Example 9 Describing a Function in a Table; Building the Table Manually

Problem Describe the function $f(x) = \sin(x)$ in a table and build the table manually using the Ask mode.

Solution To solve this problem, do the following:

1. Press

MODE

and select the Function and Degree modes.

2. Press ◆ [Y=], clear any existing functions, then enter the function

$$Y_1 = \sin X$$

by pressing

SIN X) ENTER

3. Access the TABLE SETUP menu by pressing

◆ [TBLSET]

and select the manual option [Independent: Ask]. Then press ENTER

In Ask mode, you must enter the values of the independent variable to be used in each row of the table.

4. To clear the table, press

◆ [TABLE] F1 [8:ClearTable ENTER

5. Enter the independent variables—15, 20, 30—to be used on each row of the table as follows:

15 ENTER ▼ 20 ENTER ▼ 30 ENTER ▼

(See Fig. 6.43.)

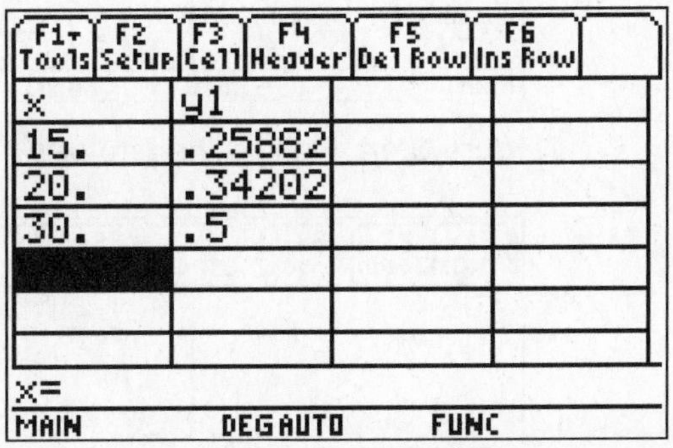

Figure 6.43 Entering the independent variable.

6. To leave the table, press

HOME

6.7 Finding Approximations to Solutions

The TI-89 includes powerful tools for finding accurate approximations to solutions of equations. Two of these are the Zero and Intersection options found in the MATH toolbar menu of the graph application. The Zero option finds real zeros of a function; the Intersection option finds the points of intersection of two functions.

Example 10 Finding the Real Zero of an Equation

Problem Find the zero of the equation $Y_1 = X^3 - 2X$.

1. Press MODE and select the default modes.

2. Press ◆ [Y=], clear any existing functions, then enter the function

$$Y_1 = X^3 - 2X$$

by pressing

X ^ 3 − 2 X ENTER

3. Graph the equation in the Standard viewing window by pressing

F2 [6:ZoomStd]

4. Select the Zero option of the MATH toolbar menu by pressing

F5 [2:Zero]

A request for a Lower Bound appears in the lower left-hand corner of the screen.

5. Press ▶ to move the cursor to just below the largest root (see Fig. 6.44).

6. To accept the Lower Bound, press

ENTER

A prompt for the Upper Bound replaces the Lower Bound prompt in the lower left-hand corner.

7. Use the cursor pad to move the cursor to just above the largest root (see Fig. 6.45).

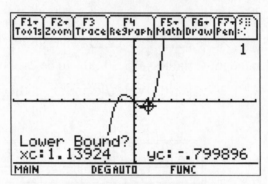

Figure 6.44 Finding the zero of $f(x) = x^3 - 2x$.

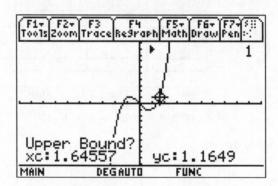

Figure 6.45 The Upper Bound.

8. To accept the Upper Bound, press ENTER.

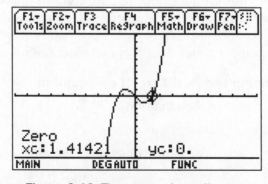

Figure 6.46 The cursor shows the zero

The TI-89 returns an accurate approximation of the zero. Compare this value with $\sqrt{2}$.

Example 11 Finding the Intersection of Two Curves

Problem Find the intersection of the equations $Y_1 = X^3 - 2X$ and $Y_2 = 2 \cos X$.

Solution Do the following:

1. Press MODE and select the default modes.
2. Press ◆ [Y=], clear any existing functions, then enter the functions
   a. $Y_1 = X^3 - 2X$; press

$$\text{X} \boxed{\wedge} 3 \boxed{-} 2 \text{ X } \boxed{\text{ENTER}}$$

   b. $Y_2 = 2 \cos X$; press;

$$2 \boxed{\cos} \text{ X } \boxed{)} \boxed{\text{ENTER}}$$

3. Graph the equations in the Standard viewing window by pressing

$$\boxed{\text{F2}} \text{ [6:ZoomStd]}$$

4. Select the Intersection option in the MATH toolbar menu by pressing

$$\boxed{\text{F5}} \text{ [5:Intersection]}$$

The graph of the equations appear on the screen, with a prompt for the first curve in the intersection (1st curve?) in the lower left-hand corner.

5. The cursor is already on the graph of Y_1, so press

$$\boxed{\text{ENTER}}$$

   to accept the graph marked by the cursor.

The cursor moves to the graph of Y_2. A prompt for the second curve (2nd curve?) replaces the first curve prompt in the lower left-hand corner.

6. As the cursor is already on the graph of Y_2, press ENTER.

A prompt for a lower bound (Lower Bound?) replaces the second curve prompt in the lower left-hand corner (see Fig. 6.47).

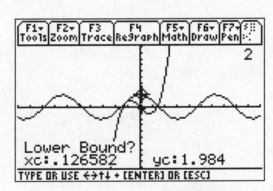

Figure 6.47 Lower Bound Prompt.

7. Move the cursor to a point in the first quadrant to the left of the intersection in that quadrant and press ENTER.

A prompt for an upper bound (Upper Bound?) replaces the lower bound prompt in the lower left-hand corner.

8. Move the cursor to a point in the first quadrant to the right of the intersection and press ENTER.

The TI-89 returns a very accurate approximation of the x- and y-coordinates for the intersection of the two curves (see Fig. 6.48).

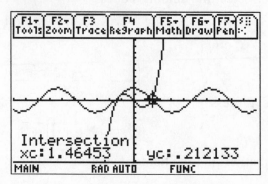

Figure 6.48 An approximation of the intersection of two curves.

6.8 Graphing Piecewise Functions

Piecewise functions like

$$f(x) = \begin{cases} 2x-1 & \text{if } x \le 1 \\ x^2-2x+2 & \text{if } x > 1 \end{cases}$$

can be graphed on the TI-89 using the WHEN function. The WHEN function can be accessed by using the CATALOG menu, press CATALOG. To graph this function, do as follows:

1. Press

MODE

and select the default modes, including Func.

2. Press [Y=], clear any existing expressions, then enter the expression

$$Y_1 = \begin{cases} 2x-1 & \text{if } x \le 1 \\ x^2-2x+2 & \text{if } x > 1 \end{cases}; \text{by pressing}$$

WHEN X [2nd] **> 1** [,] **X** [∧] **2** [−] **2 X** [+] **2** [,] **2 X** [−] **1** [ )] ENTER

The screen should look like that in Fig. 6.49.

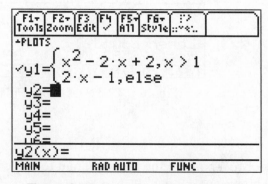

Figure 6.49 Using the WHEN function.

3. Graph the equations in a $[-2, 2]$ by $[-2, 2]$ viewing window.

The graph should look like that in Fig. 6.50.

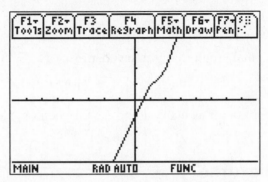

Figure 6.50 Graph of a piecewise function.

The WHEN function evaluates the first expression following the boolean expression $x >$ 1 when the boolean expression is true and evaluates the second expression following the boolean expression when the boolean expression is false. So the function Y_1 is equal to $2x - 1$ when x is less than or equal to 1 and is equal to $x^2 - 2x + 2$ when $x > 1$.

6.9 Working with Graphical Databases

The equations, viewing window, and modes used to create a graph such as that in Section 6.8 can be saved as a graphical database and then retrieved later. After you have selected the desired modes, entered the equations, and created an appropriate viewing window, save the data as follows:

1. From the $\boxed{\text{Y=}}$ editor, Window editor, Table screen, or Graph screen, press

$$\boxed{\text{F1}} \text{ [2:Save Copy As]}$$

2. Set the Type to GDB. and enter a folder and a unique variable name. For example, save the current set of equations, viewing window, and modes in the main folder as **abc**. The variable name is the information that you will need in order to retrieve the graph. A variable can use 1 to 8 characters consisting of letters and digits. This includes Greek letters (but not π), accented letters, and international letters. Do not include spaces. The first character cannot be a digit. Variables are not case sensitive, so for example, UV3, Uv3. uV3. and uv3 refer to the same variable. A variable cannot have the same name as a preassigned TI-89 name, such as abs or $y1$.

3. Quit the feature by pressing

$$\boxed{\text{ENTER}}$$

To see how graphical databases work, do the following:

1. Press

$$\boxed{\blacklozenge} \boxed{\text{Y=}}$$

and clear the equation in Y_1.

2. Retrieve the equation and settings as follows:

   a. From the $\boxed{\text{Y=}}$ editor, Window editor, Table screen, or Graph screen, press

$$\boxed{\text{F1}} \text{ [1:Open]}$$

The TI-89 displays the 'open' dialog box

b. Enter the folder and variable name for the graph that you wish to retrieve. Retrieve **abc** from the main folder. Accept your entries by pressing

$$\boxed{\text{ENTER}}$$

The TI-89 returns you to the previous screen, which now shows the retrieved information.

4. To see the original graph that was saved, press

$$\boxed{\blacklozenge} \ \boxed{\text{GRAPH}}$$

You can save the data for as many graphs as the memory available in your TI-89 will allow.

6.10 Drawing Pictures

Several tools in the TI-89 are useful for drawing pictures and diagrams. These features are found in the $\boxed{\text{F7}}$ toolbar menu.

Example 12 Drawing with Toolbar Tools

Problem Duplicate the picture found in Fig. 6.51.
Solution To draw the figure, do the following:

1. Select Func mode, press $\boxed{\blacklozenge} \ \boxed{\text{Y=}}$ and clear the equations from the edit screen.
2. Select the Decimal viewing window by pressing

$$\boxed{\text{F2}} \ [\text{4:ZoomDec}]$$

The Graph screen appears.

3. Draw a circle as follows:

   a. Select the Circle option from the toolbar menu by pressing

$$\boxed{\text{2nd}} \ \boxed{\text{F7}} \ [\text{4:Circle(}]$$

   b. Move the cursor to the point $(1, 1)$ and press $\boxed{\text{ENTER}}$.
   c. Move the cursor to the point $(3, 1)$ and press $\boxed{\text{ENTER}}$.

A circle with center (1, 1) and radius 2 is drawn on the graph.

4. Draw a diameter of the circle as follows:

   a. Press

$$\boxed{\text{2nd}} \ \boxed{\text{F7}} \ [\text{3:Line}]$$

   b. Move the cursor to the point $(-1, 1)$ and press $\boxed{\text{ENTER}}$.
   c. Use the cursor pad to drag a line across the circle to the point $(3, 1)$ and press $\boxed{\text{ENTER}}$.

5. Label the endpoints of the diameter as follows:

   a. Select the Text option by pressing

$$\boxed{\text{2nd}} \ \boxed{\text{F7}} \ [\text{7:Text}]$$

   b. Move the cursor text to the left of the left endpoint of the diameter and press

 A

   c. Move the cursor next to the right endpoint of the diameter and press

 B

The graph should resemble that in Fig. 6.51.

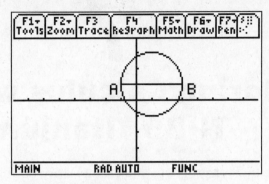

Figure 6.51 Drawing with toolbar tools.

6. Save the picture by pressing

[F1] [2:Save Copy As]

7. Change the Type to Picture, and give the picture a unique name. For example, name the picture **def**. Press [ENTER] to accept the name.

8. Clear the picture by pressing

[F6] [1:ClrDraw]

Press [◆] [GRAPH] (if you were not on the graph screen) to verify that the picture has been erased.

9. To recall the picture, press,

[◆] [GRAPH] [F1] [1:Open]

Set the Type to Picture and select the name of the picture. In this case, select **def**. Press [ENTER] to accept your settings and draw the saved picture.

CHAPTER

7

Exploring Calculus with the TI-89 Titanium

The following toolbox programs and examples are useful in exploring and visualizing concepts in calculus. In some cases, you will be given a program that must be entered in the TI-89 before you can explore a particular concept. In other cases, the program is a built-in part of the TI-89, so you will not have to enter a program in order to explore the concept. In either case, the program will be described by a name in uppercase letters and you will be given the input and output parameters. If it is built in you will be given the keys and functions necessary to execute the program.

7.1 Numerical Derivative

Program 1

NDERIV (numerical derivative)
Input: $f(x)$, x and h (step size)
Output: (approximate) value of $f'(x)$

This is a built-in program on the TI-89. It appears as the nDeriv option in the ⎡ F3 ⎤ (Calc) menu, in the Calculus submenu of the Math menu, in the CATALOG menu. To find the derivative of $f(x)$ with respect to x, enter nDeriv $(f(x), x, h)$. In order to evaluate the numerical derivative at a particular point A, use ⎡ | ⎤ as shown below. Note that the TI-89 can perform symbolic differentiation, and thus can evaluate derivatives directly, without needing a numerical approximation.

Example 1

If $f(x) = x - 2 \sin x$, then $f'(0)$ is approximated by the following key sequence:

Table 7.1 Running NDERIV

Comments	Input (keystrokes)	Screen Display
1. Select the nDeriv option from the ⎡ F3 ⎤ menu and input the derivative of $f(x)$ with respect to x, using a step size of $h = .01$ evaluated at $x = 0$.	⎡ F3 ⎤ [A:nDeriv(] X ⎡ − ⎤ 2 ⎡ 2nd ⎤ ⎡ SIN ⎤ X ⎡) ⎤ ⎡ , ⎤ X ⎡ , ⎤ ⎡ . ⎤ 01 ⎡) ⎤ ⎡	⎤ X ⎡ = ⎤ 0 ⎡ ENTER ⎤	nDeriv (nDeriv (x − 2 sin (x), x, .01) | x = 0 − .999966666833

Note: The step size h determines the accuracy of the approximation. Repeat the steps in Example 1 but set h to 0.0001 before evaluating nDer (x − 2 sin x, x, .0001). This gives a closer approximation (.−999999996667) to the exact value. The values in Table 7.2 were found by using nDeriv (x − 2 sin x, x, h) | x = A with various step sizes (h) and various values for A. Compare the results obtained using different step sizes with the exact value (to 10 decimal places) listed in the last column of Table 7.2. See if you can obtain similar results using the nDeriv option on your TI-89.

Table 7.2 Numerical derivatives of $x - 2 \sin x$.

A	nDeriv(f) $h = 0.1$	nDeriv(f) $h = 0.01$	nDeriv(f) $h = 0.0001$	EXACT $f'(A)$
−10	2.67534755118	2.67811508924	2.6781430554	2.6781430582
−7	−.505292757377	−.50777937837	−.5078045061	−.5078045087
−2	1.83090721039	1.8322798016	1.8322936717	1.8322936731
0	−.996668332937	−.999966666833	−.999999996667	−1.0000000000
1	−.07880450434	−.080586601749	−.08060461	−.0806046117
5	.433620697034	.432685084432	.43267563	.4326756291
10	2.67534755118	2.67811508924	2.6781430554	2.6781430582

7.2 Graph of Numerical Derivative

Program 2

NDERGRAF (graph of numerical derivative)

Input: $f(x)$

Output: graph of $y = f'(x)$

This is a built-in function on the TI-89, so no programming is required. To overlay the graph of $f'(x)$ on the graph of $y = f(x)$, do the following:

- Enter the function y in y_1.
- Enter $y_2 = \text{nDeriv}(y_1(x), x, h)$
- Select an appropriate viewing window.
- Graph.

If you don't want the graph of $f(x)$ to appear, unselect y_1 before you press ◆ [GRAPH]. You can increase the accuracy of the graph by reducing the step size, (h), but the graph might be drawn more slowly. Generally $h = .001$ will give accurate results.

Example 2

To graph $y = x - 2 \sin x$ and its derivative, do the following:

1. Select Radian mode, and then enter $y_1 = x - 2 \sin (x)$.
2. Enter $y_2 = \text{nDeriv}(y_1(x), x, .001)$.
3. Graph using a $[-10, 10]$ by $[-10, 10]$ window.

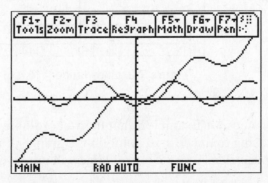

Figure 7.1 $x - 2 \sin x$ and its derivative.

These steps produce the graph shown in Fig. 7.1.

Notice the roots of the derivative have the same *x*-coordinates as the extrema of $f(x)$. Notice also that $f(x)$ is increasing on the intervals where $f'(x)$ is positive and decreasing on the intervals where $f'(x)$ is negative. To see the second derivative, enter $y_2 = \text{nDeriv}(y_1(x), x, .01)$, $y_3 = \text{nDeriv}(y_2(x), x, .01)$, and press ◆ GRAPH.

7.3 Draw a Line Tangent to a Curve

Program 3

TANLINE (draws a line tangent to a curve)
Input: $f(x), a$
Output: overlays tangent line at $(a, f(a))$ on the graph of $y = f(x)$
A function in the F5 (MATH) menu does the job directly from the graph.

Example 3

Lines tangent to the curve $y = x - 2 \sin x$ at $x = -6, -5.24$, and -4 can be overlaid on the curve.
   Directions:

1. Graph $y_1 = x - 2\sin(x)$ in the $[-10, 10]$ by $[-10, 10]$ window.

2. From the F5 menu select [A:Tangent].

3. Use the keypad to enter the *x*-coordinate of -6, then press ENTER.

A tangent line is drawn at x = −6.

4. From the F5 menu select [A:Tangent].

5. Use the keypad to enter the *x*-coordinate of -5.24, then press ENTER.

A tangent line is drawn at x = −5.24.

6. From the F5 menu select [A:Tangent].

7. Use the keypad to enter the *x*-coordinate of -4, then press ENTER.

These steps produce the graph shown in Fig. 7.2.

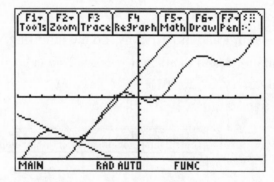

Figure 7.2 Lines tangent to $x - \sin x$.

Notice in the steps for Example 3 that the *x*-coordinate of the point of tangency can also be entered by tracing to the desired point on the graph, although since the *x*-coordinate may not be the exact value desired, the tangent line will not be exact.

7.4 Definite Integral

Program 4

NINT (definite integral)

Input: $f(x)$, a, and b

Output: (approximate) value of $\int_a^b f(x)\,dx$

This is a built-in program. It appears as the nInt option in the [F3] (Calc) menu. The expression nInt $(f(x), x, a, b)$ will return the approximate value of $\int_a^b f(x)\,dx$. The goal of the TI-89 is six significant digits of accuracy.

Example 4A

A proper integral such as $\int_0^{\pi/2} \cos x\,dx$ can be evaluated by the following key sequence in the entry line of the Home screen.

Table 7.3

Input (keystrokes)	Screen Display
[F3] [B:nInt(]	nInt (
[2nd] [COS] **X** [ )] [,] **X** [,]	nInt (cos x, x, 0, π/2)
0 [,] [2nd] [π] [÷] **2** [ )] [ENTER]	**1**

This key sequence creates the command nInt(cos (X), X, 0, $\pi/2$) on the entry line of the Home screen, with the value of the definite integral (1) as the answer in the first entry/answer pair. The first parameter in the nInt command is the function to be integrated. The second parameter is the variable with respect to which the function is to be integrated. The third and fourth parameters are the lower and upper limits of integration. Note that the TI-89 can perform symbolic integration, and thus can evaluate integrals directly, without needing a numerical approximation.

Example 4B

An improper integral such as $\int_{-1}^{3} \dfrac{\sin x}{x}\,dx$ can be approximated if we assume $\dfrac{\sin x}{x} = 1$ at $x = 0$.

Directions:

1. In the entry line of the Home screen enter nInt $(\sin (x)/x, x, -1, 3)$.

The definite integral is approximately 2.79473559837

7.5 Graph a Function Defined by an Integral

Program 5

NINTGRAF (graph a function defined by an integral)

Input: $f(x)$, a

Output: graph of $\int_a^x f(t)\,dt$

The built-in program appearing as the nInt option in the [F3] menu can be used to graph a function defined by an integral. To visualize $\int_a^x f(t)\,dt$, enter y1 = nInt $(f(t), t, a, x)$ and graph.

Example 5A

The function $\int_0^x \dfrac{\sin t}{t}\, dt$ can be graphed if we assume $\dfrac{\sin x}{x} = 1$ at $x = 0$.

Directions:

1. Enter $y_1 = \text{nInt}(\sin(t)/t, t, 0, x)$.
2. Press $\boxed{\blacklozenge}$ $\lfloor \text{WINDOW} \rceil$ and create a $[-10, 10]$ by $[-3, 3]$ viewing window.
3. Graph.

These steps produce the graph shown in Fig. 7.3.

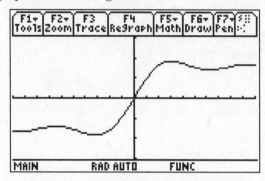

Figure 7.3 Antiderivative of $(\sin x)/x$.

If you wish to speed up the graphing, change *x*res in the WINDOW setting screen to higher number. For example, changing *x*res from 1 to 3 will triple the speed, but the function will be evaluated and graphed at every 3rd pixel, so increasing *x*res too much may affect the resolution of the graph.

This program is designed to graph functions defined by proper integrals; however, it can sometimes graph functions defined by improper integrals. You might need to make adjustments in the tolerance or in the limits of integration. If you encounter an error while attempting to graph the antiderivative, try using a different value for the tol variable in the Tolerance screen or changing the lower limit of integration by a very small amount, such as .00001. These adjustments might allow the program to avoid the cause of the discontinuity in the function that is being integrated. This is similar to the problem encountered while using nInt in Example 5B.

Example 5B

Use the TI-89 to graph $\int_0^x (1 - 2\cos t)\, dt$ and compare with the exact antiderivative.
Directions:

1. Select the Radian mode.
2. Enter $y1 = \text{nInt}(1 - 2\cos(t), t, 0, x)$.
3. Enter $y2 = x - 2\sin(x)$.
4. Press $\boxed{\text{F2}}$ from the Y = window, then select [6:ZoomStd] in the Zoom menu to create a standard $[-10, 10]$ by $[-10, 10]$ viewing window.

These steps produce the graph shown in Fig. 7.4.

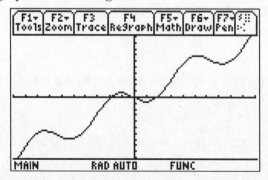

Figure 7.4 Antiderivative of $1 - 2\cos x$.

7.6 Solve an Equation

Program 6

SOLVE (solve an equation)
Input: $f(x)$ initial approximation of root
Output: (approximate) root of $f(x)$
This built-in feature is the Zero option in the [F5] (Math) menu available from the graph screen. To approximate the root of a function, do the following:

- Graph the function.
- Press [F5] and select [2:Zero] in the menu.
- Use the cursor-movement keys to select a lower bound and an upper bound. The values for the lower and upper bounds can also be entered directly from the keypad.

The TI-89 can also give approximate solutions to equations by using the Zero (command in the Home screen.

Example 6

Solve $x = 2 \sin x$ (find the roots of $x - 2 \sin x$).
   Directions:

1. Enter $y1 = x - 2 \sin x$.
2. Graph the function using a $[-10, 10]$ by $[-10, 10]$ window.
3. Press [F5] and select [2:Zero].

You will see a prompt for a lower bound.

4. Use the cursor movement keys to move the cursor to $x = -2.268908$ and press [ENTER].

Doing this marks the lower bound. You will see a prompt for an upper bound.

5. Move the cursor to $x = -1.260504$ and press [ENTER].

This selects the upper bound. The root is -1.895494.

6. Press [F5] and select [2:Zero] again.
7. Select $x = -.4201681$ for the lower bound and $x = .42016807$ for the upper bound.

Another root is 0.

   The cursor-movement keys are used to place the cursor close to a root. This provides the function with an initial estimate of the root. The TI-89 then uses a numerical method to improve significantly on the estimate.

7.7 Rectangle Approximation Method

Program 7

RAM() (rectangle approximation method)
Input: $f(x)$, a, b, and n (number of subintervals)

Output: (approximate) value of $\int_a^b f(x)\,dx$ using left, right, and midpoint rectangles

   Note that the _ indicates the spacebar. The TI-89 does not differentiate between upper- and lower-case characters. You can enter a program using all lower-case characters and after it has been run once, all the commands will show the same mixture of upper- and lower-case characters as the TI-89 manual.

Table 7.4

Comments	Input (keystrokes)	Screen Display
1. Enter the program mode.	[APPS] [Program Editor] [3:New]	New program box
2. Enter the program name in the variable box.	[▼] [▼] [ALPHA] [ALPHA] **RAM** [ALPHA] [ENTER] [ENTER]	Program screen
3. Initialize sums. Use a point after the zeros so that the result will be a decimal.	[▼] [▼] **0** [STO►] [ALPHA] **S** [2nd] [:] **0** [STO►] [ALPHA] [ALPHA] **SM** [ALPHA] [2nd] [:] **0** [STO►] [ALPHA] [ALPHA] **SR** [ALPHA] [ENTER]	:0→S: 0→SM: 0→SR
4. Enter *A, B, N*.	[F3] [3:Input] [2nd] ["] [ALPHA] **A** [=] [2nd] ["] [,] [ALPHA] **A** [ENTER]	:Input"a=",a
	[F3] [3:Input] [2nd] ["] [ALPHA] **B** [=] [2nd] ["] [,] [ALPHA] **B** [ENTER]	:Input"b=",b
	[F3] [3:Input] [2nd] ["] [ALPHA] [ALPHA] **NO** [ALPHA] . [ALPHA] [ALPHA] **SUBIN** [ALPHA] **T** [=] [2nd] ["] [,] [ALPHA] **N** [ENTER]	:Input"no.subint=",n
5. Calculate step size.	[(] [ALPHA] **B** [—] [ALPHA] **A** [)] [÷] [ALPHA] **N** [STO►] [ALPHA] **D** [ENTER]	:(b−a)/n→d
6. Initialize *x*-coordinates of rectangles.	[ALPHA] **A** [STO►] [ALPHA] [ALPHA] **RA** [ALPHA] [2nd] [:] [(] **2** [ALPHA] **A** [+] [ALPHA] **D** [)] [÷] **2** [STO►] [ALPHA] [ALPHA] **AM** [ALPHA] [ENTER]	:a→ra:(2a+d)/2→am
	[ALPHA] **A** [+] [ALPHA] **D** [STO►] [ALPHA] [ALPHA] **RR** [ALPHA] [ENTER]	:a+d→rr
7. Sum areas.	[ALPHA] [ALPHA] **LBL** _ [ALPHA] **T 1** [2nd] [:] [ALPHA] **R** [ALPHA] **A** [STO►] **X** [2nd] [:] [ALPHA] **Y1** [(] [ALPHA] **X** [)] [+] [ALPHA] **S** [STO►] [ALPHA] **S** [ENTER]	:Lbl t1:ra→x:y1(x)+s→s
	[ALPHA] [ALPHA] **RR** [ALPHA] [STO►] **X** [2nd] [:] [ALPHA] **Y1** [(] **X** [)] [+] [ALPHA] [ALPHA] **SR** [ALPHA] [STO►] [ALPHA] **S** [ALPHA] **R** [ENTER]	:rr→x:y1(x)+sr→sr
	[ALPHA] [ALPHA] **RR** [ALPHA] [+] [ALPHA] **D** [STO►] [ALPHA] [ALPHA] **RR** [ALPHA] [ENTER]	:rr+dr→rr
	[ALPHA] [ALPHA] **RA** [ALPHA] [+] [ALPHA] **D** [STO►] [ALPHA] [ALPHA] **RA** [ALPHA] [ENTER]	:ra+d→ra
	[ALPHA] **A** [ALPHA] **M** [STO►] **X** [2nd] [:] [ALPHA] **Y1** [(] **X** [)] [+] [ALPHA] **S** [ALPHA] [ALPHA] **M** [STO►] [ALPHA] **S** [ALPHA] **M** [ENTER]	:am→x:y1(x)+sm→sm
	[ALPHA] [ALPHA] **AM** [ALPHA] [+] [ALPHA] **D** [STO►] [ALPHA] [ALPHA] **AM** [ALPHA] [ENTER]	:am+d→am
	[F2] [2:If...Then][1:If...Then] **B** [—] [ALPHA] [ALPHA] **RA** [ALPHA] [2nd] [>] [·] **001** _ **THEN** [ENTER]	:If b−ra > .001 then
	[ALPHA] [ALPHA] **GOTO** _ [ALPHA] **T 1** [ENTER]	:Goto t1
	ENDIF [ENTER]	:EndIf

Continued on next page

(Continued)

Comments	Input (keystrokes)	Screen Display
8. Print results.	[ALPHA] [ALPHA] **DISP** [ALPHA] [2nd] ["] [ALPHA] [ALPHA] **LEF** [ALPHA] **T** [=] [2nd] ["] [,] [ALPHA] **D** [×] [ALPHA] **S** [ENTER]	:Disp "left=", d∗s
	[ALPHA] **DISP** [ALPHA] [2nd] ["] [ALPHA] [ALPHA] **MID** [ALPHA] [=] [2nd] ["] [,] [ALPHA] **D** [×] [ALPHA] [ALPHA] **M** [ENTER]	:Disp "mid=", d∗sm
	[ALPHA] [ALPHA] **DISP** [ALPHA] [2nd] ["] [ALPHA] [ALPHA] **RIGH** [ALPHA] **T** [=] [2nd] ["] [,] [ALPHA] **D** [×] [ALPHA] **S** [ALPHA] **R** [ENTER] [HOME]	:Disp "right=", d∗sr

Example 7A

An integral such as $\int_{-1}^{3} \frac{\sin x}{x}\, dx$ can be approximated if we assume $\frac{\sin x}{x} = 1$ at $x = 0$.
Directions:

1. Enter $y_1 = \sin(x)/x$ and select Radian mode.

2. Execute RAM() by entering **RAM** [( ] [ )] on the entry line of the Home screen.

3. Enter $-.99999$ for A, 3 for B, and 4 for the number of subintervals.

These steps produce the three approximations to the definite integral given in the first row of Table 7.5. Press [F5] *to return to the home screen.*

Repeat steps 2 and 3 in Example 7A, replacing n with 10, 50, 100, and 1000, to produce the remainder of the table.

Table 7.5 Rectangular approximations to $\int_{-1}^{3} \frac{\sin x}{x}\, dx$.

N	Left	Mid	Right
4	3.13758325638	2.82207901499	2.34315124866
10	2.94497750764	2.79904955137	2.62720470456
50	2.82615946391	2.79489969057	2.76260490329
100	2.81052957724	2.79477030735	2.77875229693
1000	2.7963151852	2.79472761487	2.79313745717

Because the integrand in Example 7A is not defined at $x = 0$, the lower limit of integration was replaced with $-.99999$. This creates a subdivision of the interval from -1 to 3 that doesn't require the program to evaluate $(\sin x)/x$ at $x = 0$. Try repeating steps 2 and 3 in Example 7A using -1 instead of $-.99999$. In this case, notice that the program returns results of "undef" for the left and right approximation methods because it attempts to evaluate $(\sin x/x)/x$ at $x = 0$.

Example 7B

Compare rectangular approximations of $\int_{0}^{\pi/2} \cos x\, dx$ using 10, 100, and 1000 subdivisions with the exact solution.

Directions:

1. First select the "Approximate" mode from the MODE screen.
2. Enter $y_1 = \cos x$.
3. Execute RAM().
4. Enter 0 for a and $\pi/2$ for b.
5. Enter 10 for the number of subintervals.
6. Repeat RAM() using 100, and then 1000, for the number of subintervals.

These steps produce the results shown in Table 7.6.

Table 7.6 Rectangular approximations to $\int_0^{\pi/2} \cos x\, dx$.

N	Left	Mid	Right	Exact
10	1.07648280269	1.00102882414	.919403170015	1.0
100	1.00783341987	1.00001028091	.992125456606	1.0
1000	1.00078519255	1.00000010281	.999214396221	1.0

Increasing the number of subintervals improves the accuracy of the approximation.

7.8 Trapezoidal Method

Program 8

TRAP() (trapezoidal method)
Input: $f(x)$, a, b, and n (number of subintervals)

Output: trapezoidal approximation of $\int_a^b f(x)\, dx$

```
:TRAP()
:Prgm
:Input "no.of subint=", n
:Input "a=", a
:Input "b=", b
:(b−a)/n→d
:a+d→ta
:0.→s
:Lbl t1: 2∗y1(ta)+s→s
:ta+d→ta
:If b−ta > .001 Then
:Goto t1
:EndIf
:y1(a)→l: y1(b)→r
:(d/2) (s+r+l)→t
:Disp "trap=", t
:EndPrgm
```

Example 8A

An integral such as $\int_{-1}^{3} \frac{\sin x}{x} \, dx$ can be approximated if we assume $\frac{\sin x}{x} = 1$ at $x = 0$.

Directions:

1. Enter $y_1 = \sin(x)/x$

2. Execute TRAP().

3. Enter 10 for the number of subintervals, $-.99999$ for a, and 3 for b.

4. Press F5 to return to the home screen. Repeat steps 2 and 3 using 100, and then 1000, for the number of subintervals.

These steps produce the results shown in Table 7.7.

Table 7.7 Trapezoidal approximations to $\int_{-1}^{3} \frac{\sin x}{x} \, dx$.

N	10	100	1000
TRAP	2.7860911061	2.79464093708	2.79472632119

A trapezoid approximation requires a partition of the interval $[A, B]$. The function is evaluated at points in the partition. Because the integrand in Example 8A is not defined at $x = 0$, the lower limit of integration was replaced with $-.99999$. Doing this creates a subdivision of the interval from -1 to 3 that doesn't require the program to evaluate $(\sin x)/x$ at $x = 0$. Try repeating the steps in Example 8A using -1 instead of $-.99999$. In this case, notice that for $N = 100$ and $N = 1000$, the program returns a result of "undef" because it attempts to evaluate $(\sin x)/x$ at $x = 0$. This is similar to the difficulty encountered in using RAM() to evaluate the same integral. However TRAP() only encounters a problem when N is divisible by 4.

Example 8B

Compare trapezoidal approximations of $\int_{0}^{\pi/2} \cos x \, dx$ using 10, 100, and 1000 subdivisions with the exact solution.

Directions:

1. Enter $y_1 = \cos(x)$.

2. Execute TRAP().

3. Enter 10 for the number of subintervals.

4. Enter 0 for A and $\pi/2$ for B.

5. Repeat steps 2–4 using 100, and then 1000, for the number of subintervals.

These steps produce the results shown in Table 7.8.

Table 7.8 Trapezoidal approximations to $\int_{0}^{\pi/2} \cos x \, dx$.

N	10	100	1000	Exact
TRAP	.997942986354	.99997943824	.999999794385	1.0

Increasing the number of subintervals improves the accuracy of approximation. The error estimate for the trapezoidal rule can be used to determine the accuracy of this program.

7.9 Simpson's Method

Program 9

SIMP() (Simpson's method)

Input: $f(x)$, a, b, and n (the number of subintervals (n) must be an even number.)

Output: Simpson's approximation of $\int_a^b f(x)dx$

```
:SIMP()
:Prgm
:Input "no. of subint=", n
:Input "a=", a
:Input "b=", b
:(b−a)/n→d
:a+d→ta
:0.→s
:Lbl t1
:4*y1(ta)+2*y1(ta+d)+s→s
:ta+2d→ta
:If b−ta > .001 Then
:Goto t1
:EndIf
:y1(a)→l: y1(b)→r
:(d/3) (s+l−r)→sim
:Disp "simp=", sim
:EndPrgm
```

Example 9A

An integral such as $\int_{-1}^3 \dfrac{\sin x}{x}\, dx$ can be approximated if we assume $\dfrac{\sin x}{x} = 1$ at $x = 0$.

Directions:

1. Enter $y_1 = \sin(x)/x$.

2. Execute SIMP().

3. Enter 10 for the number of subintervals, −.99999 for A, and 3 for B.

4. Press ⌷F5⌷ to return to the home screen. Repeat steps 2 and 3 using 100, and then 1000, for the number of subintervals.

These steps produce the results shown in the second row of Table 7.9. The trapezoidal and rectangular approximations have been included in the table for comparison.

Table 7.9 Comparison of numerical solutions to $\int_{-1}^3 \dfrac{\sin x}{x}\, dx$.

N	10	100	1000
SIMP()	2.79477378779	2.79472718825	2.79472718364
LEFT()	2.94497750764	2.81052957724	2.7963151852
MID()	2.79904955137	2.79477030735	2.79472761487
RIGHT()	2.62720470456	2.77875229639	2.79313745717
TRAP()	2.7860911061	2.79464093708	2.79472632119

Simpson's approximation requires a partition of the interval $[A, B]$. The function is evaluated at points in the partition. Because the integral in Example 9A is improper, the lower limit of integration was replaced with $-.99999$. Doing this creates a subdivision of the interval from -1 to 3 that doesn't require the program to evaluate $(\sin x)/x$ at $x = 0$. Try repeating the steps in Example 9A using -1 instead of $-.99999$. In this case, notice that for $N = 100$ and $N = 1000$, the program returns a result of "undef" because it attempts to evaluate $(\sin x)/x$ at $x = 0$. This is similar to the difficulty encountered in using RAM() and TRAP() to evaluate the same integral. Like TRAP(), SIMP() only encounters a problem when N is divisible by 4.

Example 9B

Compare trapezoidal approximations of $\int_0^{\pi/2} \cos x \, dx$ using 10, 100, and 1000 subdivisions with the exact solution.

Directions:

1. Enter $y_1 = \cos x$.

2. Execute SIMP().

3. Enter 10 for the number of subintervals.

4. Enter 0 for a and $\pi/2$ for b.

5. Repeat steps 2–4 using 100, and then 1000, for the number of subintervals.

These steps produce the results shown in Table 7.10. The trapezoidal and rectangular approximations have been included for comparison.

Table 7.10 Comparison of numerical solutions to $\int_0^{\pi/2} \cos x \, dx$.

N	10	100	1000	Exact
SIMP	1.00000339222	1.00000000034	.999999999999	1.0
LEFT	1.07648280269	1.00783341987	1.00078519255	1.0
MID	1.00102882414	1.00001028091	1.00000010281	1.0
RIGHT	.919403170015	.992125456606	.999214396221	1.0
TRAP	.997942986354	.99997943824	.999999794385	1.0

Increasing the number of subintervals improves the accuracy of the approximation in a dramatic way. Simpson's method gives a 10-place accuracy with just 100 subdivisions. The error estimate for Simpson's method can be used to determine the accuracy of this program.

7.10 Euler Table

Program 10

EULERT (Euler table)

Input: $f'(x, y)$; initial x, y; step size (h); number of ordered pairs in table (n)

Output: table of ordered pairs (x, y), where each pair is an element of $y = f(x)$ and $f(x)$ is a solution to the initial value problem.

```
:EULERT()
:Prgm
:Input "initial x=", x
:Input "y (initial x)=", y
:Input "step size=", h
:Input "no. of points=", n
```

```
:0.→j
:Lbl a
:Disp "x=", x
:Disp "y=", y
:Pause
:y+h*y1(x)→y
:x+h→x
:j+1→j
:If j≤n then        {≤ is entered using the [◆] key and the 0}
:Goto a
:EndIf
:EndPrgm
```

Example 10

EULERT() can be used to find a numerical solution to the initial value problem $\dfrac{dy}{dx} = -2xy^2$ with initial conditions $f(-2) = 0.2$

Directions:

1. Enter $y_1 = -2x*y\wedge 2$.

2. Execute EULERT().

3. Enter an initial x-value of -2.

4. Enter an initial y-value of 0.2.

5. Enter a step size of 0.1.

6. Enter 40 for the number of points.

The program will produce the ordered pairs found in Table 7.11. The x-values are in the first column and the y-values are in the third column (rounded to four decimal places). To see the next pair, you must press [ENTER] *after each ordered pair.*

The exact solution to this differential equation is $y = \dfrac{1}{1 + x^2}$. The second column of Table 7.11 contains the exact values of the solution. Compare these with the values obtained by EULERT(). As x moves away from the initial value, the difference between the exact value and the EULERT() solution increases.

Table 7.11 Numerical solutions to $\dfrac{dy}{dx} = -2xy^2$.

x	EXACT $1/(1 + x^2)$	EULERT	IMPEULT	RUNKUTT
−2.0	.20000000	.2000	.2000	.2000000
−1.9	.21691974	.2160	.2169	.2169197
−1.8	.23584906	.2337	.2357	.2358490
−1.7	.25706941	.2534	.2568	.2570692
−1.6	.28089888	.2752	.2805	.2808986
−1.5	.30769231	.2995	.3071	.3076918
−1.4	.33783784	.3264	.3370	.3378371
−1.3	.37174721	.3562	.3706	.3717462
−1.2	.40983607	.3892	.4083	.4098346
−1.1	.45248869	.4255	.4504	.4524866

Continued on next page

(Continued)

x	EXACT $1/(1 + x^2)$	EULERT	IMPEULT	RUNKUTT
−1.0	.50000000	.4654	.4972	.4999972
−0.9	.55248619	.5087	.5489	.5524824
−0.8	.6097561	.5553	.6051	.6097511
−0.7	.67114094	.6046	.6652	.6711346
−0.6	.73529412	.6558	.7279	.7352863
−0.5	.80000000	.7074	.7910	.7999905
−0.4	.86206897	.7574	.8514	.8620579
−0.3	.91743119	.8033	.9052	.9174188
−0.2	.96153846	.8420	.9480	.9615250
−0.1	.99009901	.8704	.9757	.9900849
0	1.0000000	.8855	.9852	.9999857
0.1	.99009901	.8855	.9755	.9900849
0.2	.96153846	.8699	.9477	.9615249
0.3	.91743119	.8396	.9048	.9174186
0.4	.86206897	.7973	.8510	.8620576
0.5	.80000000	.7464	.7905	.7999901
0.6	.73529412	.6907	.7275	.7352858
0.7	.67114094	.6335	.6649	.6711342
0.8	.6097561	.5773	.6048	.6097508
0.9	.55248619	.5240	.5487	.5524822
1.0	.50000000	.4746	.4972	.4999970
1.1	.45248869	.4295	.4504	.4524865
1.2	.40983607	.3889	.4083	.4098346
1.3	.37174721	.3526	.3707	.3717462
1.4	.33783784	.3203	.3371	.3378372
1.5	.30769231	.2916	.3072	.3076919
1.6	.28089888	.2661	.2806	.2808986
1.7	.2506941	.2434	.2569	.2570693
1.8	.23584906	.2233	.2358	.2358490
1.9	.21691974	.2053	.2170	.2169198
2.0	.20000000	.1893	.2001	.2000001

To see the approximation error for each ordered pair of output do the following.

1. Enter $y_2 = 1/(1 + x^2)$. This is the exact solution.

2. Edit EULERT()

3. After the x and y-values are displayed, and before the ":Pause" command, enter the following lines

   :Disp "y2=", y2(x)

   :Disp "Error=", abs(y − y2(x))

4. Execute EULERT() with parameters as stated in Example 10.

7.11 Euler Graph

Program 11

EULERG() (Euler graph)

Input: $f'(x, y)$; initial x, y; step size (h);

Output: graph of solution to initial value differential equation problem using Euler's method

```
:EULERG()
:Prgm
:0.→j: FnOff: ClrDraw
:Input "initial x=", x
:Input "y (initial x) =", y
:Input "step size =", h
:(xmax−xmin)/abs(h)→n
:Lbl a
:PtOn x, y
:y+h∗y1(x)→y
:x+h→x
:j+1→j
:If j ≤ n Then
:Goto A
:EndIf
:EndPrgm
```

Example 11A

Use EULERG to graph the solution to the initial problem $\dfrac{dy}{dx} = -2xy^2$ with $y(-2) = 0.2$ and then compare with the exact solution.

1. Enter $y_1 = -2x*y^2$.
2. Enter $y_2 = 1/(1+x^2)$.
3. Enter a $[-2, 2]$ by $[-1, 1]$ window.
4. Execute EULERG().
5. Enter an initial x-value of -2.
6. Enter an initial y-value of 0.2.
7. Enter a step size of 0.1.
8. Go to the Y = editor screen and use $\boxed{\text{F4}}$ to select y_2 for graphing, then press $\boxed{\blacklozenge}$ $\lceil \text{GRAPH} \rceil$.

These steps produce the graph shown in Fig. 7.5.

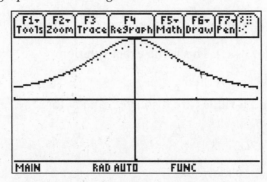

Figure 7.5 Euler's Method.

Notice the difference between the exact solution and Euler's method for x near zero.

Example 11B

Use EULERG() to graph $\int_0^x \cos t \, dt$ and compare with the exact solution.

1. Enter $y_1 = \cos(x)$.
2. Enter $y_2 = \sin(x)$.
3. Enter a $[0, 2\pi]$ by $[-2, 2]$ window.
4. Execute EULERG().
5. Enter an initial x-value of 0.
6. Enter an initial y-value of 0.
7. Enter a step size of 0.1.
8. Go to the Y = editor screen and use [F4] to select $y_2(x)$ for graphing, then press [◆] [GRAPH].

These steps produce the graph shown in Fig. 7.6.

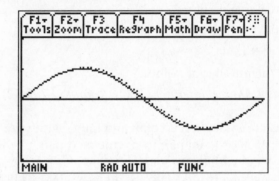

Figure 7.6 Antiderivative of cos x; Euler's Method.

Notice the difference between the exact solution and the Euler graph.

7.12 Improved Euler Table

Program 12

IMPEULT() (improved Euler table)

Input: $f'(x, y)$; initial x, y; step size (h); number of ordered pairs in table (n)
Output: table of ordered pairs (x, y), where each pair is an element of $y = f(x)$ and $f(x)$ is a solution to the initial value problem

```
:IMPEULT()
:Prgm
:0.→J
:Input "initial x=", x
:Input "y (initial x)=", y
:Input "step size=", h
:Input "no. of points=", n
:Lbl a
:y→z
:Disp "x=", x
:Disp "y=", y
:Pause
:h∗y1(x)→d
:y+d→y
:x+h→x
:z+(d+h∗y1(x))/2→y
```

```
:j+1→j
:If j ≤ n Then
:Goto a
:EndIf
:EndPrgm
```

Example 12

IMPEULT() can be used to find a numerical solution to the initial value problem $\dfrac{dy}{dx} = -2xy^2$ with initial conditions $f(-2) = 0.2$.

Directions:

1. Enter y1 $= -2x*y\verb|^|2$.
2. Execute IMPEULT().
3. Enter an initial x-value of -2.
4. Enter an initial y-value of 0.2.
5. Enter a step of 0.1.
6. Enter 40 for the number of points.

The program will produce the ordered pairs found in Table 7.11 (in Example 10).

The x-values are in the first column and the y-values are in the fourth column. You must press ENTER after each ordered pair to see the next pair. Compare the results of IMPEULT() with EULERT() and with the exact results.

The approximation error can also be added to IMPEULT(). Follow the steps at the end of Section 7.10.

7.13 Improved Euler Graph

Program 13

IMPEULG() (improved Euler graph)
Input: $f'(x, y)$; initial x, y; step size (h)
Output: graph of solution to initial value differential equation problem using the improved Euler's method

```
:IMPEULG()
:Prgm
:0.→j: FnOff: ClrDraw
:Input "initial x=", x
:Input "y (initial x)=", y
:Input "step size=", h
:(xmax−xmin)/(abs(h))→n
:lbl a
:y→z
:PtOn x,y
:h*y1(x)→d
:y+d→y
:x+h→x
:z+(d+h*y1(x))/2→y
:j+1→j
:If j ≤ n Then
```

```
:Goto a
:EndIf
:EndPrgm
```

Example 13A

Use IMPEULG() to graph the solution to the initial value problem $\frac{dy}{dx} = -2xy^2$, with $y(-2) = 0.2$, and then compare with the exact solution.

Directions:

1. Enter $y_1 = -2x*y\char`\^2$.

2. Enter $y_2 = 1/(1 + x\char`\^2)$.

3. Enter $[-2, 2]$ by $[-1, 1]$ window.

4. Execute IMPEULG().

5. Enter an initial x-value of -2.

6. Enter an initial y-value of 0.2.

7. Enter a step size of 0.1.

8. Go to the Y = editor screen and use ⌑ F4 ⌑ to select y_2 for graphing, then press ⌑◆⌑ ⌑GRAPH⌑.

These steps produce the graph shown in Fig. 7.7.

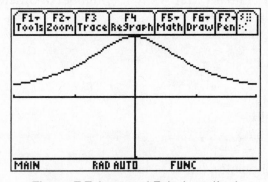

Figure 7.7 Improved Euler's method.

Compare this graph with the graph produced by Euler's method in Example 11A. Notice the improved agreement with the exact solution.

Example 13B

Use IMPEULG() to graph $\int_0^x \cos t \, dt$ and compare with the exact solution.

Directions:

1. Enter $y_1 = \cos x$.

2. Enter $y_2 = \sin x$.

3. Enter a $[0, 6.28]$ by $[-2, 2]$ window.

4. Execute IMPEULG().

5. Enter an initial x-value of 0.

6. Enter an initial y-value of 0.

7. Enter a step size of 0.1.

8. Go to the Y = editor screen and use ⌑ F4 ⌑ to select y_2 for graphing, then press ⌑◆⌑ ⌑GRAPH⌑.

These steps produce the graph shown in Fig. 7.8.

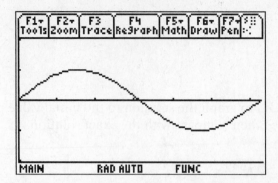

Figure 7.8 Antiderivative of cos x; improved Eulers' method.

Compare this graph with that produced by Euler's method in Example 11B. Notice the improved agreement with the exact solution.

7.14 Runge-Kutta Table

Program 14

RUNKUTT() (Runge-Kutta table)

Input: $f'(x, y)$; initial x, y; step size (h); number of ordered pairs in table (n)

Output: table of ordered pairs (x, y), where each pair is an element of $y = f(x)$ and $f(x)$ is a solution to the initial value problem.

```
:RUNKUTT()
:Prgm
:0.→m
:Input "initial x=", x
:Input "y (initial x)=", y
:Input "step size=", h
:Input "no. of points=", n
:Lbl a
:y→z
:Disp "x=", x
:Disp "y=", y
:Pause
:h*y1(x)→i
:x+h/2→x
:z+i/2→y
:h*y1(x)→j
:z+j/2→y
:h*y1(x)→k
:x+h/2→x
:z+k→y
:h*y1(x)→l
:z+(i+2*j+2*k+l)/6→y
:m+1→m
:If m ≤ n Then
:Goto a
:EndIf
:EndPrgm
```

Example 14

RUNKUTT() can be used to find a numerical solution to the initial value problem
$\frac{dy}{dx} = -2xy^2$ with initial conditions $f(-2) = 0.2$.

Directions:

1. Enter y1 $= -2x*y^2$.

2. Execute RUNKUTT().

3. Enter an initial x-value of -2.

4. Enter an initial y-value of 0.2.

5. Enter a step size of 0.1.

6. Enter 40 for the number of points.

The program will produce the ordered pairs found in Table 7.11 (in Example 10).

The x-values are in the first column and the y-values are in the fifth column. You must press [ENTER] after each ordered pair to see the next pair. Compare the results of RUNKUTT() with IMPEULT(), EULERT(), and the exact results. The Runge-Kutta method is analogous to Simpson's method, while the improved Euler's method uses trapezoidal approximations and Euler's method uses rectangular approximations. It is not surprising that the Runge-Kutta method is the most accurate of the three numerical techniques.

The approximation error can also be added to RUNKUTT(). Follow the steps at the end of Section 7.10.

7.15 Runge-Kutta Graph

Program 15

RUNKUTG() (Runge-Kutta graph)

Input: $f'(x, y)$; initial x, y; step size (h)
Output: graph of solution to initial value differential equation problem using the Runge-Kutta method

```
:RUNKUTG()
:Prgm
:0.→m:FnOff:ClrDraw
:Input "initial x=", x
:Input "y (initial x)=", y
:Input "step size=", h
:(xmax−xmin)/(abs(h))→n
:Lbl a
:y→z
:PtOn x,y
:h∗y1(x)→i
:x+h/2→x
:z+i/2→y
:h∗y1(x)→j
:z+j/2→y
:h∗y1(x)→k
:x+h/2→x
:z+k→y
```

```
:h*y1(x)→l
:z+(i+2*j+2*k+l)/6→y
:m+1→m
:If m ≤ n Then
:Goto a
:EndIf
:EndPrgm
```

Example 15A

Use RUNKUTG() to graph the solution to the initial value problem $\dfrac{dy}{dx} = -2xy^2$ with $y(-2) = 0.2$ and then compare with the exact solution.

1. Enter $y_1 = -2x*y\text{^}2$.
2. Enter $y_2 = 1/(1 + x\text{^}2)$.
3. Enter a $[-2, 2]$ by $[-1, 1]$ window.
4. Execute RUNKUTG().
5. Enter an initial x-value of -2.
6. Enter an initial y-value of 0.2.
7. Enter a step size of 0.1.
8. Go to the Y = editor screen and use ⎡F4⎤ to select y_2 for graphing, then press ⎡◆⎤ ⎡GRAPH⎤.

These steps produce the graph shown in Fig. 7.9.

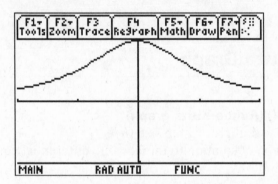

Figure 7.9 Runge-Kutta Method.

Compare this graph with the graphs produced by Euler's method in Example 11A and the improved Euler's method in Example 13A. Notice the close agreement between the Runge-Kutta graph and the exact solution.

Example 15B

Use RUNKUTG() to graph $\displaystyle\int_0^x \cos t\, dt$ and compare with the exact solution.

1. Enter $y_1 = \cos(x)$.
2. Enter $y_2 = \sin(x)$.
3. Enter a $[0, 6.28]$ by $[-2, 2]$ window.
4. Execute RUNKUTG.
5. Enter an initial x-value of 0.
6. Enter an initial y-value of 0.
7. Enter a step size of 0.1.
8. Go to the Y = editor screen and use ⎡F4⎤ to select y_2 for graphing, then press ⎡◆⎤ ⎡GRAPH⎤.

These steps produce the graph shown in Fig. 7.10.

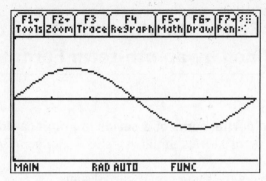

Figure 7.10 Antiderivative of cos x; Runge-Kutta method.

Compare the graph with the graphs produced by Euler's method in Example 11B and the improved Euler's method in Example 13B. Notice the close agreement between the Runge-Kutta graph and the exact solution.

7.16 Make a Table of the Sequence of Partial Sums of a Series that Is Defined by an *n*th-term Formula

Program 16

> **PARTSUMT (partial sums of a series in tabular form)**
> Input: *n*th term of a series, initial value of *n*, number of terms in the sequence of partial sums
> Output: sequence of partial sums
> You can make the table without a program by using the sum and seq commands.

Example 16

Make a table of the first 10 partial sums of the series

$$\sum_{n=1}^{10} 1/2^n.$$

Directions:

1. Enter the following key sequence on the entry line of the Home screen:

Note that you have to use a decimal point in the command in order to ensure that the result is a decimal.

The SUM command adds up the terms in a sequence. The SEQ (sequence) command makes a sequence. The first parameter in the SEQ command is the formula for the *n*th term of the sequence. The second parameter is the index. The third and fourth parameters are the initial and final values of the index. The last parameter is the amount by which the index will change between terms in the sequence.

2. Press ENTER repeatedly to see the sequence of partial sums.

These steps produce the following output:

N	Nth partial sum
1	.5
2	.75
3	.875
.	.
.	.
.	.
10	.99902

7.17 Graph the Sequence of Partial Sums of a Series that Is Defined by an *n*th-term Formula

Program 17

PARTSUMG (partial sums of a series in graphical form)
Input: *n*th term of a series, initial value of *n*, number of terms in the sequence of partial sums
Output: graph of the sequence of partial sums
You can draw the graph without a program with the SUM and SEQ commands in Parametric mode, as follows:

$$x_{t1} = t$$

$$y_{t1} = \text{sum}(\text{seq}(a_n, n, 1, t, 1))$$

and using a *t*step of 1.

Example 17

Graph the first 10 partial sums of the series $\sum\limits_{n=1}^{10} 1/2^n$.

Directions:

1. Press MODE and select the Parametric mode.

2. Enter the following equations in the Y = edit screen for parametric functions.

$$x_{t1} = t$$

$$y_{t1} = \text{sum}(\text{seq}(1/2^{\wedge}n, n, 1, t, 1))$$

Use ⎡F6⎤ [2:Dot] to have the function graphed as a series of dots, rather than having the TI-89 connect the terms of the sequence with line segments.

3. Enter the following WINDOW values:

*t*min = 1	*x*min = 0	*y*min = 0
*t*max = 10	*x*max = 10	*y*max = 1
*t*step = 1	*x*scl = 1	*y*scl = 0

4. Graph.

These steps produce the graph shown in Fig. 7.11.

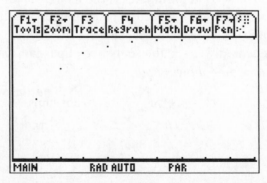

Figure 7.11 Sequence of partial sums for $\sum 1/2^n$.

7.18 Make A Table of the Sequence of Partial Sums of a Series that Is Defined Recursively

Program 18

PSUMRECT() (sequence of partial sums of a recursive series in tabular format)
Input: recursive definition of nth term of the series, initial n, initial term in series, number of terms in the sequence of partial sums
Output: sequence of partial sums

```
:PSUMRECT
:Prgm
:Input "initial n=", i
:Input "initial term=", a
:Input "no. of terms=", m
:i→n
:a→s
:Lbl a
:Disp "n=", n
:Disp "partial sum=", s
:Pause
:1+n→n
:y1(x)+s→s
:y1(x)→a
:If (n−i)<m Then
:Goto a
:EndIf
:EndPrgm
```

Example 18A

Use PSUMRECT() to make a table of the sequence of partial sums for the series
$\dfrac{1}{2}+\dfrac{1}{4}+\dfrac{1}{8}+\dfrac{1}{16}$ ... defined recursively as $\sum a_n$ where $a_n = \left(\dfrac{1}{2}\right)a_{n-1}, a_1 = \left(\dfrac{1}{2}\right)$.

1. Enter $y_1 = (1/2.)a$ in the Y= edit screen (You must be in Function Mode). *Note that you must put a decimal point in the function to ensure that the results are decimals rather than fractions.*

2. Execute PSUMRECT().

3. Enter 1 for the initial n-value.

4. Enter 1/2 for the initial term.

5. Enter 10 for the number of terms.

6. Press

[ENTER]

to see each element in the sequence of partial sums.

These steps produce the values listed at the end of Example 16.

Example 18B

Find the sequence of partial sums for the series $1^2 + 2^2 + 3^2 + 4^2 + ...$, which can be recursively defined as $\sum a_n$, where $a_n = a_{n-1} + 2n - 1, a_1 = 1$.

Directions:

1. Enter $y_1 = a + 2n - 1$ in the Y = edit screen.
2. Execute PSUMRECT().
3. Enter 1 for the initial n-value.
4. Enter 1 for the initial term.
5. Enter 10 for the number of terms.
6. Press

ENTER

to see each element in the sequence of partial sums.

These steps produce the values listed below:

N	Nth partial sum
1	1
2	5
3	14
4	30
.	.
.	.
.	.
10	385

7.19 Graph the Sequence of Partial Sums of a Series that Is Defined Recursively

Program 19

PSUMRECG() (graphs a sequence of partial sums of a recursive series)
Input: recursive definition of the nth term of the series, initial n, initial term in series, number of terms in the sequence of partial sums
Output: graph of the sequence of partial sums

```
:PSUMRECG
:Prgm
:FnOff: ClrDraw
:Input "inital n=", i
:Input "initial term", a
:Input "no. of terms=", m
:i→n
:a→s
:Lbl a
:PtOn n,s
:1+n→n
:y1(x)+s→s
:y1(x)→a
:If (n−i) < m Then
:Goto a
:EndIf
:EndPrgm
```

Example 19

Use PSUMRECG() to graph the sequence of partial sums for the series $\dfrac{1}{2} + \dfrac{1}{4} + \dfrac{1}{8} + \dfrac{1}{16} \dots$ defined recursively as $\sum a_n$, where $a_n = \left(\dfrac{1}{2}\right)a_{n-1}, a_1 = \dfrac{1}{2}$.

Directions:

1. Enter $y_1 = (1/2)a$ in the Y = edit screen.
2. Set the viewing window to $[0, 10]$ by $[0, 1]$.
3. Execute PSUMRECG().
4. Enter 1 for the initial n-value.
5. Enter 1/2 for the initial term.
6. Enter 10 for the number of terms.

These steps produce the same graph as Fig. 7.11.

7.20 Graph the *n*th Partial Sum of a Power Series

Program 20

GRAPHSUM() (graph *n*th partial sum of a power series)
Input: *n*th term of series, initial *n*, number of terms in the series
Output: graph of the *n*th partial sum of the series
The graph can be drawn using the SUM and SEQ commands.

Example 20

Graph the power series for sin x, $\displaystyle\sum_{N=1}^{10} \dfrac{(-1)^{N+1}X^{2N-1}}{(2N-1)!}$ and overlay with sin x.

Directions:

1. Select dot mode.
2. Enter $y_1 = \text{sum}(\text{seq}((-1)^\wedge(N + 1)x^\wedge(2N - 1)/(2N - 1)!, N, 1, 10, 1))$.
3. Enter $y_2 = \sin(x)$.
4. Graph in the $[-10, 10]$ by $[-2, 2]$ viewing window.

These steps produce the graph shown in Fig. 7.12.

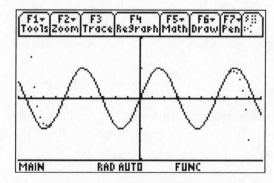

Figure 7.12 Power series for sin *x*.

This is the tenth partial sum of the MacLaurin series for sin x overlaid on the graph of sin x.

The first parameter in the seq function in Step 1 is the *n*th term of the series. The second parameter is the index for the series. The third parameter is the beginning value of the index and the fourth is the end value for the index. The last parameter is the increment for the index.

7.21 Graph a Slope Field for a Differential Equation

Program 21

SLOPEFLD() (graph the slope field for a differential equation $y' = f(x, y)$)
Input: Differential equation $y' = f(x, y)$
Output: Slope field for the differential equation

```
:SLOPEFLD
:Prgm
:10→l
:10→w
:(ymax−ymin)/l→v
:(xMax−xMin)/w→h
:ClrDraw
:FnOff
:ymin+v/2→y
:For r, 1, l
:xmin+h/2→x
:For c, 1, w
:y1(x)→m
:−m∗h/4+y→s
:m∗h/4+y→t
:If abs (t−s)>v Then
:y+v/4→t
:y−v/4→s
:(t−y)/m+x→q
:(s−y)/m+x→p
:Else
:x−h/4→p
:x+h/4→q
:EndIf
:y→z
:Line p,s,q,t
:z→y
:x+h→x
:EndFor
:y+v→y
:EndFor
:EndPrgm
```

The variables 1 and w are both initialized to 10 in the first two lines of the program. These initial values can be adjusted to change the number of rows and columns in the output of the Slopefld program.

Example 21A

Use SLOPEFLD() to illustrate the family of solutions to the differential equation $y' = \sin x/x$.

1. Enter $y_1 = \sin x/x$
2. Enter a $[-7, 7]$ by $[-2, 2]$ viewing window.
3. Execute SLOPEFLD().

These steps produce the slopefield shown (see Fig. 7.13).

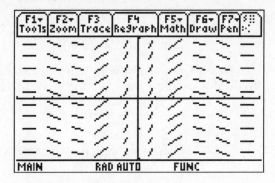

Figure 7.13 Slope field for $y' = \sin x/x$.

Example 21B

Graph the slope field for the differential equation $y' = x + y$.

1. Enter $y_1 = x + y$.
2. Enter a $[-2, 2]$ by $[-1, 1]$ viewing window.
3. Execute SLOPEFLD.

You should see the following slope field (see Fig. 7.14).

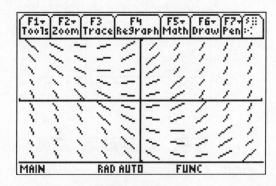

Figure 7.14 Slope field for $y' = x + y$.

Example 21C

Graph the slope field for $y' = -2xy^2$.

1. Enter $y_1 = -2x*y^2$.
2. Enter a $[-2, 2]$ by $[-1, 1]$ viewing window and execute SLOPEFLD().

Compare this slope field (Fig. 7.15) with the results of Prgms EULERG(), IMPEULG(), and RUNGKUTG() in Examples 11A, 13A, and 15A.

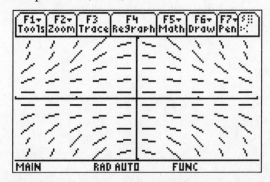

Figure 7.15 Family of solutions to $y = -2xy^2$.

Example 21D

Graph the slope field for $y' = -2xy^2$, then use EULERG() to superimpose the solution to the initial value problem $\dfrac{dy}{dx} = -2xy^2$ with $y(-2) = 0.2$.

The TI-89 will overlay the Euler graph onto a slope field automatically if you assign the initial conditions. To do this on the TI-86 you need to edit your EULERG() program.

1. Enter $y_1 = -2x*y\textasciicircum2$.
2. Enter $y_2 = 1/(1 + x\textasciicircum2)$.
3. Enter a $[-2, 2]$ by $[-1, 1]$ viewing window and execute SLOPEFLD().
4. Edit EULERG().
5. Delete the :ClrDraw command from line 3.
6. Execute EULERG().
7. Enter an initial x-value of -2.
8. Enter an initial y-value of 0.2.
9. Enter a step size of 0.1.

***Note:** This example will also work with IMPEULG() and RUNKUTG().*

These steps produce the graph shown in Figure 7.16.

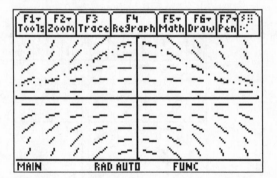

Figure 7.16 Slope field for $y' = -2xy^2$ and Euler's method.

7.22 Visualizing Rectangular Approximation Methods for Areas

Program 22

AREA() (graph left, right, and midpoint rectangles used for area approximation)
Input: $f(x), a, b, n$ (number of rectangles)
Output: numeric results and graphs of rectangles used to approximate areas bounded by $f(x), a, b,$ and the x-axis

```
:AREA
:Prgm
:Prompt a
:Prompt b
:Input "no. of subint =", n
:(b - a)/n→h
:h/2→d
:0→l
:0→m
:0→r
```

```
:ClrDraw
:DispG
:0→j
:a→x
:While j < n
:y1(x)+l→l
:Line x, 0, x, y1(x)
:Line x, y1(x), x+h, y1(x)
:Line x+h, 0, x+h, y1(x)
:x+h→x
:j+1→j
:EndWhile
:Pause
:Disp "left=",h∗l
:Pause
:ClrDraw
:DispG
:0→j
:a+h→x
:While j < n
:y1(x)+r→r
:Line x−h,0,x−h,y1(x)
:Line x−h,y1(x),x,y1(x)
:Line x,0,x,y1(x)
:x+h→x
:j+1→j
:EndWhile
:Pause
:Disp "right=",h∗r
:Pause
:ClrDraw
:DispG
:0→j
:a+d→x
:While j < n
:y1(x)+m→m
:Line x−d,0,x−d,y1(x)
:Line x−d,y1(x),x+d,y1(x)
:Line x+d,y1(x),x+d,0
:x+h→x
:1+j→j
:EndWhile
:Pause
:Disp "midpoint=",h∗m
:EndPrgm
```

Example 22

Graph the left, right and midpoint rectangles that approximate the area bounded by the function $y = 4x - x^2$.

Directions:

1. Enter $y_1 = 4x - x^2$
2. Enter a $[-1, 5]$ by $[-1, 4]$ viewing window.
3. Execute AREA().
4. Enter 0 for a.
5. Enter 4 for b.
6. Enter 4 for the number of subintervals.

You should see a graph like Fig. 7.17 that illustrates the left-hand rectangles.

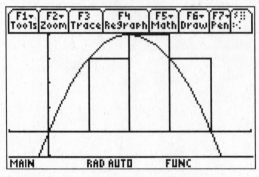

Figure 7.17 Left-rectangles.

7. Press [ENTER] to see the sum of the areas of the left-hand rectangles (10) and then press [ENTER] again to continue.

Now you should see the right-hand rectangles (see Fig. 7.18).

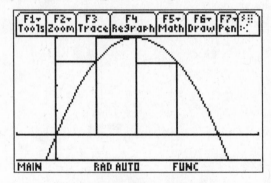

Figure 7.18 Right-rectangles.

8. Press [ENTER] to see the sums of the left-hand and right-hand rectangles (10 again) and then press [ENTER] to continue.

You should see midpoint rectangles like those in Fig. 7.19.

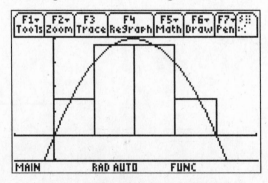

Figure 7.19 Midpoint rectangles.

9. Press [ENTER] once more to see the numerical results of the summations.

7.23 Investigating Limits

Example 23A

Graphically investigate $\lim\limits_{x \to -\infty} \tan^{-1}x$, $\lim\limits_{x \to \infty} \tan^{-1}x$.

Directions:

1. Enter $y_1 = \tan^{-1} x$.
2. Enter $y_2 = -\pi/2$.
3. Enter $y_3 = \pi/2$.
4. Graph in a $[-100, 100]$ by $[-3, 3]$ viewing window.

These steps produce the graph shown in Fig. 7.20.

This graph provides evidence that $\lim\limits_{x \to -\infty} \tan^{-1}x = -\dfrac{\pi}{2}$ and $\lim\limits_{x \to \infty} \tan^{-1}x = \dfrac{\pi}{2}$.

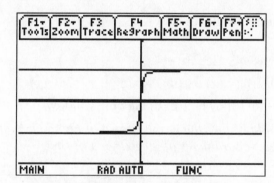

Figure 7.20 End behavior of arctan *x*.

Example 23B

Graphically investigate $\lim\limits_{x \to 0+} (1 + x)^{1/x}$.

Directions:

1. Enter $y_1 = (1 + x)^{\wedge}(1/x)$.
2. Graph in a $[-1, 5]$ by $[-1, 4]$ viewing window.

These steps produce the graph shown in Fig. 7.21.

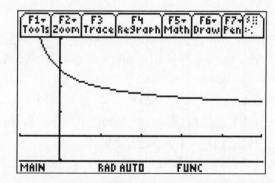

Figure 7.21 $y = (1 + x)^{\wedge}(1/x)$.

Zoom in several times on the *y*-intercept of the graph and then trace towards the *y*-intercept from the positive side. Zoom-in produces something similar to the graph shown in Fig. 7.22.

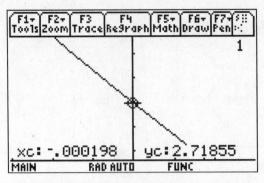

Figure 7.22 Zoom in on $y = (1 + x)^\wedge(1/x)$.

This graph provides evidence that $\lim\limits_{x \to 0+} (1 + x)^{1/x} = e$. This limit is the y-coordinate of a removable discontinuity in the graph.

Example 23C

Find a local minimum value of $f(x) = x^3 - 4x^2 + 3x - 4$.
Directions:

1. Enter $y_1 = x^\wedge 3 - 4x^\wedge 2 + 3x - 4$.

2. Enter $y_2 = \text{nDeriv}(y_1(x), x, .01)$.

3. Graph in a $[-10, 10]$ by $[-10, 10]$ viewing window.

These steps should produce the graph shown in Fig. 7.23. Notice that the zeros of the derivative correspond to the x-coordinates of the extrema of $f(x)$.

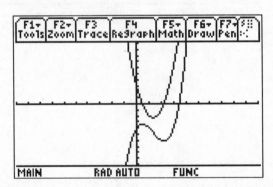

Figure 7.23 $y = x^3 - 4x^2 + 3x - 4$ and its derivative.

4. Select [2:Zero] from the $\boxed{\text{F5}}$ menu to find the zero of y_2 near $x = 2.2$.

   (Remember to use the up direction on the cursor pad to move the cursor to y_2 before you enter the lower and upper bounds.)

The value of the zero should appear to be 2.21523153859.

5. You can evaluate $f(2.2152315386)$ by printing the current value of y_1 on the Home screen. (Type **y1** $\boxed{(}$ **xc** $\boxed{)}$ and press $\boxed{\text{ENTER}}$.)

The value of y_1 should be -6.11261178998.

The exact local minimum is $f\left(\dfrac{8 + \sqrt{28}}{6}\right)$ which is -6.11261179092 (to 11 decimal places).

Note the high degree of accuracy of the local minimum value! Changing h to 0.0001 in the nDeriv method used in y_2 will improve accuracy even more.

7.24 Find Local Extrema

Local extrema can be found using the fMin and fMax options from the [F3] menu on the Home screen or the Miniumum and Maximum commands on the [F5] menu from the graph screen. The fMin option returns the x-value where the minimum value of $f(x)$ occurs, and the fMax option returns the x-value for the maximum value of $f(x)$. Using the Minimum and Maximum commands gives both the x-value and the y-value of the local extrema.

Example 24

Find local minimum and maximum values of $f(x) = x^3 - 4x^2 + 3x - 4$.
Directions:

1. Enter $y_1 = x^3 - 4x^2 + 3x - 4$.
2. Graph in a $[-10, 10]$ by $[-10, 10]$ viewing window.
3. Press [F5] and select [3:Minimum].
4. Use the cursor pad to set the lower bound at $x = 1.4285714$ and the upper bound at $x = 2.9411765$, then press [ENTER].

The output on the screen should be $x = 2.2152504$, $y = -6.112612$. These are the coordinates of the local minimum. Compare these results with those of Example 25.

5. Press [F5] and select [4:Maximum].
6. Use the cursor pad to set the lower bound at $x = .08403361$, the right bound at $x = 1.092437$, then press [ENTER].

The output should be $x = .45141635$, $y = -3.36887$. These are the coordinates of the local maximum.

You can also enter lower and upper bounds from the keypad.